GRESLEY'S LEGACY

LOCOMOTIVES AND ROLLING STOCK

David McIntosh

Ian Allan
PUBLISHING

First published 2015

ISBN 978 0 7110 3461 7

Published by Ian Allan Publishing Ltd, Addlestone, Surrey KT12 2SF

Printed in Bulgaria

Visit the Ian Allan Publishing website at www.ianallanpublishing.com

Picture credits
Every effort has been made to identify and correctly attribute photographic credits. Should any error have occurred this is entirely unintentional.

FRONT COVER TOP PICTURE In 2012 preserved 'B12/3' No 8572 visited the Severn Valley Railway, permitting this re-creation of the 'Day Continental' boat train using the SVR's beautiful rake of eight preserved Gresley teak-bodied carriages. Here the train approaches Highley *en route* for Bridgnorth. *Steve Allen*

FRONT COVER BOTTOM PICTURE Pioneer 'V2' No 60800 *Green Arrow* poses outside its home shed at King's Cross in 1961. Barring six weeks at Woodford Halse in 1953 the former No 4771 was allocated to King's Cross for its entire BR career, until withdrawal for preservation in August 1962. Here, more than a year after its last overhaul (at Darlington in January 1960), it still presents the smart appearance that typified 'Top Shed' locomotives, contrasting with the rather grubby prototype 'A4', No 60014 *Silver Link*, alongside.
W. Potter/Kidderminster Railway Museum

BACK COVER Preserved 'A4' No 4468 *Mallard* is seen at Giggleswick on 16 May 1987 (see page 109). *D. S. Lindsey/Gresley Society collection*

ENDPAPERS Gresley 'A4' Pacific No 4491 *Commonwealth of Australia* (Doncaster, July 1937) is seen speeding through Hitchin with the Up 'West Riding Limited' streamliner in the late 1930s. *George Heiron*

CONTENTS

INTRODUCTION

Herbert Nigel Gresley was unique in his unparalleled 36 years of continuous service as a railway All-Line Chief Officer. His career encompassed the positions of Carriage & Wagon Superintendent to the Great Northern Railway (from 1905, at the age of 28), Locomotive Engineer to the GNR (from the age of 35) and, ultimately (from 1923, at the age of 47, until his untimely death in office in 1941), Chief Mechanical Engineer of the London & North Eastern Railway.

Gresley established a reputation as a brilliant and innovative engineer, not afraid to learn from others and apply their ideas to produce creative yet practical solutions to problems, often through the application of science and research. He was an excellent leader and created devoted teams of men, many of whom went on to lead teams on other railways, both pre- and post-nationalisation. He was in the vanguard in developing such items as locomotive valve gear, poppet valves, feed-water pre-heating, the use of high-pressure water-tube boilers and Kylchap exhaust systems, the streamlining of internal steam passages and the application of external streamlining on locomotives and trains; he also championed the use of locomotive-testing stations. In the field of passenger carriages he was an early pioneer of articulation (for weight saving), still employed by the Eurostar and TGV trains, and the use of buckeye knuckle couplers and Pullman gangways, which over the years have saved many lives in keeping derailed trains upright and in line.

Gresley designed many successful and graceful locomotives and carriages, including the world's most famous steam locomotives, *Flying Scotsman* and *Mallard*, and the LNER's three streamlined trains, the 'Silver Jubilee', the 'Coronation' and the 'West Riding Limited'. He designed many carriages which demonstrated the ultimate in style and comfort with excellent riding qualities delivered by Gresley bogies, some of which were still being fitted to new BR electric multiple-units as late as 1961.

In this book I have sought to reflect upon Gresley's many achievements, with particular reference to the many items of Gresley rolling stock that have survived into the 21st century.

ABOVE A portrait of Nigel Gresley aged 35 in 1911, on his appointment as Locomotive Engineer to the Great Northern Railway. *Gresley Society collection*

We are fortunate that, almost three quarters of a century after his death, these vehicles can still be admired by all of those who have come to appreciate the beauty and efficiency of his designs.

In my researches I have been greatly assisted by Gresley family papers to which I was given access by Sir Nigel's grandsons, Tim and Ben Godfrey, by numerous articles in the Gresley Society Journal, *The Gresley Observer*, and by access to the photographic libraries of Ian Allan Publishing, the Gresley Society, the LNER (SVR) Carriage Group and the Kidderminster Railway Museum; to all of the foregoing I owe a debt of gratitude. Any errors or omissions are, of course, entirely my own responsibility.

Herbert Nigel Gresley and his family

Herbert Nigel Gresley, fifth child of the Rector of Netherseal, Derbyshire, the Reverend Nigel Gresley, was born on 19 June 1876. His grandfather was the Reverend Sir William Gresley, Bart, ninth holder of the baronetcy conferred originally on Sir George Gresley in 1611, when King James I instituted hereditary baronetcies. Unlike his siblings the future Sir Nigel Gresley was born not at Netherseal but at 14 (now 34) Dublin Street, Edinburgh. Apparently his mother was in fragile health, having previously lost a baby, and was visiting Edinburgh in order to consult a prominent female Scots obstetrician, Nigel arriving rather sooner than expected. In the city of his birth Sir Nigel is commemorated by a memorial plaque located in the main concourse area at Waverley station in Edinburgh.

The Gresley family can claim family connections back to the Norman Conquest, when the Duke of Normandy's entourage included the three sons – Ralph, Robert and Nigel – of one Roger de Toeni, Lord of the Manor of Conches. Robert received considerable gifts of appropriated English land, staying in England for the remainder of his life and becoming known as Robert de Stafford. Robert's successor was his younger son, Nigel, whose own son, William Fitz-Nigel de Stafford, settled in Derbyshire, at Drakelowe. When this village was ravaged by plague *c*1095 the de Stafford family hurriedly moved to the neighbouring village of Gresley, now known as Church Gresley. By 1129 William was known, as was the custom of the time with landowners, as William Fitz-Nigel de Gresley. Sometime in the 14th century the Gresleys returned to Drakelowe, which remained the family seat until it was sold in 1933. Many of the Gresley family members, including Sir Nigel and his wife, Ethel, are interred in the old graveyard opposite the village church in Netherseal, where a descriptive panel gives brief details of his illustrious career, and his childhood home at the old rectory is honoured with a blue plaque affixed early in 2013.

It is certain that Nigel's first railway journey was made within a few weeks of his birth, when he returned home to Derbyshire with his mother. The route chosen is unknown, but the simplest would have been by direct Midland Railway service from Edinburgh via the Waverley and Settle & Carlisle routes to Trent and thence to the local station at Donisthorpe (on the joint LNW/Midland line linking Burton and Nuneaton). Nigel was an excellent example of the strong affinity between the Church and railway engineering. 'Sons of the Manse' who became successful locomotive engineers include not only Gresley but H. A. Ivatt, Patrick and James Stirling, F. W. Webb, C. J. Bowen-Cooke and Sir Vincent Raven.

As was the custom of the time the young Herbert Nigel, having attained in 1884 the tender age of eight years, was sent away from home to Preparatory School at St Leonards-on-Sea. Then, in 1890, having attained the age of 14 years, he began schooling at Marlborough College, leaving at the age of 17 in July 1893, preferring to take up a practical training rather than stay in the sixth form. Marlborough had been founded in order to undertake the education of sons of the clergy and was coincidentally the birthplace of his successor at the LNER, Edward Thompson, whose father was a master. Herbert Nigel had shown an early aptitude for practical work by becoming an accomplished woodworker, and a lectern he constructed whilst at Marlborough survives in his father's church (St Peter's) in Netherseal. Another survivor from his early days is a highly prophetic detailed Gresley drawing, made at the age of 13, of a Great Northern 2-2-2 express engine, Stirling single No 234.

BELOW Stopwatch in hand, for the purpose of checking the train speed, Sir Nigel sits in a First-class seat in the 'Coronation' high-speed Edinburgh–King's Cross service. The stopwatch survives in the possession of the Gresley Society Trust. *Gresley Society collection*

1

EARLY YEARS AT CREWE

On 17 October 1893, aged 17, Gresley was enrolled as a premium apprentice at the Crewe works of the London & North Western Railway. Crewe was at that time known to be Britain's 'premier' locomotive works, under the LNWR's CME, Francis Webb, and Works Manager, Henry Earl. Gresley's Crewe notebooks have been preserved and show him to have been an attentive student not only of locomotive details but also of ancillary machinery. These notebooks and his many Crewe drawings confirm that Gresley had a most particular grasp of attention to detail.

Nigel's wages as an apprentice were four shillings per week, rising after four years to 24 shillings as an 'improver' in the fitting and erecting shops at Crewe by March 1897. His father had died on 29 January 1897, which must have placed a further strain on family finances. Although Crewe Works was the centrepiece of the 'Premier Line' locomotive engineering the same could not be said of its design side under the ageing Webb, and it is not surprising that Gresley should have sought drawing-office training elsewhere.

Horwich and the LYR

Aged 22 in 1898, Gresley was engaged as a pupil by J. A. F. (later Sir John) Aspinall, CME of the Lancashire & Yorkshire Railway, commencing work in the Drawing Office at Horwich. An interesting letter, dated 24 March 1899, survives in the family archives, written by Aspinall in reply to a letter from Gresley's mother seeking regular employment for her son. This tends to confirm the view that after the death of his father the family's finances were under some strain and that paid employment for Nigel was of some priority for his mother. Aspinall regretted 'that it will not be possible to find work for your son at these works [i.e. Horwich] when he is out of his time, but if I find it possible to allow him to remain here for one month after his pupilage I shall be willing to consider that question if your son sees me personally on the subject'. This led to a six-month period in charge of the Materials Test Room at Horwich, confirming a lifelong interest in materials and locomotive testing which was to lead ultimately to the establishment in 1948 of the Rugby Locomotive Testing Plant; Gresley would also arrange for all of his own pupils to spend a period in the test room at Doncaster.

In 1899 Aspinall's large-boilered Atlantic-type locomotives with inside cylinders emerged from Horwich, this notable advance in the use of big boilers no doubt impressing the young Gresley as he completed his design-initiation course in the Drawing Office. Another design feature destined to appear in Gresley's designs was the swing-link locomotive bogie, which had appeared at Inchicore Works in Dublin during the era of Alexander McDonnell and been imported to Horwich by Aspinall, the latter's successor in Ireland, H. A. Ivatt, subsequently taking this design feature to Doncaster. It is scarcely surprising, therefore, that Gresley, having come across such bogies at Horwich and then Doncaster, should have used them on his own bogie locomotives.

A contemporary of Gresley at Horwich was H. Fowler, later Sir Henry Fowler, CME of the London, Midland & Scottish Railway from 1925, while another to spend time as a pupil under Aspinall at Horwich (following a pupilage at Inchicore Works) was one R. E. L. Maunsell, destined to become Chief Mechanical Engineer of the South Eastern & Chatham Railway in 1913 and of the Southern in 1923. Thus it was that between 1925 and 1931 three of the 'Big Four' railways had CMEs who were former Horwich men.

In 1899 Gresley was appointed for the summer season to an arduous position as running-shed foreman at Blackpool. This appointment clearly did not occupy all his time, for it was here that he met his future wife, Ethel Frances Fullager, daughter of W. P. Fullager, a well-known solicitor of St Annes, the couple marrying in October 1901. In the meantime he had been promoted again (in the autumn of 1900) to Outdoor Assistant to the Carriage & Wagon Superintendent, supervising carriage repairers at sidings and large passenger stations and checking the work of wagon examiners and repair staff in goods yards. Further promotion soon followed, Gresley being appointed in 1901 (at the age of 25) Assistant Works Manager of the Carriage & Wagon Works at Newton Heath, where just one year later, on 1 April 1902, he became Works Manager. Two years later he became Assistant Carriage & Wagon Superintendent, at a salary of £450 per annum. During his brief tenure he had created a firm impression amongst the staff at Newton Heath, and this was reflected in the presentation of a silver rose bowl from the LYR's Carriage & Wagon staff 'with the good wishes of a host of friends' on the occasion of his departure in 1905 for the Great Northern Railway at Doncaster.

2

CARRIAGE & WAGON SUPERINTENDENT, GREAT NORTHERN RAILWAY

In the autumn of 1904 the Great Northern Railway's Carriage & Wagon Superintendent, Frank Howlden, had decided to retire, having attained the age of 60 years, whereupon the GNR's directors interviewed six applicants in November but failed to find a suitable candidate. The GNR CME, Henry Ivatt, then wrote to his old Crewe and Inchicore friend and colleague, Aspinall, seeking help in finding a suitable candidate. Aspinall recommended his recently promoted and highly talented junior colleague, and, after interviewing Gresley, Ivatt informed the directors in January 1905 that he had appointed the now 28-year-old, at an annual salary of £750.

Among the unsuccessful candidates was Francis Wintour, who at the time was Locomotive Superintendent at King's Cross. He had not long to cope with his disappointment, as he was soon appointed to the post of Works Manager, Doncaster (and Assistant Locomotive Engineer), also at £750 per annum. However, a minute of the GNR Locomotive Committee records a statement from Ivatt that at Doncaster Gresley was to be regarded as senior to all, save Ivatt himself! Despite this apparent insult Wintour and Gresley worked closely together until Wintour's retirement in 1927. (Indeed, the esteem in which he was held by Gresley is evidenced by the fact that he was subsequently invited back to join the select group for the naming at Marylebone of No 4498 as *Sir Nigel Gresley* in November 1937, where he was photographed at Gresley's right hand.)

When they moved to Doncaster, to 'Milford', in Thorne Road, Mr and Mrs Gresley had two small children, Nigel and Violet, both born in Lancashire. Soon the family would be complete, Roger being born on 15 July 1906, and Marjorie on 15 September 1908. The boys were given family names (unlike the girls), though none was given a second Christian name. In 1910, while staying with his widowed mother, Nigel suffered an injury which nearly proved fatal. His elder brother, Nigel Bowyer Gresley, was also visiting from his home in Canada, and the two had been out shooting when H. N. got a black-thorn in his right leg. His brother managed to remove it with a penknife, but the wound became infected, and phlebitis set in. The local doctor thought that the leg might have to be amputated, but the GNR Chairman, Lord Allerton, on hearing of the matter, arranged for a specialist to be sent down from London, and the wound was cleansed by the application of medical leeches. H. N. always was subject to a very tender spot on his right leg, and his desk had a felt pad attached in order to prevent any painful reminders of this incident. It is interesting – and indicative of the esteem in which Nigel was held by the Chairman – that Lord Allerton should take such an interest in the welfare of the Carriage & Wagon Superintendent, and this tends to confirm the view sometimes expressed that by this time Gresley was already regarded as Ivatt's 'heir apparent'.

Carriage design, 1905-23

GNR carriage and wagon design had been in the direct control of Howlden since 1877, and he had been responsible for a number of significant developments, the first being the introduction in 1879 of dining cars, initially for First-class passengers only but extended to Third-class passengers from 1896. They were followed in 1881 by side-corridor carriages and then, in 1896, by the most significant and long-lasting innovation – the standardisation of Pullman gangways and the buckeye centre coupler. Originally developed in USA, this vestibule and coupler provide a stronger and safer connection between corridor coaches than the screw coupling and bellows of the British Standard gangway arrangement. Because of its enhanced safety features – keeping derailed vehicles upright and in line, with consequently much-reduced capacity for telescoping – this design would eventually become the standard for all new construction by British Railways from 1951, despite its being recommended in numerous accident reports for many years beforehand. Since 1896 it must have been responsible for saving the lives of many passengers travelling in, successively, GNR, LNER and BR Mk 1, 2, 3 and 4 stock. Clerestory roofs were used on all Howlden's vestibuled corridor stock, as they were on other British railways until 1904, when the GWR began building coaches with the now-universal semi-elliptical roof.

The partners in the East Coast route – the Great Northern, North Eastern and North British railways – had for many years produced East Coast Joint Stock for the operation of Anglo-Scottish expresses. Much of the earlier stock had been designed by David Bain of the North Eastern and had been built in the North Eastern carriage shops at York, but progressively Doncaster took over the construction of this 'premier' fleet. One notable survivor is ECJS Third-class dining car No 189 of 1894, currently being restored by the LNER Coach Association at Pickering, on the North Yorkshire Moors Railway.

For several months after Gresley's appointment the Doncaster carriage shops continued to turn out clerestory-roofed corridor stock to Howlden's designs. The first signs of the new regime appeared early in 1905 in the form of two 'steam rail motor-cars', Nos 1 and 2, which featured Gresley-designed elliptical roofs. A further four steam-powered cars were built by contractors, and an additional two petrol-engined cars at Doncaster. In the spring of 1906 Doncaster built an ECJS bogie luggage van, No 126. This had an elliptical roof with bowed ends, Pullman gangways and buckeye couplers; it was also the first Doncaster vehicle to have an underframe, solebars and truss-rods built entirely of steel, with a body of teak with pine roof boards. This was Gresley's prototype for all future main-line stock. Later in 1906 new coaches were built for the GNR 'Manchester fliers', each being supplied with three sets of four coaches. This was typical GNR practice, perpetuated by the LNER, whereby complete trains were supplied with all-new stock as a single set. The two afternoon departures were worked by GCR motive power between Manchester and Grantham, whence they had the fastest timings on the GNR to and from King's Cross.

The new elliptical-roofed stock, stronger and lighter than the older clerestory type, gave more light and air inside the coach and was far neater in appearance, while the teak finish was enhanced by white-painted roofs. Another innovation was electric lighting, then a novelty in a British carriage. Four-wheel bogies were fitted to the first three vehicles of each set, but to afford especially smooth riding the dining cars were mounted on six-wheel bogies, a practice which ceased when four-wheeled compound-bolster bogies came into use. These 1906 sets, despite operating through to Manchester, were known as 'Sheffield stock' and marked an important stage in the development of GNR express-passenger-train construction. Externally they set a pattern for future construction which lasted with but minor changes until Gresley's death in 1941.

Another early innovation associated with the new regime was the January 1906 experiment at King's Cross, where a rake of GNR stock equipped with the GNR stem-storage heating system was compared with a rake of North Eastern stock heated by the now-familiar low-pressure steam drawn directly from a locomotive. The North Eastern stock reached the required temperature in 15 minutes, compared with 75 for the GNR set. Henceforth direct locomotive heating became standard for GNR and ECJS carriages.

In 1907 the locomotive chiefs of the East Coast partners recommended that all future ECJS carriages should follow the Gresley exterior pattern, whether built at Doncaster or York. This was probably a reaction to the construction by the North Eastern in 1906, as part of an economy drive, of some rather ugly straight-sided ECJS carriages. The external design adopted for all future ECJS stock followed that of the 'Sheffield stock', again showing the significance of this particular design. A project initiated at an ECJS meeting in 1906 and completed in 1908 was the construction of two new Royal carriages, one each for the King and the Queen – No 395, the King's saloon, being built at Doncaster and No 396 at York. Both of these most impressive vehicles have survived, No 395 at the National Railway Museum and No 396 at Bressingham.

A further wide-ranging innovation appeared in 1907 with the introduction of articulated coaches. Ever seeking innovation and economy, Gresley arranged for some elderly Stirling/Howlden carriages with bodies which were capable of life extension to be mounted in pairs with three bogies between the two coaches, the centre bogie forming an articulated unit beneath the inner ends of the carriages. Brakes had originally been fitted to alternate axles only; now all the wheels were braked. A weight reduction of 14cwt was achieved with improved braking power. Gresley took out a patent for articulation of carriages, which soon became common practice on the GNR, being perpetuated by the LNER and copied on a smaller scale by both the LMS and GWR.

Combined with buckeye couplers and Pullman gangways, articulated vehicles provide a significant safety enhancement, the downside being that a technical problem with one vehicle often affects all vehicles in the set. The weight saving achieved through articulation is quite significant, as is evident from preserved 1924 'Quad-Art' set No 74 (now resident on the North Norfolk Railway), which in the standard eight-carriage formation provides more than 600 seats in a train weighing only 180 tons tare. Articulation is still used by the TGV and Eurostar sets, and these have proved their safety features in several high-speed derailments in which no passengers have been killed or seriously injured.

There are now only a handful of survivors from this era. In addition to the two Royal Train vehicles, Nos 395 and 396, only a further two ECJS vehicles survive – a beautifully restored gangwayed full brake, No 82, part of the National Collection at York, and No 377, a Corridor Third, partially restored at Llangollen. The GNR is represented by eight vehicles, of which 1909 Doncaster-built Invalid Saloon No 3087 is fully restored

ABOVE Built at Doncaster in 1922 as a Diagram 164K Corridor Composite, carriage No 2701 was used on King's Cross–Cambridge services until 1958, when it was converted as a camping coach at Mundesley, Norfolk. Further converted in 1963 for departmental service, it ended up as an office at Boston, finally being sold in the 1980s for use as a pub dining room at Swineshead (Lincolnshire) and then Heanor, whence it was rescued by the LNER (SVR) Coach Fund in 1994. Acquired as an empty shell, it was painstakingly restored over many years, the work not being completed until 2008. The result is seen here at Bewdley, on the Severn Valley Railway. *Richard Hill*

and operational on the North Yorkshire Moors Railway and 1912 First family saloon No 807 is beautifully restored at Carnforth. The most recent full restoration is 1922 Corridor Composite No 2701, an authentic vehicle magnificently restored after more than 10 years' work by the LNER (SVR) Coach Fund at the Severn Valley Railway. Partially restored are 1912 Brake Composite Corridor No 229 at Llangollen and 1912

Open First No 397 in use, much modified, at the Valley Junction Restaurant in Jesmond. The other three have survived unrestored in poor condition; two 1906 examples are Open Brake Third (rebuilt as full brake) No 1798, currently at Kirkby Stephen, and Corridor Third (later Tool Van) No 2440, at the Colne Valley Railway, the other being 1910 Brake First (later packing Van) No 3178, currently at Mangapps Farm. All of these vehicles exhibit the classic Gresley features of elliptical roof, Pullman gangways and buckeye couplers.

Wagon design, 1905-23

Despite the predominance of privately owned contractor-built wagons in the movement of coal traffic, wagon design was an important part of Gresley's responsibilities. At the Grouping the GNR bequeathed the LNER some 38,000 wagons, the third-largest total, after the NER's 123,000 and the NBR's 56,000 (the NER figure reflecting its large fleet of company-owned mineral hoppers). It was a innovation in wagon

ABOVE The restoration of No 2701 won the Heritage Railway Association's 2009 Rolling Stock award, and the vehicle carries a plaque to this effect. It is seen here at Bridgnorth. *Richard Hill*

ABOVE Interior of one of No 2701's First-class compartments. *Richard Hill*

design that first brought Gresley's talents to the attention of a wider audience, in an article in the July 1906 edition of *The Railway Engineer*. This featured an experimental bogie brick wagon with a capacity of 35 tons, built at Doncaster and featuring swivelling bogies for use with wagon turntables, the design being correctly attributed to H. N. Gresley. The wagons were fitted with vacuum brakes, and two or three soon became a frequent sight at the head of Peterborough–London brick trains next to the Ivatt 'Long-Tom' 0-8-0 locomotive, providing a useful addition to the braking power of these heavy trains. A further 25 wagons, of enhanced (50-ton) capacity, were introduced in 1921, another 25 being introduced by the LNER in 1930. One of these bogie brick wagons featured in the models

offered by Hornby Dublo in the 1940s and '50s, in addition to an 'A4', an 'N2' and tinplate 'teak' carriages.

Another design innovation appearing in 1907 were two bogie girder well-wagons, coded 'Flatrol S', for the conveyance of heavy machinery and large boilers. As part of the testing of the 40-ton capacity of this wagon Gresley arranged for Stirling 4-2-2 No 221 to be loaded and photographed being moved about the Doncaster Works yard. Railways were then still 'common carriers' and had to provide special vehicles for a wide variety of exceptional loads, some out-of-gauge, which demanded great ingenuity in coping with the demands being placed, in terms of size and capacity, within the constraints of Britain's very restricted loading gauge.

3

LOCOMOTIVE ENGINEER, GREAT NORTHERN RAILWAY

Like Howlden, Ivatt decided to retire early, on 16 September 1911, his 60th birthday. When this news became known there was considerable speculation amongst the railway community as to his possible successor. The GNR's directors had not previously selected a candidate from within the company, Sturrock, Stirling and Ivatt himself having all come from other railways. However, Ivatt had come to appreciate Gresley's capabilities and advised the Board that they need look no further for his successor. Indeed during the last few years of Ivatt's term of office Gresley had come to be regarded as his chief assistant, despite Frances Wintour's holding the title of Assistant Locomotive Engineer in addition to his substantive post of Works Manager, Doncaster. The issue had in part been complicated by Gresley's phlebitis, from which he did not fully recover until well into 1911. At

the age of 35 he was, however, well enough to succeed Ivatt as Locomotive Engineer with effect from 1 October 1911, at the greatly enhanced salary of £1,800 per annum.

The locomotive situation facing Gresley in 1911 was far more satisfactory than that with which Ivatt had been confronted in 1896. For express passenger work Ivatt's 94 large Atlantics were to remain masters of their task until the increased loads experienced after the onset of World War 1 required pilot assistance, at least as far as Potters Bar. The Ivatt fleet comprised a range of standardised locomotives perfectly adequate for the tasks required of them, the only obvious need being for a large mixed-traffic design to work the increasingly important fast freight services whilst having the capability to cope with passenger trains at times of peak demand. Indeed one of the first reports (dated 23 January 1912) made by Gresley made to the Locomotive Committee would comment on the significant freight-train mileage being worked by passenger locomotives, with adverse consequences for train loading and coal consumption. Accordingly his first design was for a mixed-traffic Mogul, the 'H2'.

The 'J22' (later LNER 'J6') 5ft 2in 0-6-0 tender engines

The need for a new mixed-traffic type notwithstanding, the first locomotives to emerge under the new regime were (as would be the case many times during Gresley's 40-year tenure) an enhancement of an existing successful design,

LEFT Colwick-allocated 'J6' No 3628 (Doncaster, March 1920) arrives at Nottingham Victoria with an excursion train bound for Skegness, formed of Gresley articulated suburban stock.
Gresley Society collection

the 20 5ft 2in Ivatt 'J22' 0-6-0s of 1909/10, enhanced with Schmidt superheaters, twin anti-vacuum valves and a modified cab design, while the boiler was set back further in the frames. In all some 95 locomotives of this '536 series' were turned out by Doncaster before class construction ceased in 1922. They quickly took over the main-line goods duties across the GNR network, examples being allocated to all the principal sheds, including Manchester Trafford Park, where they replaced Ivatt 4-4-0s on the arduous fast goods service to Colwick, and Colwick itself, the latter's allocation working through to Manchester and Liverpool via both the Midland and Great Central routes (over which the GNR had running powers) to Manchester and thence via the Cheshire Lines route to Liverpool. Following the introduction from 1912 of the 'H2' and 'H3' 2-6-0s the 'J22s' were seen less often on the main line and in the London area apart from limited use on the Dunstable branch.

Rebuilds of the 'J15', 'J16' and 'J17' (later 'J54', 'J55' and 'J56') 0-6-0 tank engines

Among the early tasks undertaken by Gresley was to pick up the rebuilding in more modern form of the Stirling shunting saddle tanks of Classes J15, J16 and J17. Ivatt had rebuilt a couple of these locomotives in 1897 and three more, at the rate of one per year, in 1906, 1907 and 1908. Gresley took a more active line, and from 1913 a further 23 locomotives were rebuilt, to be followed by another 28 after the Grouping. As with the 'J23s', existing 4ft 5in-diameter boilers (rendered surplus by new 4ft 8in standard boilers being fitted to larger locomotives) were utilised, supplemented by some new 4ft 5in construction, although there were to be no new domeless boilers. Only three locomotives,

Nos 3859, 3908 and 4990, would survive to be renumbered in 1946, as 8317, 8318 and 8319, of which only Nos 8317 and 8319 would pass into BR ownership, No 68319 finally being withdrawn from Departmental service in July 1950.

The 'H2' and 'H3' (later 'K1' and 'K2') two-cylinder 2-6-0s

The GNR had some previous experience with locomotives with the 2-6-0 wheel arrangement. At the turn of the century British locomotive works had been suffering a shortage of capacity, and several railways had resorted to purchasing locomotives from overseas, among them the GNR, which in 1899 had purchased 20 2-6-0s from the Baldwin Locomotive Co, of the USA. These were intended primarily for everyday goods work; three had been tried for a short period on London suburban trains, but, being non-standard in many ways, they did not last long in service once the urgency had passed. However, the American Moguls had clearly impressed the British railway authorities and led indirectly to a number of developments, of which the first significant example was the Great Western Railway's '43xx' 2-6-0 introduced by Churchward in 1911.

Just over a year after the Churchward Mogul came the first true Gresley design in the form of No 1630, a 2-6-0 with 5ft

8in-diameter driving wheels and two 20in-diameter cylinders with a 26in stroke and 10in piston valves operated by outside Walschaerts valve gear, in the first British application for a main-line locomotive. As the design was prepared with some speed an existing boiler design – as fitted to Ivatt's Class K1 0-8-0 mineral engine, complete with Schmidt superheater – was used, of 4ft 8in diameter, but with a shorter barrel. The order for the first locomotive was issued in March 1912, and No 1630 appeared in August, to be followed by a further nine locomotives. Early experience of the performance of No 1630 when working at sustained maximum power indicated that the boiler lacked the capacity to meet the highest demands being placed upon it, and a larger (5ft 6in-diameter) boiler, fitted with the Robinson design of superheater, was designed in 1913, being fitted to Nos 1640-9 in 1914. These and subsequent locomotives were designated 'H3', the class ultimately numbering 75 examples – 20 built by Doncaster, 20 by the North British Locomotive Co and 25 by Kitson & Co.

The 'H2' and 'H3' Moguls proved to be highly capable mixed-traffic locomotives, equally at home on express goods and ordinary passenger and excursion work. The first 'H2s' were allocated to King's Cross, taking charge of both fast good trains to Peterborough and passenger services as far as Cambridge. They also appeared on excursions to such destinations as Skegness.

After the arrival of the larger-boilered 'H3' class the 'H2s' moved north to Colwick, Doncaster and Peterborough. The 'H3s' worked in the same areas on the more arduous duties and in addition appeared at Ardsley. Here they were frequently used on express passenger work, their extra adhesion giving them a distinct advantage on the severe gradients out of both Leeds and Bradford. Two 'H2s' were re-boilered in 1920/1 with 5ft 6in boilers, being redesignated 'H3', releasing spare 4ft 8in boilers to provide spares for the 'H2s'. All would pass into LNER stock, being designated 'K1' and 'K2', the remaining eight 'H2s' ('K1s') being rebuilt as 'K2s' during the 1930s. The locomotives gained an early reputation for lively riding characteristics and soon acquired the collective nickname 'Ragtimers', after a popular dance craze of the time.

By 1924 the first of the new 'K3' 2-6-0s had begun to take over the hardest duties, allowing six 'K1s' and six 'K2s' to be

BELOW Class K2 2-6-0 No 1699 (Kitson, August 1921) on shed at King's Cross in 1921. New to New England shed, as LNER No 4699 this locomotive was destined to be transferred to Eastfield in 1925, being modified to comply with the North British loading gauge; fitted with a side-window cab and named *Loch Laidon* in June 1934, it would be withdrawn in September 1959 as BR No 61789 and cut up at Cowlairs in December of the same year. *Gresley Society collection*

ABOVE Smart-looking Colwick-allocated 'K2' No 61771 (Kitson & Co, June 1921) rests on shed at its home depot in the early 1950s. The former No 4681/1771 was a Colwick resident between 1945 and 1958 and would be again for its last three months before withdrawal on 16 December 1960, ultimately being cut up at Doncaster early in 1961. *J. Tarrant/Kidderminster Railway Museum*

BELOW 'K2' No 61772 *Loch Lochy* (Kitson, June 1921) on shed at Parkhead on 30 July 1954. New as GNR No 1682 and later LNER No 4682 and 1772, it had been modified to meet the NB loading gauge in 1931 and named April 1933. Withdrawn from Parkhead in November 1959, it would be cut up at Cowlairs in January 1960. *P. Groom*

transferred to the Great Eastern Section, both types appearing at March and Stratford and the 'K2s' additionally Cambridge. In 1925 14 'K2s' were transferred to the Scottish Area, while in 1927/8 a further 13 moved to the GE Section. All of these transfers necessitated some physical changes to the locomotives, as both the GE and Scottish areas had a more restrictive loading gauge than that of the generous GNR, to which they had been constructed. Although they had been designed specifically for fast-freight work Stratford, in particular, soon exploited the locomotives' wider abilities, such that they could be observed on express passenger trains throughout East Anglia and as far north as Lincoln.

The Scottish locomotives were initially concentrated at Eastfield, where they took over West Highland line services from the 'D34' 4-4-0s in an attempt to reduce the instances of double-heading on the regular passenger services, on which the permitted load for a 'K2' load was 220 tons, compared with the 190 tons for a 'D34'. The number of 'K2s' north of the border was increased to 20 in 1931/2, allowing them to be allocated to St Margarets in addition to Eastfield. Postwar, in 1951, another 10 would be transferred to Scotland, being allocated to Parkhead, Dunfermline and Thornton sheds, while a further transfer, in 1952, would see nine locomotives working on the former GNoS Section, from Kittybrewster and Keith. Despite the discomfort of their GN cabs (addressed by 1935 with the provision of side-window cabs), rough ride, right-hand drive and pull-out regulators the Scottish 'K2s' would remain hard at work on the West Highland line until 1961. In 1933/4 the 13 'K2s' that worked regularly over the West Highland line were graced with the names of various lochs close to the line. Elsewhere the 'K2s' demonstrated their versatility by remaining on virtually the same work into the 1960s. All passed into BR stock in 1948, the final survivor, No 61756, lasting until June 1962.

Developments in superheating
The GNR had begun to experiment with superheating as early as 1905, with an experimental fitting of a Schmidt-design superheater to a 'Long-Tom' 0-8-0 coal engine. This had been followed in 1908 by the first application to an express passenger locomotive, a 'Small Atlantic'. The economies in fuel consumption thereby achieved were sufficiently great that in 1910 the final 10 'Large Atlantics' were all fitted with Gresley's own-design equipment, further development of the Schmidt design being hampered by the poor bolted design of the attachment of the elements to the header in the smokebox – and the patent fees required for each installation. Robinson of the Great Central then produced a design whereby the elements were expanded directly into the header; this proved to be a much more robust arrangement and would be widely used, including by Gresley in his larger locomotives. In 1913, however,

Gresley patented his own design of twin-tube superheater, which was used initially in one of the 'H2' Moguls and then in three 'Small Atlantics' and 10 'Large Atlantics'. Apart from the effects on lubrication, one of the problems introduced by the use of higher-temperature steam was the potential for overheating of the elements when coasting. Initially damping apparatus was used, but Ivatt's solution was to insert a 'snifting' valve on the inlet side of the header, to allow the ingress of cooling air. Gresley's design, in the shape of a mushroom and fitted immediately behind the chimney, became one of the distinctive features of his locomotives.

The 'O1' (later 'O3') two-cylinder 2-8-0s
Mixed-traffic requirements having been met, the next priority was for a heavy-freight locomotive to supplement the 55-strong fleet of Ivatt 'K1'/'K2' 0-8-0s. By 1913 the 'Long-Toms' were fully extended in coping with the increasing volumes of coal traffic originating in Yorkshire and the East Midlands. Rather than resorting yet again to double-heading Gresley produced a large 2-8-0 design, classified 'O1', with two cylinders, of 21in diameter and 28in stroke, fed by a 5ft 6in-diameter boiler, fitted with a 24-element superheater, that set the standard for future construction of all his larger locomotives. Outside Walschaerts valve gear was employed, driving 10in piston valves, as on the 'H2' Moguls. The front end was supported by a Gresley-designed double-bolster swing-link pony truck.

In February 1913 Doncaster received orders for six boilers – five for the 'O1s' and one for the prototype three-cylinder 'O2'. It was anticipated that further locomotives would be built at Doncaster in 1916, but the pressure of armaments work left insufficient capacity, and eventually an order for a further 15 'O1s' was completed by the North British Locomotive Co in 1919, giving a final fleet of 20 locomotives.

The first five 'O1' locos were allocated initially to Peterborough (New England) shed where they worked 80-wagon block loads of coal up the GN main line to Ferme Park, returning north with the empties; this represented an increase of 20 wagons over the load permitted for their predecessors, the 'Q1' and 'Q2' 0-8-0s. They also worked north with coal empties to Doncaster via the GN&GE Joint line through Spalding and Lincoln, returning with loaded coal trains and also regularly worked two 80-wagon daily trains of potatoes from Spalding to King's Cross.

From the second batch four locomotives were delivered to Colwick, where they were responsible for working two daily 80-wagon coal trains to New England, returning with the empties. With occasional short-term changes the 'O1s' remained on this work until reallocation of 10 locomotives to Grantham in November 1942 to work iron-ore trains on the steeply graded branches from High Dyke to Stainby and Sproston and the subsequent block loads to Frodingham via Lincoln and Barnetby.

In February 1944 the 'O1s' were reclassified 'O3', the 'O1' classification henceforth being applied to the Thompson rebuilds of Robinson Class O4 2-8-0s. From June 1945 the Grantham ore workings were taken over by 'O2s' transferred from New England, and the entire class (now as 'O3') was concentrated at Doncaster, a further move to Frodingham between 1946 and 1948 being followed by a return to Doncaster and Retford. Withdrawals commenced in 1947; by the start of 1952 only four remained in service, and the class became extinct with the withdrawal of No 63484 in December of that year.

The 'J23' (later 'J50') 0-6-0 tank engines

The steeply graded branch lines in the West Riding were in urgent need of something with greater power and adhesion than the motley collection of elderly 0-6-0 tender engines currently in use. Gresley's third new design was therefore an 0-6-0 tank designed specifically for these routes, with cylinders enlarged to 18½in and the greater adhesion and flexibility of a 56-ton tank engine. As the intended work comprised mainly short trips and shunting, a large-capacity boiler was not required, so a useful economy was achieved by utilising the 4ft 2in boilers rendered surplus by re-boilering the 'L1' 0-8-2s. Instead of the traditional saddle tank the locomotives were provided with side tanks with a distinctive tapered front end to give an enhanced forward view for shunting and with apertures in the sides for ease of

access to the motion. Between 1913 and 1919 three batches of 10 locomotives each were delivered from Doncaster, followed by another 10 with 4ft 5in boilers in 1922. The design became a Group Standard, a further 52 locomotives being constructed between 1926 and 1939 and the originals rebuilt to the same standard between 1929 and 1935, providing an ultimate fleet of 102 'J50' locomotives.

As the locomotives were designed specifically for work in the West Riding their allocations were initially all to Ardsley and Bradford, Copley Hill gaining a couple in 1922 for marshalling passenger stock. Once expanded as a Group Standard design the 'J50' became more widespread across the LNER's Southern Area, with allocations to Immingham and Stratford, where hump shunting at Goodmayes and Temple Mills became regular work. An unusual move in 1926 was of seven locomotives to Eastfield, where they found work shunting at Cadder and Sighthill yards. In 1938 'J50s' arrived at Hatfield, King's Cross and Hornsey. Between 1942 and 1945 four locomotives were loaned to the War Department for use at military ports in Scotland. In 1952 a further 30 'J50s' were transferred to

Hornsey, where they took over cross-London trip workings to the Southern Region via the Widened Lines and trips to Temple Mills, taking enhanced loads over the previously employed 'J52s' and 'N1s'.

Withdrawal commenced in 1958, the last 'J50' in normal service being withdrawn in September 1963, but between 1961/2 and 1965 seven examples were used on Departmental shunting work in the Doncaster area (replacing 'J52s'), thus becoming the last survivors of the class.

Development of the Ivatt Atlantic

Despite the diversion of much works capacity to the requirement to produce munitions for World War 1 it is clear that Gresley's innovative mind was engaged in plans to produce more-powerful passenger designs, given greater prominence by the much-increased passenger train loads brought by the onset of war. Despite the generous height permitted by the GNR loading gauge, width restrictions imposed by platforms and other structures restricted the size of outside cylinders, and the space between locomotive frames imposed similar limitations on the size of inside cylinders. One solution would be to increase boiler pressure, but apart from the extra costs imposed by the heavier plates required to meet strength requirements

this also brought forth problems caused by excessive formation of boiler scale, in an era before the application of water treatment. The chosen route was therefore to develop the multi-cylinder layout with which Ivatt had already conducted experiments in 1905 and 1907. Involving three four-cylinder compound Atlantics, these had been inconclusive, so the design produced in 1913 was for a four-cylinder simple, and two years later 'Large Atlantic' No 279 was rebuilt in this form, for evaluation as a possible prototype. No 279 had two sets of Walschaerts valve gear, with the valves of the inside cylinders driven by an arrangement of rocking shafts. The arrangement of a single slide-bar cross-head for the inside cylinders was the first application of what was to become another Gresley 'standard' fitting. The standard Robinson 18-element design superheater was used, subsequently enlarged to the 24- and then 32-element size which became standard for the whole class.

BELOW By now in its final form, with piston valves (from 1923) and 32-element superheater (fitted 1929), Ivatt 'C1' Atlantic No 4413 (Doncaster, March 1906) passes Huntingdon North No 1 signalbox with a parcels train in 1935. Originally GNR No 1413, this locomotive would survive until January 1946 – not long enough to receive its intended new number of 2846. *A. Butler/Kidderminster Railway Museum*

ABOVE Preserved original GNR 'Large Atlantic' No 251 (Doncaster, December 1902) draws into Lincoln with the 3.5pm from Retford on 26 August 1954. This train, along with the return 5.31pm Lincoln–Sheffield Victoria, was used for two weeks' running in for No 251 before Alan Pegler used it in September for specials to Liverpool and Farnborough, which duties it shared with 'D11' 4 4 0 No 62663 *Prince Albert*. Restored by the LNER in 1947 but latterly stored in Doncaster's paint shop, No 251 had been resurrected in September 1953 for use with 'Small Atlantic' No 990 *Henry Oakley* on the 'Plant Centenarian' specials from King's Cross to Doncaster and back. After the 12 September trip No 251 would return to the Doncaster paint shop, remaining there until moved to the original York Museum in March 1957. *P. J. Lynch/ Kidderminster Railway Museum*

BELOW Preserved 'C1' No 251 returns light-engine to Doncaster shed in August 1954 after a running in turn to Lincoln and Sheffield prior to working two railtours to Liverpool and Farnborough organised by Alan Pegler, the future owner of *Flying Scotsman*. *J. M. Jarvis/Kidderminster Railway Museum*

ABOVE Prototype GNR 'O2' No 461 (Doncaster, May 1918) rests at its home shed of New England in 1923. The locomotive would be renumbered 3461 in 1924 and again as 3921 in 1946 but would be withdrawn, from Langwith Junction in May 1948, before gaining its intended BR number of 63921. *R. H. Whitworth collection/Kidderminster Railway Museum*

Given the subsequent Gresley Pacific design of 1922, these developments provide significant pointers to the way in which Gresley's design thoughts were being developed. The Ivatt Atlantic in its final form as enhanced by Gresley is fortunately represented in preservation by the prototype 'Large Atlantic', No 251, currently at Locomotion, Shildon.

The 'O2' three-cylinder 2-8-0s

As described above, the 1913 order for five Diagram 13 boilers for the 'O1' 2-8-0s was supplemented by a sixth order for first of the new three-cylinder 'O2' class. It is indicative of the pressure of war work on Doncaster's capacity that this locomotive, to be No 461, was not actually ordered until February 1916 and did not appear until May 1918. Given the 1915 rebuild of Atlantic No 279 with the use of rocking shafts to drive the inside cylinder's valves and Gresley's 1915 patent for a conjugated valve gear for three-cylinder locomotives, it is hardly surprising that the design of the 'O2' which emerged in December 1916 incorporated this design detail, another distinctive feature of the classic Gresley-designed locomotive. The first patent for conjugated valve-gear operation had been taken out by Joy as early as 1884, for marine application, followed by a much more relevant design by Holcroft in 1909, which Gresley had been assured had expired in 1913. The collaboration with Holcroft, initially Churchward's technical assistant at Swindon and later Maunsell's assistant at the SECR, was significant and

continued for many years. Indeed, Holcroft having presented a paper on the subject at the Institute of Locomotive Engineers in November 1918, Gresley invited him to a meeting at King's Cross in January 1919 and followed this up with an offer of employment on the Great Northern, which Maunsell frustrated refusing to release him.

No 461 was Gresley's first three-cylinder design and embodied the alternative form of his conjugated valve gear, with the middle-cylinder valve operated by rocking shafts. The three-cylinder design brought significant advantages, three smaller cylinders together producing comparable power yet suffering less wear from the lighter pistons thereby made possible – and, more significantly, producing a much-reduced hammer-blow for each revolution, with six, lighter piston strokes rather than the four delivered by a two-cylinder locomotive. Railway civil engineers had begun to express disquiet over the effects of increased axle weights and severe hammer-blow on track and structures, and the weight saving and reduced hammer-blow of three cylinder designs provided an effective response to these

ABOVE Grantham-allocated 'O2' No 63940 (Doncaster, February 1924) rests on shed at Sheffield Darnall on 19 September 1954; Grantham having no regular mineral workings to Sheffield, the locomotive was presumably still being run in following a General Overhaul at Doncaster (completed 1 September) and had yet to return home or, alternatively, had been borrowed by Frodingham shed. Originally numbered 495N, then 3495 and 3940, it would be withdrawn from Doncaster in September 1963. *L. W. Perkins/Kidderminster Railway Museum*

BELOW Grantham-allocated 'O2' 2 8 0 No 63934 (Doncaster, November 1923) rests on shed at Grantham on 3 May 1960. Originally numbered 3489, the locomotive had been allocated initially to New England and was destined to be withdrawn from Retford, in July 1962. *P. Groom/ Gresley Society collection*

concerns. After the appearance of No 461 Gresley announced his intention of concentrating on three-cylinder designs for future construction.

A further order for 10 'O2s' was placed in March 1919, initially from Doncaster. However, as the latter was still heavily engaged in recovering arrears of wartime maintenance the order was transferred to the North British Locomotive Co's Atlas Works in Glasgow, materials and second-hand tenders being supplied by Doncaster. The cylinder and steam-chest layout was redesigned, permitting the use of the simpler design of the conjugated valve gear with two-to-one levers, as used on the 'H4' 2-6-0s of 1920. Following the Grouping another 15 locomotives were ordered from Doncaster in February 1923, delivery commencing in November of that year but not being completed until June 1924 and a further 16 being delivered in 1932 and 1933/4 for work between the new Whitemoor Yard at March and Temple Mills, in East London. The final batch of 25 locomotives was ordered to meet wartime requirements and delivered after Gresley's death, in 1942/3.

As the principal mineral traffic flow of the GNR was coal from the Nottinghamshire and South Yorkshire coalfields to London it was inevitable that the 'O2s' would be concentrated at New England shed for this huge and increasing traffic. Indeed, of the initial 26 locomotives only two (both delivered after the Grouping) were *not* sent new to New England, No 3496 being allocated to Doncaster for 10 months before joining the others and No 3501 to Newport, Teesside, in the North Eastern Area, for 10 months before the call to New England. Of the next batch 13 went straight to March, the other three going to Doncaster, which would be the initial home for all of the final batch. Wartime moves saw major reallocations to Colwick, many moving on to Langwith in 1946/7 before being transferred to Mexborough, Grantham and Retford sheds. The Langwith and Mexborough locomotives were engaged in the trans-Pennine coal flows over the Woodhead route before electrification, following which they moved to the iron-ore flows from south Lincolnshire to Scunthorpe and Teesside.

All the 'O2s' survived to pass into BR stock, and although prototype No 461 (latterly No 3921) was withdrawn in May 1948 the 66 production-series locomotives all continued into the 1960s, the last GNR example, No 479, surviving (as BR No 63924) until November 1963 along with five from the 1942/3 batch.

The 'H4' (later 'K3') 2-6-0s

In December 1918 Gresley produced an outline drawing for a new three-cylinder express goods 2-6-0 based on the 'H3' but having 18½in cylinders with 26in stroke and 180lb boiler pressure. This provided a 36% increase in tractive effort over the two-cylinder 'H3' locomotives. One development over the three-cylinder arrangement of 2-8-0 No 461 was a steeply inclined inside cylinder, in order to clear the leading coupled axle, whilst the two outside cylinders were almost horizontal. Such a layout was facilitated by an adjustment to the valve gear in line with Holcroft's January 1919 suggestions. Gresley also decided to use two-to-one levers ahead of the cylinders instead of a rocking shaft behind them. The new Diagram 9 boiler had a maximum diameter of 6ft, the largest that could be accommodated within the loading gauge, ensuring that – as with all Gresley designs – there was never any question regarding its ability to boil water.

The introduction of the 'H4' Moguls in 1920 coincided with the importation of jazz music, and because of their syncopated exhaust beat and swaying motion the locomotives quickly acquired the nickname 'Jazzers'. The first example, specially given the prestige number 1000, was allocated to New England and was employed on a diagram which took it daily from Peterborough to Grimsby and thence with a fast fish train to London before returning to Peterborough with fish empties for Grimsby. Another service to be allocated one of the new locomotives was the most prestigious of the three daily King's Cross–Manchester/Liverpool services, running in competition with both the Midland and LNWR, the 'H4' working between King's Cross and Colwick, sometimes with an engine change at Peterborough. The first 10 locomotives were allocated to King's Cross (two), Peterborough (five) and Doncaster (three).

The debut of the 'H4s' in service coincided with the coal strike from May to July 1921. The GNR's response was to combine numerous services in order to reduce coal consumption, and the loadings of many expresses soon outstripped the ability of the Atlantics, even with the provision of pilots as far as Potters Bar. Many services began to load to 16 or 17 coaches, and instances of 20 coaches were recorded. The 'H3' and 'H4' Moguls were soon transferred from their express goods work to take over the premier East Coast passenger trains, which they worked single-handed with great distinction.

Following the Grouping the 'H4', redesignated 'K3', became an LNER Group Standard design for mixed-traffic operation, and between 1924 and 1937 a further 183 locomotives were constructed. The only significant design alteration was the provision of a Darlington-style side-window cab in lieu of the rather austere GNR design seen on the first 10. The later locomotives were also built to the composite LNER loading gauge, being just a 13ft in height (in contrast to the 13ft 5in of the first 10, which were themselves altered to comply by 1940).

The first LNER-built locomotives, ordered in 1923 and 1924 in batches of 25, 25 and 10, were constructed by Darlington, appearing between August 1924 and December 1925. These were allocated 44 to the Southern Area, 10 to the North Eastern Area and six to the Scottish Area, these last being concentrated at Carlisle Canal shed for working express freight trains over the Waverley route; the North Eastern

TOP LEFT Overtaking an 'N2'-hauled local, a very smart GNR 'H4' 2-6-0, No 1003 (Doncaster, October 1920), storms past Holloway with a down express in 1921. Allocated initially to New England shed, this locomotive, reclassified 'K3' by the LNER and successively renumbered 4003, 1803 and 61803 (by BR), would be withdrawn from Doncaster in July 1961. *H. Gordon Tidey*

BOTTOM LEFT Passing a fine NER signal gantry, 'K3' No 4005 (Doncaster, April 1921) brings a down express into York on 21 August 1937. New to Doncaster shed as GNR No 1005, this locomotive would be withdrawn from Lincoln as BR No 61806 in March 1960 and cut up at Doncaster. *H. C. Doyle/Gresley Society collection*

TOP An official works photograph of 'K3' No 33 (Darlington, September 1924). Sent new to Blaydon shed, it would, as BR No 61813, be withdrawn from Hull Dairycoates in April 1962, to be cut up at Doncaster. *Ian Allan Library*

ABOVE 'K3' No 200 (Darlington, April 1925) had the distinction of being exhibited at the 1925 British Empire Exhibition at Wembley before being placed in traffic from Eastfield shed. Still showing signs of its special exhibition finish, the locomotive is seen heading a Cadder–Niddrie freight past St Margarets later that same year. Latterly numbered 61859, it would be withdrawn from Lincoln in November 1962 and broken up by T. W. Ward in Sheffield. *Gresley Society collection*

ABOVE 'K3' No 134 (Darlington, January 1925) on shed at Doncaster in the late 1920s. Allocated new to Ardsley, it would end its days at Doncaster, where, as BR No 61839, it was withdrawn and cut up in January 1962. *Ian Allan Library*

locomotives went mainly to Blaydon for similar work over the Newcastle–Carlisle route. Of the Southern Area allocation 34 went to the GN main-line sheds at King's Cross, New England and Doncaster (many after initial brief spells at Ardsley), Gorton being allocated the remaining 10, of which six soon moved on to March, the other four to Neasden. The arrival of these powerful new locomotives allowed a cascade of 'K1s' and 'K2s' (a total of 12 locomotives) to the Great Eastern Section and 14 'K2s' to the Scottish Area.

In 1927 a further 20 locomotives were ordered from Doncaster, topped up in 1928 by nine from Darlington and in 1930 by 20 from Armstrong Whitworth. All of the Doncaster batch were fitted with Westinghouse brakes and allocated to the North Eastern sheds at Heaton, Tweedmouth and York, which also gained most of the Blaydon allocation from the 1924 batch. The 18 examples received by the Southern Area led to further cascades of a further eight 'K2s' to the GE Section and six to the Scottish Area. By the end of 1930 there were 15 'K3s' based at King's Cross, allowing all of the 'No 1 Express Goods' services to be 'K3'-hauled, with increased loads and accelerated timings. The additional Scottish locomotives went to Carlisle, although St Margarets and Eastfield would later gain small allocations.

The final 74 'K3s' were ordered in 1934 and 1935 and were built by Armstong Whitworth (20 locomotives, construction of the first batch of 10 having been transferred from Darlington), Robert Stephenson (10), North British (20) and Darlington

(24). Of these the Southern Area received 43, of which Doncaster initially received all 43 before passing on 11 to Gorton, seven to New England, five to King's Cross and single examples to March, Mexborough and Colwick. The North Eastern received 23 examples, most of which went initially to Darlington and Heaton before moving to Gateshead (six), Tweedmouth (eight) and York (four), five remaining at Heaton. The Scottish Area received a further eight locomotives, shared between Carlisle (three) and St Margarets (five). Although engaged principally on the fast freight services for which they were designed, such useful locomotives appeared increasingly (particularly at weekends) on excursion and relief passenger services, at the head of long-distance Cup Final specials, at East Coast resorts and even, in cases of emergency, at the head of the 'Queen of Scots' and the 'Flying Scotsman'.

In 1931 the use of 'K3s' on GC lines saw an allocation of three locomotives to Annesley, where they were put to work on the reorganised service of fast block coal train loads (later known as 'Windcutters') to Woodford Halse, which they worked successfully until 1935. Despite their extensive use from 1925 over the GN&GE Joint line between Doncaster and March it was 1938 before the GE Section south of March was cleared for the

ABOVE An official works photograph of 'K3' No 2939 (Robert Stephenson & Hawthorn, December 1934), penultimate locomotive of a batch of 10 delivered in 1934. It was sent new to Carlisle Canal and, save for an eight-month spell at March in 1959/60, would remain a Carlisle engine, being withdrawn from the same shed in February 1960 (as BR No 61937) and ultimately cut up at Cowlairs. *W. Haigh Parry*

BELOW New England 'K3' No 61811 (Darlington, August 1924), originally LNER No 28, heads a fitted freight composed entirely of loaded container flats north of Hadley Wood in September 1953. New to Blaydon shed, it would be withdrawn from Lincoln in November 1962, being broken up at Doncaster Works. *Brian Morrison*

ABOVE Gorton-allocated 'K3' No 61870 (Doncaster, April 1929), originally LNER No 1300, tackles the climb to Woodhead Tunnel near Crowden with an up express on 4 July 1953. Note the 1,500V DC overhead-line equipment ready to be energised in 1954. Delivered new to York shed, the locomotive would be withdrawn from Colwick in July 1962 and cut up at Doncaster. *N. Fields*

LEFT Carlisle Canal-based 'K3' No 61858 (Darlington, April 1925) draws a long southbound freight out of Niddrie Yard. As LNER No 195 the locomotive had been new to Carlisle Canal and, barring eight months spent at St Margarets in 1939 and six months at Sheffield Neepsend in 1941, would be a lifelong resident, finally being withdrawn from the same shed in April 1961 and cut up at Cowlairs. *Ian Allan Library*

operation of 'K3s', because of weight restrictions over bridges. As soon as the restrictions were lifted three locomotives moved to Stratford to work the overnight fast fitted goods services to and from Whitemoor plus several passenger trains between Liverpool Street and Cambridge. In October 1938 Norwich gained three locomotives from March, and the use of 'K3s' in East Anglia grew after World War 2 such that by the time of nationalisation 38 locomotives were based at GE sheds. The class would be particularly associated with the seasonal herring specials operated out of Yarmouth and Lowestoft, remaining thus until replaced by diesels in 1960.

In March 1939 Berwick-on-Tweed marshalling yard closed, and of the Tweedmouth allocation of 17 'K3s' seven moved north to St Margarets, four to Heaton and four to York in order to continue their involvement in the revised through workings between Niddrie and Heaton. The St Margarets locomotives had regular work to Perth and Thornton, also making occasional appearances at Aberdeen. In 1924/5 the West Highland line to Fort William was visited by two 'K3s' running light, but the Civil Engineer vetoed the type's use over the line, and, aside from one recorded 1946 instance of a working at Crianlarich, they never worked beyond Glen Douglas.

Withdrawal of the 193 'K3s' took effect between February 1959 (No 61898, from Carlisle) and December 1962, when the North Eastern Region withdrew its last 22 examples – three from Ardsley and 19 from Hull (Dairycoates). Three locomotives withdrawn in September 1962 saw further service as

ABOVE March-allocated 'K3' No 61826 (Darlington, November 1924) is seen fresh from a General Overhaul at Doncaster Works on 20 April 1958. The former No 92 had a varied career, being allocated to GC Section sheds from 1939 to 1953 and then March and Norwich between 1953 and 1960 before returning to the GC at Staveley and spending a final three months at Colwick from June 1962, ultimately being withdrawn in September of that year, to be cut up at Cashmore's, Great Bridge. *W. Potter/Kidderminster Railway Museum*

stationary boilers at King's Cross (No 61912), New England (61835) and Colwick (61943), the last-mentioned becoming the final example to be condemned, in October 1965.

The 'N2' 0-6-2 passenger tank engines

Shortly after the end of World War 1 Gresley was able to give his attention to the pressing need for more powerful suburban tank engines, particularly for London commuter services operating over the Metropolitan Widened Lines out of Moorgate. These were being worked by the 1907-designed Ivatt 'N1' 0-6-2 tank engines, supplemented by the 1898-design 4-4-2 tanks of Class C2 (later C12). The severe weight and loading-gauge limitations imposed by the Metropolitan Railway for working over the Widened Lines were exacerbated by the severely restricted platform lengths over the section to Moorgate, which would be the limiting factor in locomotive design for this service until the end of steam. Despite preparing schemes for larger

2-6-2 and 2-6-4 tank designs, all of which were rejected by the Metropolitan, Gresley eventually solved the problem in typical fashion, coming up with an enhanced version of the successful Ivatt 'N1'. The resultant 'N2' became the standard locomotive for this work for almost 40 years until the advent (from 1959) of diesel locomotives and multiple-units. The regular combination of an 'N2' and two 'Quad-Art' sets just fitted the restricted platforms at Moorgate and provided capacity to move up to 900 passengers per train, which has not been exceeded by any subsequent diesel or electric service right up to the present day with the final closure of the Faringdon–Moorgate section as part of the Thameslink upgrade.

The enhancements introduced with the 'N2' class were piston valves, requiring a higher pitch of the boiler, cylinders increased to 19in bore and superheating. The limitations of the Metropolitan loading gauge produced a locomotive with a squat but powerful appearance. All of the original batch of 60 locomotives (50 from North British and 10 from Doncaster) were fitted with condensing gear and constructed to the restricted loading gauge for working to/from Moorgate.

In 1925 the LNER added a further 18 (12 from Beyer Peacock and six from Doncaster); all were non-condensing locomotives for the Scottish Area, these differing from the GNR engines in having left-hand drive, the Doncaster-built sextet being additionally fitted with dual (Westinghouse and vacuum) brakes. Further batches were constructed in 1928/9,

Newly delivered GNR 'N2' No 1763 (NBL, April 1921) seen shortly after arrival at King's Cross shed in April 1921. Sent new to Hatfield, it would return to King's Cross in 1924, thereafter (as LNER No 763 and 9542 and BR No 69542) maintaining until withdrawal in 1959 a continuous association broken only by a five-month spell at Neasden in 1943. *Gresley Society collection*

20 being supplied by Hawthorn Leslie and nine by the Yorkshire Engine Co (all condenser-fitted for use in the London area save for the last six YEC-built examples, which were intended for use in Scotland), giving a final fleet of 107 locomotives.

All of the condenser-fitted locomotives were delivered with Westinghouse steam-driven water pumps, as, when condensing, the water in the side tanks tended to heat up and could thus not used by conventional injectors. The feed-water pumps proved to be expensive to maintain and unreliable, so from 1925 hot-water injectors were made available and gradually replaced the feed-water pumps. By the autumn of 1927 the production of new 'N7' 0-6-2 tanks, some of which had been allocated to Hatfield and King's Cross, permitted the transfer to Scotland of 20 of the original NBL-built 'N2s'. Of these, 12 – in addition to their vacuum brakes – were specially fitted (three at Doncaster and nine at Cowlairs) with Westinghouse brakes, necessary because many of the ex-NBR local services still relied on Westinghouse-fitted stock; when, in 1929 and 1932, five of these locomotives were transferred to the GE Section their Westinghouse brakes proved useful, but the equipment was removed when, between 1939 and 1940, they were transferred back to the GN Section. Three of these Scottish area Westinghouse-fitted locomotives went on loan to Stratford

between January and October 1941. The remaining seven had their Westinghouse pumps removed by Cowlairs between 1945 and 1946. From July 1925 the 'N2s' based in the London area were fitted with trip cocks for working over the Widened Lines. Initially these were located in front of the driving wheels, but in 1947 the trip cocks on the right-hand side were moved in order to comply with an LPTB requirement that they be not more than 5ft behind the leading coupled wheels; this was because the lineside equipment with which they engaged was always on the left-hand side of the line so that when running bunker first into Moorgate the gear was initially too far back.

All of the initial batch of 60 locomotives had been delivered to King's Cross by August 1921, five being based at Hatfield, one at Hitchin and a further six at Hornsey. The Hatfield engines were put to work on the Dunstable branch, where their weight caused derailments on the poor LNWR track at Dunstable station. This was the first manifestation of a problem that was to dog the 'N2s' throughout their existence when running on less-than-top-quality track. Significant derailments were recorded in 1929 at Gartmore, on the Aberfoyle branch, in 1941 at Bramley, between Leeds and Bradford, and in 1950 at Forest Town, near Mansfield. Whilst some experiments were conducted with revised springing arrangements it was considered that the locomotives rode well on well-maintained track, although this conclusion did prompt speed restrictions or complete bans from some secondary branches in both England and Scotland. Recent experience with preserved 'N2' No 1744 has confirmed that the locomotive rides well on good-quality track, crews frequently commenting on the good ride of the locomotive, admittedly at the lower speeds applicable in the preservation era.

By 1925 King's Cross had 40 'N2s' diagrammed to the regular Metropolitan links, a further four diagrams being worked by Hornsey. Each locomotive was treble-shifted with regular crews, which led to a high standard of performance, most services being tightly timed and requiring sprightly running. In addition to suburban services the 'N2s' covered most workings of empty stock from/for main-line expresses into and out of King's Cross. On these duties it was common for an 'N2' to take trains of up to 500 tons unassisted to Hornsey carriage sidings. By 1932 there were 45 weekday diagrams for King's Cross 'N2s' and a further six worked by Hornsey.

In April 1924 No 4737 was sent to Eastfield for trials on the heavy suburban trains being operated between Helensburgh and Airdrie via Glasgow Queen Street Low Level. This was obviously a success, as another 12 'N2s' were transferred to Dundee, St Margarets and Eastfield in the spring of 1925, to be followed later in the same year by a further six locomotives, allocated to Parkhead, Eastfield, Kipps and St Margarets. In August 1927 the transfer of 20 more 'N2s' to Scotland began with allocations to Dunfermline and Haymarket sheds, bringing the type to the North Berwick, Bathgate, St Boswells and Hawick services. At their peak, until displaced from 1930 by new 'V1' 2-6-2 tanks, some 44 'N2s' were at work in Scotland; indeed some 'N2s' would remain in Scotland throughout their working lives, 15 examples being withdrawn from Scottish sheds between 1955 and 1961, the last (No 69518) surviving (just) into the 'Blue

BELOW GNR 'N2' No 1754 (NBL, March 1921) pictured in Hornsey yard with 'N1' No 1571 (Doncaster, November 1910). The two locomotives would remain allocated to Hornsey until the 1950s, both being fitted with condensing apparatus for working over the Metropolitan Widened Lines to Moorgate. The 'N2' (later LNER No 4754 and 9533 and finally BR No 69533) would be transferred in November 1959 to King's Cross, where it would be withdrawn on 26 June 1961; the 'N1' (later LNER No 4571 and 9451 and finally BR No 69451), after two months' loan to King's Cross in 1953, would move to Colwick in 1954 and thence to Bradford the following year, being condemned on 12 October 1955. *Gresley Society collection*

ABOVE In the late 1930s several 'N2s' found work from Stratford on outer-suburban services from Liverpool Street. Here No 4740 (NBL, February 1921), non-condensing and dual-braked, heads a Shenfield–Liverpool Street local near Brentwood. The former GNR No 1740 would be further renumbered as 9519 in 1946 and again by BR as 69519 in 1948. It proved something of a nomad, being allocated to no fewer than 11 sheds during the course of a 36-year career that saw it spend four years in Scotland (1928-32) and eight at Stratford, following these with brief spells at Hatfield, Mexborough and Neasden before settling in June 1948 at its final shed, King's Cross, where it would remain until withdrawal in October 1957. *H. C. Casserley/Gresley Society collection*

TOP RIGHT King's Cross-allocated 'N2' No 69535 (NBL, March 1921) heads through Potters Bar on 2 June 1951 in charge of a Hatfield train formed of the inevitable pair of 'Quad-Art' sets, the 'Main Line' destination board denoting a limited-stop service after Finsbury Park. Formerly numbered 1756, 4756 and 9535, this locomotive had, aside from two months at Ardsley in 1926, always been allocated to King's Cross and would remain thus until a final move to New England in May 1962, withdrawal following in September of the same year. *G. Goslin/Gresley Society collection*

BOTTOM RIGHT King's Cross allocated 'N2' No 69536 (NBL, March 1921) passes Harringay in the early 1950s with a northbound commuter train formed of two Gresley 'Quad Art' sets. The former No 1757/4757/9536 had been new to King's Cross, where it was to remain, save for 10 months at Neasden in 1946, until transferred to Hitchin in February 1959. Withdrawal (from Hitchin) would come in June 1959. *Gresley Society collection*

Train' era, being withdrawn from Kipps in January 1961. The arrival of the 'V1s' nevertheless allowed the transfer of 33 'N2s' from Scotland to the Southern Area, 22 vacuum-only examples finding work on the GN Section (among them 12 at Hatfield and King's Cross), nine also on the GN at Bradford and Ardsley and two briefly at Gateshead before returning to Kipps. Prior to this two examples had been tried out at Marylebone for eight months in 1926, a further pair spending a similar period in the West Riding. (It should also be noted that, whilst it was not until 1931 that 'N2s' found permanent employment at Bradford and Ardsley sheds, the 20 Hawthorn Leslie-built locomotives were all run in from Ardsley in 1928/9.)

Seven dual-braked examples all went to Stratford, No 4737 in May 1929, the others following early in 1932. Nos 4731 and 4732 were, however, back at Kipps by November, leaving 28 locomotives permanently transferred, having been replaced in Scotland by the first batch of 'V1s'.

Although the 'N2s' were employed on some GE suburban services, notably the 6pm Liverpool Street–Buntingford, their

LEFT Between 1966 and 1987 the Gresley Society Trust's preserved 'N2' displayed its LNER identity as No 4744, being seen here posing outside Loughborough station on the Great Central Railway shortly after its first overhaul in preservation in 1980. *Gresley Society Trust*

BELOW Between 1987 and 1999 the Gresley Society's preserved 'N2', No 1744, displayed its latter-day identity of BR No 69523. In June 1994, in a change of scenery from its usual home on the Great Central Railway, it participated in 'Steam on the Met', being seen here running round at Watford (Met) ahead of a trip to Amersham. For these workings the locomotive was fitted with through air pipes and control valve in order to control train brakes and a London Underground reporting-number frame. *Gresley Society collection*

ABOVE In 2010 preserved 'N2' No 1744 visited the North Norfolk Railway, permitting a first reunion with the M&GN Society's preserved Gresley 'Quad-Art' set. Here the full Gresley ensemble departs Sheringham for Holt. *Gresley Society Trust*

ABOVE During a visit to the Severn Valley Railway in 2010 preserved Gresley 'N2' climbs Erdington Bank *en route* to Bridgnorth with a full rake of seven Gresley carriages in tow. *Phil Jones*

ABOVE In September 2012 No 1744 visited the North Yorkshire Moors Railway, being seen here storming the 1 in 49 gradient between Grosmont and Goathland with a six-coach rake of preserved Gresley carriages. *P. Benham/Gresley Society Trust*

5ft 8in driving wheels allowed them a much better turn of speed than the 4ft 10in 'N7s', so they tended to be used on the longer-distance services as far as Colchester and Witham. Unlike their counterparts the GN, however, the GE 'N2s' began to experience regular problems with 'hot boxes' and soon gravitated to less-demanding duties. By the late 1930s the remaining GE 'N2s' had been swapped for 'N7s' from the GN suburban area and soon lost their Westinghouse brake fittings. Apparently on the GE Section the 'N2s' acquired a reputation for mediocre performance, which was also reported in some areas away from their traditional haunts of GN suburban area, the Glasgow area and the West Riding. Recent discussions with the former shedmasters at King's Cross and Woodford Halse and the former Divisional Motive Power Superintendent

at Stratford have confirmed that the 'N2s' performed best when worked hard with good loads and that when worked gently with light loads they could be shy for steam (an experience repeated with the preserved No 1744), and this goes a long way towards the varied reputation of the 'N2s' in different parts of the network.

In the West Riding the 'N2s' were used on the same local passenger diagrams as the 'N1s', and the improved acceleration they demonstrated was much appreciated by crews. Between 1937 and 1939 the streamlined 'West Riding Limited' was worked between Bradford and Leeds by a pair of 'N2s', usually bunker-first in the up direction. Again, however, questions arose about the locomotives' riding qualities on less-than-perfect track, and a derailment at Bramley in 1941 precipitated their departure from the West Riding.

Extension of the London Underground's Piccadilly and Northern lines led to some reduction in the available work for the 'N2' fleet, and wartime service reductions in 1942 saw 10 examples sent to Mexborough, where they found employment on surprising work for locomotives with 5ft 8in driving wheels – banking coal trains from Wath to Penistone, sometimes in double harness with the LNER Garratt. No 4758, meanwhile, spent 18 months at Frodingham, where it was used on banking duties from Keadby. By 1946 all had returned to the King's Cross district, Neasden or Colwick.

In July 1945 the peak-hour commuter service from GN suburban stations to the ex-NLR Broad Street station, suspended in 1941, was reinstated, the difference being that trains were now worked by LNER locomotives and stock rather than by the LMS, which had provided these services since their inception by the former North London Railway. Thus Broad Street station became another regular venue for the standard GN combination of an 'N2' and two 'Quad-Art' sets.

At nationalisation in 1948 the 'N2' fleet was distributed between King's Cross (58), Hornsey (10), Hatfield (14), Hitchin (two), Colwick (five), Neasden (two), Parkhead (eight) and Kipps (eight). By July Neasden had lost its allocation to King's Cross, and the next three years saw brief allocations of odd locomotives to Woodford Halse, Lincoln and Grantham. In 1952 the GE Section again gained some 'N2s' with the allocation of five locomotives to Parkeston and three to Colchester, one from each shed soon moving to Stratford. The Parkeston examples soon proved popular locally and monopolised the Manningtree–Harwich local service for four years.

During 1958 the route into Broad Street was cleared for operation by 'L1' 2-6-4 tanks, and the beginning of the end for the 'N2s' came on 1 December, when diesel locomotives took over some Moorgate services, the entire operation being scheduled for diesel operation from 15 June 1959. The 1958-60 period was, however, marked by frequent steam substitution of the unreliable new Type 2 diesel-electrics; the new Clarence Yard at Hornsey diesel depot was blessed with early allocations of both the English Electric 'Baby Deltic' 'D59xx' and North British 'D61xx' diesel-electrics, all of which proved to be amongst the least successful diesel classes and indirectly contributed to the survival of the 'N2s' well into the 1960s, the last five King's Cross 'N2s' finally departing for storage at New England in May 1962.

This was not to be the end of the story of the 'N2s', as No 1744/4744/9523/69523, constructed by North British in February 1921, which prior to withdrawal in September 1962 had spent almost all of its working life at King's Cross shed, was purchased by the Gresley Society on 31 October 1963, for £900. Moved initially in November 1963 to Harworth Colliery, it was eventually found a home on the Keighley & Worth Valley Railway, where it moved in February 1965. Initially restored as LNER No 4744, it was first steamed on 31 July. Almost every steaming brought problems with leaking tubes or elements, so that, apart from a brief starring role as the 'Scots Flyer' in the film of *The Railway Children*, it saw little use, and in 1975 it was relocated to the Great Central Railway for a full overhaul, returning to traffic in 1979. Further overhauls were completed in 1994 and 2009, when the locomotive resumed its original identity as GNR No 1744. To its pre-preservation mileage of 1.1 million have now been added a further 72,000 miles in preservation. Although still based at the Great Central Railway it has toured the country, visiting the National Railway Museum sites at York and Shildon as well as more than a dozen heritage railways, proving a popular attraction, particularly at the North Norfolk Railway when paired with the preserved 'Quad-Art' set which it hauled for almost 40 years out of King's Cross.

The 'A1' Pacifics

Engineering carried a series of articles in 1916 describing the design, construction and performance of the Pennsylvania Railroad's 'K4' Pacific locomotives. There is some evidence from subsequent documents that Gresley took great interest in these articles and the proven capacity of the 'K4' boiler design to generate copious quantities of steam. The coned boiler adopted for his first Pacific owed much to the 'K4' design, as did the adoption of nickel-chrome steel for connecting and side rods. Also of significance was the report of the 1919 Government-promoted Bridge Stress Committee, which led to a revision of previous thinking regarding the combination of axle weight and reciprocating mass and its impact on track and structures. This confirmed Gresley in his opinion that the combination of lighter alloy use for reciprocating motion and three-cylinder drive would permit a 20-ton axle loading without detrimental effects on structures. The weight-saving requirement also dictated the (by then) relatively low boiler pressure of 180lb, any higher pressure requiring stronger boiler plates, with an inevitable increase in weight.

On 10 January 1921 Doncaster received Order No 293 for the construction of two Pacific locomotives. Contrasting with the later speed at which the 'A4' order was fulfilled, Doncaster took 15 months to deliver No 1470 *Great Northern*, a reflection of the extent to which the works was still recovering from the effects of World War 1 new-build capacity reductions and material shortages. Three months later, on 10 July 1922, the second Pacific, No 1471, soon named *Sir Frederick Banbury*, was placed in traffic, and at the same time an order was placed for another 10 Pacifics. A further 40 locomotives were ordered in 1923 – 20 from Doncaster and 20 from North British – with the result that no fewer than 52 'A1'-class Pacifics were in traffic by July 1925.

The quoted specification for the new locomotives was the ability to haul passenger trains of up to 600 tons (a weight unprecedented other than at the height of World War 1), Gresley showing great foresight in anticipating the extent to which passenger demand and on-board facilities would increase the average weight of Britain's express trains.

The frames for the first locomotive of the second batch were laid in October, and No 1472 entered traffic on 24 February 1923, thus becoming the first locomotive to be delivered by Doncaster after the Grouping on 1 January. Despite being designed on the eve of the Grouping, no provision was made for the loading gauge which prevailed away from the generous clearances that applied on the GNR; this required some early alterations to facilitate the use of these new locomotives north of Doncaster, a full three inches being taken from the locomotives' overall height, by cutting down the chimney and other fittings, including the cab, and cutting away the front corners

ABOVE The sixth Gresley Pacific, unnamed No 1475, appears on the newly installed 70ft turntable at King's Cross early in 1924. Delivered in April 1923, the locomotive was the last to enter service carrying the 'L&NER' (with ampersand) branding and retained its GNR number until February 1925. The locomotive is in its original condition, constructed to the GNR loading gauge. Later to be named *Flying Fox*, it survived, rebuilt as an 'A3' in 1947, as 60106, until withdrawn from New England in December 1964. *Real Photographs/Gresley Society collection*

of the front buffer-beam in order to clear certain curved platform edges.

Great Northern was, of course, not Britain's first Pacific, that honour belonging to Churchward's *The Great Bear* of 1908 for the Great Western Railway. But whereas the GWR Pacific could hardly be regarded as a successful design and remained the sole representative of its class, Gresley had produced a design which, with later modifications, was to extend to a total of 114 locomotives. He incorporated all that he considered best in contemporary British and US practice – a large boiler, with wide firebox, three cylinders and high running plates, all contributing to a well-proportioned locomotive. The original 'A1' Pacific had a front end designed along lines which at the time were more-or-less orthodox in Britain. The valve motion was arranged with a maximum travel of $4^9/_{16}$in at 75% cut-off; this was the biggest cut-off at which the locomotives could be worked. This limitation was due to the fact that the earlier 'K3' 2-6-0s had been found to damage the covers of their inside cylinder-valve chests by overrunning of the valve spindle when coasting at their full 75% cut-off with regulator shut. With such a valve setting the 'A1s' had to be worked at long cut-offs, often up to 45 or 50% with the fastest and heaviest trains, and with partially closed regulators. Their well-designed boilers and sharp blast resulting from such methods of working always guaranteed plenty of steam but at a cost of average coal consumption on all duties, heavy and light, as high as 50lb per mile.

4

CHIEF MECHANICAL ENGINEER, LONDON & NORTH EASTERN RAILWAY

With the passing of the Railways Act 1921 the constituent companies of the East Coast group held a series of meetings to decide on the structure and senior staffing of the new London & North Eastern Railway Co. One of the early decisions was to adopt a devolved structure with three Areas, each under a Divisional General Manager responsible to the Chief General Manager, to be based in London. Although the North Eastern was the largest constituent company it did not have an outstanding personage to claim the office of Chairman, so this post went to the North British Chairman, William Whitelaw. The NER General Manager, Ralph Wedgwood, was appointed Chief General Manager. Early discussions concluded that there should be an all-line Chief Mechanical Engineer to look after

the 7,392 locomotives, approximately 21,000 carriages and 300,400 goods wagons owned by the new company. Of the constituent companies the CMEs (or equivalent) of the Great Eastern (Alfred Hill), North British (Walter Chalmers) and Great North of Scotland (Thomas Heywood) either decided

BELOW Class D11 'Enlarged Director' 4-4-0 No 6394 *Lord James of Douglas* (Armstrong Whitworth, October 1924), as allocated new to Dundee. Note the tablet-catcher affixed to the leading edge of the tender, for use on the Usan–Montrose section. Renumbered 2687 by the LNER in 1946 and again as 62687 by BR, the locomotive would be withdrawn from Eastfield shed in August 1961.
F. Moore/Gresley Society collection

to retire or were not considered for the post, the choice lying between John Robinson (66) of the Great Central, Sir Vincent Raven (63) of the North Eastern and Nigel Gresley (46) of the Great Northern. Diplomatically, Raven resigned to join Metropolitan-Vickers, leaving the choice between Robinson and Gresley. Robinson was by far the senior, having been in office since 1900, but was only two years away from retirement. Robinson claimed after Gresley's death that he had been offered the CME post but had declined and recommended Gresley, although there are different versions from several sources who were all personally involved at the time. It was therefore the 46-year-old Gresley who took up the post, being confirmed at a Board meeting held on 23 February 1923, some seven weeks after the formation of the company, at a salary of £4,500 per annum. Gresley decided to continue with his Principal Assistant from the GNR, Oliver Bulleid. There was no post of Carriage & Wagon Superintendent, although in effect Bulleid fulfilled this role. The new CME's empire included some 30,000 staff and the works at Cowlairs, Inverurie, Gateshead, Shildon, Darlington, York, Springhead, Dukinfield, Gorton, Doncaster and Stratford.

Inevitably the varying locomotive and workshop practices of the constituent companies came under early examination, and a series of comparative trials was soon underway, a Great Central 'Director' 4-4-0 being trialled between King's Cross, Cambridge and Peterborough, three designs of Atlantic (from the GNR, NER and NBR) operating between Newcastle and Edinburgh, and GNR and NER Pacifics operating between King's Cross and Doncaster. Results were inconclusive, all the participants claiming victory for their own locomotives!

In the immediate post-Grouping period there was an urgent need for more locomotives in a number of areas. After the order for 40 additional 'A1' Pacifics for express passenger

service the highest priority was for the former NBR, and here Gresley showed yet again that he was prepared to adopt effective designs from his predecessors by ordering 24 Robinson-designed 'Director' 4-4-0 locomotives, suitably modified to fit the more restrictive NBR loading gauge. These were supplemented by a much less successful transfer to the Scottish Area of 20 ex-GNR 'D1' 4-4-0s. The need for more mixed-traffic locomotives was met by an order in October 1923 for 25 slightly modified 'K3' 2-6-0s from Darlington Works, the order being doubled one month later and increased by a further 10 locomotives the following year. The North Eastern Railway had, when the inevitability of the Grouping became clear, ceased ordering new construction (apart from the prestige project of the Raven Pacifics), and the LNER thus had an early requirement for additional locomotives to serve the North Eastern Area. This was met in similar style to the NB requirement, suitable pre-Grouping designs being selected for replication, modified to fit the new LNER composite loading gauge.

The 'P1' three-cylinder 2-8-2s

In 1922 Gresley had considered heavy-freight designs able to haul loads exceeding the capabilities of his 'O2' 2-8-0, and there emerged initially a 2-10-2 design, subsequently revised to 2-8-2, the latter being put to the Locomotive Committee in August 1923. The proposed design was estimated to be able to haul a load 25% greater than could an 'O2', authorisation being granted for a pair of locomotives at a total cost of £8,000, with the proviso that 'loads can be found for them', although this prerequisite, significantly, was omitted from the final minutes of the meeting. In order to provide extra starting power for the heavy trains the 'P1' was intended to haul Gresley arranged for the fitting of a 'booster' engine to the Cartazzi truck under the cab. No 2393 was completed just in time for an appearance at the Stockton &

RIGHT The first 'P1', No 2393, at Doncaster on 26 June 1925. Note the steam-supply pipe to the booster (fitted under the cab), which would be removed May 1938. Following display at the Stockton & Darlington Centenary event the locomotive was sent new in July 1925 to New England shed, whence it would be withdrawn precisely 20 years later, in July 1945, to be broken up at Doncaster the following month. *LNER*

ABOVE The second 'P1', No 2394 (Doncaster, November 1925), hauling a 102-wagon train up the gradient towards Potters Bar, with booster in use. The locomotive would have its booster removed in April 1937 and, like its sister, would be withdrawn from New England in July 1945 and cut up that August at Doncaster. *F. R. Hebron*

Darlington Centenary celebrations in June 1925, No 2394 appearing five months later. These large and puissant new locomotives could be gainfully employed only on the New England–Ferme Park coal hauls, on which the established special loading was 1,600 tons in 100 wagons. Special Working Instructions had to be issued for the single daily service diagrammed for a 'P1' between New England and Ferme Park, reflecting the fact that such a train was longer than many block sections and goods loops and therefore required very careful regulation if delays were not to be caused to the nine passenger trains scheduled to overtake the 'P1'-hauled service during its journey south. No 2394 was tested on a northbound stopping passenger train during design work on the 'P2' and achieved speeds of up to 65mph – highly respectable for a locomotive with 5ft 2in driving wheels.

The boosters generated a significant additional maintenance requirement and were eventually removed in 1937/8. Given the particular problems associated with such a small fleet and the difficulties in finding suitable work for such powerful

machines it is not surprising that the 'P1s' gained the doubtful distinction in being the first Gresley-designed class to be withdrawn from service, in 1945.

The 'U1' 2-8-8-2 Garratt

Locomotive builder Beyer, Peacock & Co had for many years maintained a close relationship with John Robinson of the GCR, and its main works was close to the latter's Gorton Works. Indeed Sir Sam Fay, formerly the GCR's General Manager, became Chairman of Beyer Peacock. Apparently the company was short of work in the early 1920s, and it seems reasonable to assume that Fay used his connections to pursue a previous interest in the provision of Garratt-type locomotives, the GCR having developed two Garratt designs in 1910 (0-8-8-0) and 1912 (2-8-8-2), neither of which had been proceeded with. Thus it was that in 1923 the LNER began discussions with Beyer Peacock over the purchase of two 2-8-8-2 locomotives, each power bogie having a three-cylinder layout similar to that of the 'O2'. This produced the most powerful locomotive in the British Isles, the most powerful Garratt design produced to that date and the first Garratt produced for a British main-line railway. However, as the quotation from Beyer Peacock of £14,395 took up most of the £20,000 budget set for the two locomotives, only one ever appeared. No 2395 was assembled

ABOVE 'U1' 2-8-8-2 Garratt No 9999 (Beyer Peacock, June 1925) awaits its next banking assignment at Wentworth Junction on 18 April 1947. The former No 2395 had been renumbered in March 1946 and would assume its BR identity of 69999 in November 1948. The locomotive was built for banking trains up the Worsborough Incline, a task to which it would remain dedicated throughout its life, excepting brief spells at Bromsgrove in 1949/50 and 1955. *H. C. Casserley/Kidderminster Railway Museum*

BELOW Between March 1949 and November 1950 No 69999 was tried out at Bromsgrove, taking turns with the resident MR 0-10-0, No 58100, to bank trains up the Lickey Incline, both locomotives being seen here between duties at Bromsgrove. Converted to oil-firing in 1952 but made redundant by electrification at Worsborough in 1954, No 69999 would see a final spell at Bromsgrove between July and September 1955, finally being withdrawn in December and cut up early in 1956. *Roy F. Burrows/Midland Collection, Kidderminster Railway Museum*

ABOVE One surviving part of the LNER Garratt No 2395 (Beyer Peacock, June 1925) is a builder's plate, here posed with a works photograph of the locomotive. *Gresley Society Trust collection*

at great speed in order for it to appear at the Stockton & Darlington Railway Centenary celebrations in July 1925, where it caused quite a stir. Its intended use was not revealed at the time, its tractive effort, at over 72,000lb, being too great for it to be sensibly employed on main-line work (even the 'P1' 2-8-2s producing a tractive effort of only 38,000lb), and its eventual use for banking was unprecedented for a Garratt. Indeed the LNER already possessed several large tank engines (of Classes Q1, R1, S1 and T1, all much better suited to heavy

BELOW Pictured on 26 June 1958, 'T1' 4-8-0T No 69918 (Darlington, November 1925) rests on shed at Goole, where it had been transferred in 1957 from Stockton . The former LNER No 1656 had shunted at the new Whitemoor Yard between 1929 and 1932 before a spell at Tyne Dock, until 1943, when it moved to the reopened yard at Stockton, being transferred thence to Dairycoates in 1949. *A. N. H. Glover/ Kidderminster Railway Museum*

banking work), so the acquisition of this locomotive with fuel and water capacity much greater than required for its intended use must be regarded as a mystery. Put to work in August on the 3½-mile, 1-in-40 Worsborough Incline, it displaced two 2-8-0s but often worked in harness with another locomotive.

With no alternative work available the 'U1', renumbered 9999 in 1946 and again as 69999 following nationalisation, remained at Mexborough until March 1949. Although it would ultimately be displaced by electrification, this was still almost five years away, so its transfer to the London Midland Region at Bromsgrove, for banking on the 1-in-37 Lickey Incline, came as a surprise, the intention presumably being to assess its suitability for this work following electrification of the Woodhead route. By November 1950 No 69999 was back at Mexborough, being initially placed in store before resuming banking work in February 1951 but returning to store a year later. Clearly the physical effort required of firemen feeding the 56sq ft of firegrate was now a significant factor, and in late 1952 the locomotive entered Gorton Works for conversion to oil-firing. Testing the new arrangement at Gorton was undertaken fitfully through 1953 and 1954, the locomotive eventually returning to Bromsgrove in July 1955. After just over two months' use No 69999 was put aside and eventually withdrawn on 23 December 1955, being broken up at Doncaster Works early in 1956.

Other pre-Grouping designs
Ex-NER Worsdell Class X (LNER 'T1') three-cylinder heavy-shunting 4-8-0 tank engine
As stated earlier, Gresley was happy to resort to a success-ful pre-Grouping design if it met a specific requirement, and in 1925 Darlington produced a further five 'T1' 4-8-0 heavy-shunting tank engines to supplement the 10 existing examples built to the 1909 Worsdell design. These locomotives worked in the same areas as their earlier counterparts – York, Stockton, Newport (Teesside) and Dairycoates – and continued

ABOVE Class A5 4-6-2T No 1771 (Hawthorn Leslie, January 1926) pictured when new and allocated to Blaydon. Later renumbered 9839 and, in BR days, 69839, it would be withdrawn from Darlington shed and cut up at Darlington Works in September 1958. *LNER*

BELOW Class A5 4-6-2T No 69842 (Hawthorn Leslie, March 1926) is seen near Thirsk with a local train for Stockton in June 1954. New to Blaydon shed as No 1790, it would be withdrawn from Thornaby in October 1958 and cut up at Darlington in 1959. *P. Ransome-Wallis*

ABOVE Colwick-allocated Robinson 'A5' 4-6-2T No 69805 (Gorton, June 1911) rests on shed at Doncaster on 20 April 1958 *en route* to its last General Overhaul at Darlington Works, where it would arrive three days later. Gresley sponsored a batch of 13 'A5s' built by Hawthorn Leslie in 1925 for use in the North Eastern Area, but the former No 5170 was always a GC Section locomotive, aside from two months spent at Ardsley early in 1924. *W. Potter/Kidderminster Railway Museum*

their basic work of shunting loaded coal trains until displaced by diesel shunters in the late 1950s, the last survivor, No 69921, finally being withdrawn in June 1961.

Ex-GCR Robinson (LNER 'A5') 4-6-2 passenger tank engine

The North Eastern requirement for further large passenger tank engines was met by an order for 13 locomotives placed with Hawthorn Leslie in early 1925. These were standard GCR passenger tanks, suitably modified to meet the new composite loading gauge, the NE having no suitable designs available prior to the rebuilding, from 1931, of the 45 'H1' 4-4-4 tanks as 'A8' 4-6-2Ts. All of the new locomotives were allocated to traditional Tyneside sheds at Gateshead, Heaton and Blaydon until 1927, when seven moved to Saltburn to replace 'H1' 4-4-4Ts on services to Darlington and along the coast to Scarborough – a route with which they would be associated

until 1958. Most of the Tyneside allocation was moved south to Teesside in 1930, and by 1939 all were concentrated at Darlington. The next transfer of any significance came early in 1951, when five moved to Norwich. Shortly afterwards the reconstruction of the Liverpool Street turntable to accommodate the new 'Britannia' Pacifics saw four of the Norwich 'A5s' and a further six from Teesside drafted into Stratford to cover Southend-line workings, all 10 returning home upon completion of the turntable work in August. (None of the much closer ex-GCR 'A5s' at Marylebone was suitable, as these were out of gauge for the Great Eastern Section.) In 1952 two 'A5s' (to be joined by a third in 1954) were reallocated to Botanic Gardens depot in Hull, where they monopolised the heavy workmen's trains to Brough. Withdrawal began in 1957, No 69833 succumbing in April, the other 12 being condemned between August and December 1958, having been displaced by the arrival of DMUs to work the services which they had covered for almost 20 years.

Ex-GER Hill (LNER 'N7') 0-6-2 tank engine

Although numbering just 22 examples of which 10, ordered by the GER, were built after the Grouping, the Hill 'N7' 0-6-2 tank engines were of sufficient merit for the type to be adopted as an LNER Group Standard design. Accordingly further batches of 50 (built 1925/7) and 62 (1927/8) were ordered from Gorton, Doncaster, W. Beardmore and Robert Stephenson; curiously Stratford Works, which originated the design, was not involved, being no longer used for new construction, although it retained responsibility for overhauls throughout the lives of the 'N7s'. All of the 112 additional locomotives were constructed with left-hand drive and to the Metropolitan loading gauge, progressively incorporating series of detailed improvements that included long-travel valves, superheating and round-topped fireboxes.

The Liverpool Street inner-suburban services were almost monopolised by the 'N7s', Stratford and its sub-sheds being responsible by 1931 for an allocation of 114 locomotives, the other 20 finding work in the King's Cross district. With their relatively small (4ft 10in) driving wheels the 'N7s' were ideally suited to suburban services with frequent stops and were capable of achieving timings that would be only marginally improved by their electric successors. They were also capable, when pushed, of achieving surprising bursts of speed, instances of up to 71mph being reported. Over time they gradually spread their work across the GE Section, particularly as larger tank engines appeared at Stratford, so many country branches became home to these

versatile locomotives, although 73 examples spent their entire careers at London-area sheds.

In the 1950s 'N7s' were to be found in Lincolnshire at Boston and Lincoln; there was also a small stud at Colwick. Early in the decade 10 'N7s' were fitted with push-pull equipment, and this led to a variety of uses including the Annesley 'Dido', the Finsbury Park–Alexandra Palace shuttle, on the Romford–Upminster–Grays branch and on Yarmouth–Lowestoft/Beccles services. For a period in 1954 four of these locomotives were sent to cover for non-available DMUs in the West Riding, where, working with push-pull carriage sets, they successfully matched the accelerated diesel timings. In the London area suburban electrification was taking over, displacing the 'N7s' from Shenfield and Loughton–Epping services in 1949 and the remainder of the suburban network in 1960, No 69685 working the last steam-hauled suburban service out of Liverpool Street on 20 November.

Particularly memorable was the use in the period 1956-60 of No 69614 as the West Side pilot at Liverpool Street station, the locomotive being kept in immaculate condition, with all brightwork burnished, matching 'J69' No 68619, maintained in similar condition as the East Side pilot. Steam workings on the GE Section south of March ceased with effect from 9 September 1962, whereupon the last eight 'N7s' at Stratford were all condemned. Their story was not over, however, as one of these, the last Stratford-built locomotive, No 69621, was purchased for preservation by Dr Fred Youell and stored at Neville Hill shed until moved in 1973 to the East Anglian Railway Museum at Chappel & Wakes Colne. Following Dr Youell's death it was acquired by the museum, and this remains its home, notwithstanding long spells in recent years on the Churnet Valley Railway.

RIGHT The North Yorkshire Moors Railway's Autumn Gala of September 2012 featured planned double-heading by the two preserved Gresley 0-6-2 tank engines, BR-liveried 'N7' No 69621 (built Stratford, March 1924) being attached behind GNR-liveried 'N2' No 1744 (NBL, February 1921) with a rake of Gresley carriages, the train being seen here on the climb to Goathland. By this time, however, the 'N7' had already failed, being dragged about by the 'N2' for the rest of the day but failing to reappear thereafter. *M. Crawford/ North Yorkshire Moors Railway*

The British Empire Exhibition and the 1925 Locomotive Exchanges

The LNER was justifiably proud of its new Pacifics and in 1924 arranged for the third locomotive and first post-Grouping example, No 4472, specially named *Flying Scotsman*, to appear as an exhibit in the Palace of Engineering at the British Empire Exhibition at Wembley. Next to No 4472 was the newly completed GWR 4-6-0 No 4073 *Caerphilly Castle*. Noticeably smaller and of an earlier, Edwardian appearance, the 'Castle' displayed a prominent notice proclaiming it as the most powerful locomotive in the British Isles. As the 'Castle' was of modest size in comparison with the 'A1' this became a talking-point. The matter was to be settled by trial when, in 1925, exchanges were arranged whereby the LNER Pacific was to run on the Great Western in comparative tests with a native 'Castle', the two types being similarly pitted against one another on the LNER. Surprisingly, Gresley was not, apparently, consulted before the trials were instituted, and these were said to have been the result of a social conversation between Sir Felix Pole, the GWR's General Manager, and (depending which source one believes) either Ralph Wedgwood or Alex Wilson, the LNER's Southern Area Divisional General Manager. Gresley had agreed with his opposite number at the GWR, Charles Collett, that the results would not be publicised until both had had the opportunity to analyse them properly. Paddington, however, had other ideas and made much of the claimed 'victory' of its locomotives. Indeed the 'Castles', with Churchward's valve setting and 225lb pressure, had proved that they could make better times than the 180lb Gresley locomotives and on lower fuel consumption, whether with Welsh or Yorkshire coal.

O. S. Nock relates the story that Gresley visited Paddington early in the week of the trials with the 'Cornish Riviera Express' to meet 'A1' No 4474 (as yet unnamed but soon to become *Victor Wild*) and its crew on arrival. The LNER footplate representative was E. D. Trask, later to become Locomotive Running Superintendent for the Southern Area of the LNER. In response to a query as to how they were doing, Trask is reported to have replied: 'All right, but not as well as the GW.' Gresley is supposed to have responded: 'Oh, but you must,' to which Trask replied: 'I don't see how we can. They've got a better valve gear than ours.' Gresley apparently rejoined: 'Mr Wintour [Locomotive Works Manager at Doncaster] is getting out a modified form of ours,' to which Trask retorted: 'Well, that won't be much good to us this week!'

On the LNER the tests were conducted between London and Grantham or Doncaster, the locomotives involved being GWR No 4079 *Pendennis Castle* and 'A1' No 4475 *Flying Fox*. On its very first down run No 4475 failed with a 'hot box' and had to be replaced by No 2545 *Diamond Jubilee*. The result was not all bad for the LNER, however, as Gresley was forced to reconsider

aspects of his Pacific design, particularly the poor valve events given by the short-travel valve gear, so that ultimately the losers came to benefit more from the experience.

Later development of the 'A1' Pacifics

Bert Spencer, Gresley's chief technical assistant and the man responsible for the design of the characteristic Gresley cab, had already (in 1924) tried to persuade his boss to introduce long-lap, long-travel valve gear without success. Not afraid of a little industrial espionage, the LNER had had the valve-gear arrangements of No 4079 *Pendennis Castle* examined at Doncaster shed before the trials in April 1925, and in June of the same year No 4082 *Windsor Castle* was similarly examined while stabled in Faverdale Wagon Works prior to exhibition at the Stockton & Darlington Railway centenary celebrations. The CME's reluctance to alter a design still comparatively new and which, despite with some concerns regarding fuel consumption, was master of the tasks it was being set, was understandable. Eventually, in 1926, Spencer was allowed to fit his own design of valve gear, first to 'A1' No 4477 *Gay Crusader*, with 1½in instead of 1¼in lap, and then to 'A1' No 2555 *Centenary*, which also had its maximum valve travel increased to 5¾in. New narrow-ring piston valves were also fitted, and the locomotive was tested on the road, where it showed remarkable fuel economy, average fuel consumption falling to 38lb per mile from the original 50lb per mile. Having taken the opportunity to observe this more economical working personally from the footplate, Gresley instructed that all of the class be so altered. He had also been convinced that the higher boiler pressure of the GWR locomotives had something to do with their economy, and so it was that in 1927 a higher-pressure (220lb/sq in) boiler, which also had a much larger superheater, was fitted to Nos 4480 *Enterprise* and 2544 *Lemberg*. Despite the 4-ton increase in weight of the higher-pressure boiler, the locomotives were an instant success and extremely powerful, so much so that future 'A3s' (for which these were the prototypes) were built with smaller, 19x26in cylinders. Between August 1928 and February 1935 Doncaster turned out 27 new 'A3s', and in due course all but the first of the 'A1s' would be rebuilt to conform. All valve-gear modifications were completed by 1931, but the higher-pressure boiler conversions took much longer, being completed only after nationalisation, the LNER's typical thrift ensuring that new boilers were constructed only when the useful life of the originals had expired.

As of 25 April 1945 the 17 locomotives as yet unrebuilt were reclassified 'A10' so that the 'A1' designation could be applied to a 'new' Thompson Pacific. On 1 May 1945, having been in traffic for 16 months since its last overhaul, the original Gresley Pacific, newly redesignated 'A10' No 4470 *Great Northern*, entered Doncaster Works for a General Overhaul and programmed 'A3' conversion. By now Thompson had been in office for four years and had already rebuilt the 'P2' 2-8-2s as 'A2/2' Pacifics and

arranged for the last four of the planned 'V2s' to emerge as 'A2/1' Pacifics, and No 4470 was controversially selected for a more detailed reconstruction. Many commentators have expressed the view that Gresley's first Pacific was specially selected by Thompson for this drastic reconstruction as a deliberate slight to the memory of his predecessor. I do not subscribe to this view, and the chronology suggests that it was pure accident that it was in works when the decision was made to undertake a more radical reconstruction of an 'A10' as the prototype for Thompson's proposed new 'A1' class. What cannot be denied is that the Thompson reconstruction destroyed the graceful lines of the locomotive and produced an 'ugly duckling' which nevertheless gained a reputation as a powerful and capable free-steaming machine. The 'A10' (original 'A1') class became extinct with the conversion to 'A3' in December 1948 of No 60068 (originally LNER No 2567) *Sir Visto*.

Subsequent development of the 'A3' design is recorded under that heading

The 'J-38' goods 0-6-0s

Although on 30 October 1924 the Locomotive Committee had proposed the construction of 103 0-6-0 goods locomotives, to be allocated 48 to the Southern Area, 20 to the North Eastern Area and 35 to the Scottish Area, within a month the purchase of 48 ex-ROD 2-8-0s caused the order that was actually placed in March 1925 to be reduced to 55; then, in June, the 20 intended for the North East were deleted, leaving Darlington with an order for just 35 locomotives, all destined for Scotland, which duly appeared in the first five months of 1926.

The construction order description of this new Group Standard class as 'J27 Modified' was, in fact, singularly

ABOVE The first 'J39', No 1448 (Darlington 9/26), poses for its official picture. Note the non-standard fittings later removed including steam reversing gear, cover at base of safety valves and tender. The first 12 were allocated to North Eastern sheds which allowed an equivalent number of 'J27s' to be transferred to the GE Section. The later 4700/64700 was always a North Eastern area locomotive until withdrawn in April 1961, curiously being broken up at Cowlairs.
Gresley Society collection

inappropriate, the only similarity with the original Worsdell 'J27s' of 1906-9 or Raven's modified version of 1921-3 being the wheel arrangement. Wheelbase was lengthened, and wheel diameter, at 4ft 8in, was larger, as were the cylinders and journals. The grate area was also increased, from 20 to 26sq ft. The Stephenson Link Motion valve gear was a slightly modified version of that fitted to the original 'A5' 4-6-2 tank engines, which had been immediately applied to the new batch of 13 'A5s' being constructed by Hawthorn Leslie (and would be replicated on the 'J39s' and for several subsequent rebuilding of Classes D11, D16/3 and J11/3). The result was a much larger and more powerful locomotive than the 'J27', admittedly at the price of greater weight and a consequent reduction in route availability, the rating for which increased from 5 to 8.

Throughout their existence the 'J38s' were only ever allocated to the Scottish Area and, apart from brief spells, to only the sheds at Dunfermline, Thornton, Dundee and St Margarets. They spent their entire working lives engaged in the same local coal hauls and main-line freight for which they were designed, only rarely appearing on passenger trains. The 'J38' class also had the distinction of being the last LNER steam class to remain intact – until December 1962, when the first two examples were withdrawn. The last survivors,

Nos 65901 and 65929, finally succumbed in April 1967, having been the very last Gresley locomotives still in regular service with BR.

The 'J39' goods 0-6-0s

Although declared a Group Standard design the 'J38' class only ever comprised 35 locomotives, and in September 1926 there appeared a modified 'J39' design, with 5ft 2in driving wheels, which would eventually number 289 examples and become the most numerous of all Gresley types. The design closely followed the 'J38', and, apart from a batch of 28 locomotives constructed by Beyer Peacock in 1936/7, all were assembled at Darlington. After the initial 44 locomotives, orders were placed in batches: 52 were ordered in 1927, 27 in 1928, 25 in 1929, 12 in 1933, 39 in 1934, 6 plus 28 from Beyer Peacock in 1935, 38 in 1936 and a final 18 in 1940. Slightly shorter frames than the 'J38' and some minor weight-saving improvements resulted in a Route Availability rating of 6, which meant that the class could be used much more widely.

As a Group Standard design the 'J39' was supplied to all LNER Areas, although the presence of the 'J38s' in Scotland meant that the 'J39s' were less numerous there, only 24 examples being allocated to Scottish sheds at the time of nationalisation. The North Eastern Area had been well provided with freight locomotives, so there was less need here for the 'J39s', and it was the Southern Area that became the principal user of these powerful and versatile machines. Its numerous heavy seasonal flows of fruit, vegetables, sugar beet and fish traffic all provided plentiful employment for 'J39s', this being supplemented by a supporting role to larger locomotives in the South Yorkshire and Nottinghamshire coalfields. By virtue of an agreement to supply motive power to the Cheshire Lines Committee 'J39s' also saw widespread use in Lancashire and Cheshire, being allocated to

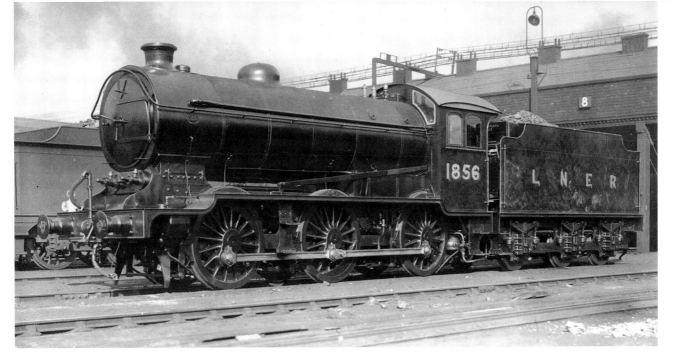

ABOVE In 1936/7 Beyer, Peacock & Co was contracted to build 28 'J39s', of which the sixth example, No 1856, is pictured in September 1936 while being run in from Gorton shed, ahead of allocation to Colwick (from 24 October). Interestingly Beyer Peacock enhanced the livery of its locomotives by adding red lining, a detail dropped by the LNER in 1928. Renumbered 4910, this machine would be reallocated to Doncaster in August 1946 before moving to the North Eastern Region in 1951, ultimately being withdrawn from Alnmouth in November 1962. *W. H. Whitworth/Gresley Society collection*

BELOW Retford-allocated No 64898 (Darlington 10/35) heads a freight south from Retford in this late 1950s view. The former No 2994 was withdrawn in February 1960 and cut up at Stratford. *Gresley Society collection*

Gorton, Trafford Park and Brunswick sheds besides spending short periods at Heaton Mersey, Northwich and Bidston. In the late 1950s I frequently observed a Gorton 'J39' on a daily working from Mottram to Wrexham, so the type's sphere of influence extended as far as Wales. The Great Eastern Section, meanwhile, made extensive use of 'J39s' on its many long-distance freight flows, some 74 locomotives being allocated to GE Section sheds in 1939, although by 1947 the total had fallen to 66, including 30 at Stratford and 14 at Norwich. Between 1949 and 1958 the M&GN line had small allocations of 'J39s' at Norwich and Melton Constable, where they apparently worked only on freight trains.

Although principally goods locomotives the 'J39s' soon demonstrated their suitability for local stopping trains, reliefs and excursion work, particularly to seaside resorts in the summer months, when demand for freight was at its lowest. On the Great Eastern Section, shortly after the arrival of dual-braked examples at Stratford in 1927 (and following a test run on an express from Liverpool Street to Ipswich and back, apparently organised by the redoubtable Stratford District Locomotive Superintendent, L. P. Parker), 'J39s' regularly appeared on main-line express passenger trains, particularly at times of extreme pressure, when the locomotives' versatility proved a Godsend to hard-pressed locomotive foremen. Between 1933 and 1933 the 6.0pm service from Liverpool Street to Buntingford (on which no less a figure than the Governor of the Bank of England regularly returned home) was allocated to a 'J39', virtually eliminating the previous erratic timekeeping of this high-profile service. The last Eastern Region 'J39', No 64901, was

withdrawn from March shed in October 1961, but it was not until December 1962 that the class became extinct, with the withdrawal of 38 locomotives from the North Eastern Region and the final eight Scottish examples.

The 'D49' secondary passenger 4-4-0s

With the impending completion early in 1925 of the 52nd 'A1' Pacific attention had turned to the needs of secondary passenger services. Having in 1924 placed orders with outside contractors for 24 new Robinson 'D11' 4-4-0s for service in Scotland, Gresley in April 1926 ordered the first examples of a new design of three-cylinder 4-4-0, Class D49, to be built at Darlington and used where route restrictions still precluded the use of Pacifics but where the pre-Grouping Atlantics required supplementing. The initial order was for 28 (13 for the North East and 15 for Scotland), with tenders supplied by Doncaster; boilers were interchangeable with those fitted to the Darlington-built 'J38' and 'J39' 0-6-0s – a useful economy. The first 20 locomotives, classified 'D49/1', were equipped

BELOW An official works photograph of 'D49/2' No 336 *Buckinghamshire* (Darlington, March 1929), fitted with Lentz rotary-cam poppet valves and dual brakes. Allocated initially to York, it would subsequently have its Westinghouse pump removed and would be renamed *The Quorn* in May 1932, thereby changing from a 'Shire' to a 'Hunt'. Later renumbered 2727 and again by BR as 62727, it would be withdrawn from Hull Dairycoates shed in January 1961 and cut up at Darlington. *Ian Allan Library*

ABOVE Class D49/1 No 253 *Oxfordshire* (Darlington, November 1927) brings the Newcastle–Harwich boat train into Northallerton in 1933; the fireman has clearly overfilled the tender at Wiske Moor troughs and has drenched the front coach. The locomotive had been new to Neville Hill shed, whence (as BR No 62702) it would be withdrawn in November 1958, notwithstanding a spell in Scotland from 1943 to 1952. *H. Gordon Tidey*

with conventional piston valves and Walschaerts valve gear; the next six, designated 'D49/3', had Lentz poppet valves and oscillating cams, also driven by Walschaerts gear, while the final two (curiously referred to as 'compounds' until 1927 but not completed until 1929) were also fitted with Lentz poppet valves, but rotary-cam-operated, and were described as 'D49/2'. Initial experience with the new design was satisfactory, such that further examples were ordered – another eight 'D49/1s' in February 1928 and further 'D49/2s' in December 1929 (15) and October 1933 (25) to complete a class of 76 locomotives.

The first British application of the Lentz poppet valves with oscillating cams had been in 1925 to a 'J20' 0-6-0, this being followed in 1926 by ex-GER 'B12' 4-6-0 No 8516 and then in 1928 by a batch of 10 additional 'B12s' built by Beyer Peacock and therefore fitted from new, although the equipment would be removed in 1931/2. The oscillating cam gear fitted to the 'D49/3s' did not prove satisfactory, so all six locomotives were fitted with new cylinders fitted with piston valves in 1938, being consequently reclassified 'D49/1'. The decision to experiment with Lentz poppet valves is believed to have been taken after a meeting at the Colchester premises of the UK licensee, Davey Paxman, between Gresley and André Chapelon, of the Paris–Orléans Railway, which led to collaboration and a strong

personal friendship between kindred spirits. This in turn led to the first British experiments with the newly patented Kylchap design of blastpipe and exhaust-draughting system to 'D49s' Nos 251 and 322, both retaining the single-chimney arrangement. However, some difficulties were experienced with fitting the equipment at Darlington, and no significant improvements were achieved.

When class leader No 234 *Yorkshire* appeared in October 1927 it was the first LNER-designed passenger locomotive but also the first example of the last 4-4-0 type to be constructed by the LNER. The first 36 examples to be built were named after English and Scottish counties and thus became known as 'Shires'; curiously, although all were constructed in County Durham, no 'D49' would be so named, and, perversely, *Cheshire* and *Rutlandshire* were always allocated to Scottish Area sheds. In 1929 the naming theme was changed to English Hunts, and

the 40 locomotives that constituted these final two batches were all allocated to the North Eastern Area. As the 'D49/1s' were 'Shires' and the 'D49/2s' 'Hunts', Nos 352 *Leicestershire* and 336 *Buckinghamshire*, the first two 'D49/2s', were renamed in 1932 as *The Meynell* and *The Quorn* respectively, to be consistent with this theme.

The first 15 locomotives allocated to the Scottish Area went to just four sheds – Haymarket, St Margarets, Perth and Dundee. In 1929 a further eight locomotives, Nos 2753-2760, were sent new to Eastfield, and thereafter the Scottish Area allocation remained stable until June 1943, when, in exchange for a pair of ex-NER Atlantics, two more were transferred to Haymarket, bringing the Area total to 25. In 1950 Carlisle lost five locomotives to the North Eastern Region, but two quickly returned. Further transfers in 1936 and 1937 saw four of Eastfield's 'D49s' transferred to Carlisle to replace withdrawn North British Atlantics.

When the 'D49s' first appeared in Scotland the Pacifics were restricted in their sphere of operation, but the larger

ABOVE No 365 *The Morpeth* (Darlington, December 1934) had been built as a 'D49/2' but is shown here as modified by Darlington late in 1939 with infinitely variable rotary-cam poppet gear. The experiment was not successful, and in 1941 the locomotive would be rebuilt by Thompson with two inside cylinders, as Class D. New to Gateshead shed, it would be withdrawn from Starbeck (as BR No 62768) in 1952 after sustaining collision damage. *LNER*

locomotives were gradually permitted over all the principal routes and were later joined by the 'V2s', so that the 'Shires' were progressively displaced from express passenger work onto local passenger turns, mainly on the main lines owing to their restricted (RA8) route availability, which also kept them off most branch lines.

The North Eastern's initial allocation of 13 'D49s' was based at York or Neville Hill, but by May 1932 Hull Botanic Gardens had gained seven examples, and these three sheds acquired further locomotives until October 1933, when York transferred two to Heaton, primarily to work the 'Queen of

ABOVE Pictured on 3 August 1950, 'D49/2' No 62740 *The Bedale* (Darlington, June 1932) awaits departure from Whitby with the 6.50pm to Malton and York, over what is now the North Yorkshire Moors Railway. New to York shed as No 235, the locomotive would be withdrawn from Hull Dairycoates in August 1960. *W. S. Garth*

BELOW 'D49/1' No 62729 *Rutlandshire* (Darlington, April 1929) emerges from Kinghorn Tunnel on Saturday 6 October 1951 with an Edinburgh–Thornton stopping train. The locomotive was originally numbered 2754 and, despite its name, was always allocated to Scottish sheds, being new to Eastfield and withdrawn from St Margarets, in May 1961. *W. Oswald*

TOP LEFT York-allocated 'D49/2' No 62774 *The Staintondale* (Darlington, February 1935) passes Kirkham Abbey station with a York–Scarborough train in April 1954. The former No 376 was always allocated to sheds between Scarborough and Leeds and was destined to be withdrawn from Neville Hill in June 1957. *J. M. Jarvis/Kidderminster Railway Museum*

BOTTOM LEFT Dundee-allocated 'D49/1' No 62744 *The Holderness* stands on shed at Perth in September 1954. New (as LNER No 273) to Neville Hill, the locomotive moved to Scotland in 1952 and would be withdrawn from Hawick in December 1960, being cut up at Cowlairs in March 1962. *J. Robertson*

ABOVE Starbeck's 'D49/2' No 62773 *The South Durham* (Darlington, January 1935) leaves Leeds for Harrogate in the early 1950s, being seen passing Whitehall Junction. Originally numbered 2773, this locomotive had been new to Neville Hill shed, where, after a 10 year sojourn (1947 57) at Starbeck, it would be withdrawn in October 1958. *Ian Allan Library*

TOP LEFT In charge of the 4.27pm Newcastle–Hawick on 9 June 1956, Blaydon's 'D49/2' No 62771 *The Rufford* (Darlington, January 1935) waits for the road onto the single line at Reedsmouth. The former NB route from Hexham to Riccarton Junction was destined to close in October. New to Neville Hill shed as LNER No 370, the locomotive would be withdrawn from York in October 1958. *I. S. Carr*

BOTTOM LEFT For its September 2010 gala the National Railway Museum's base at Shildon had two apple-green visitors. Here in the yard at Shildon preserved 'D49' *Morayshire* (Darlington, February 1928) raises steam alongside preserved 'N2' No 1744 before sharing duties on the demonstration line. *D. McIntosh/Gresley Society*

BELOW Preserved 'D49' No 246 *Morayshire* poses at Bo'ness on its home railway, the Bo'ness & Kinneil Railway, in July 2012. *Gresley Society Trust collection*

ABOVE In October 2010 *Morayshire* visited the Great Central Railway for a gala, being seen here heading a Leicester North train near Swithland. *Gresley Society Trust collection*

Scots' Pullman to Leeds. In the opposite direction Neville Hill used its 'D49s' to work the daily Leeds–Glasgow express to Newcastle and back, although the later allocation of new locomotives to Neville Hill saw older 'D49s' transferred to Scarborough, Bridlington and Gateshead. In May 1939 a wholesale reallocation was implemented in order to concentrate locomotives of the same sub-class at as few sheds as possible, so all the Area's 11 'D49/1s' were all based at Botanic Gardens, the 'D49/2s' at Leeds, York, Gateshead and Scarborough, as well as Botanic Gardens. In 1947 Starbeck gained its first five 'D49s' as increasing numbers of the new 'B1' 4-6-0s elsewhere displaced the 4-4-0s onto secondary work. Although the 'English' examples were all confined to the North Eastern Area (Carlisle being part of the Scottish Area) they did occasionally stray, particularly on excursions, and there are recorded instances of 'D49s' at King's Cross. Indeed No 245 had a spell on loan to 'Top Shed' between September 1928 and April 1929, during which period it regularly worked 370-mile turns on the 'West Riding Pullman' and the Sunday Leeds excursion from King's Cross.

Early in 1942 No 365 *The Morpeth* was admitted to Doncaster Works for reconstruction, two inside cylinders and piston valves replacing the original three cylinders and poppet valves, the locomotive emerging in August 1942 as the sole member of Class D (later D49/4). Apparently the rebuilding was not considered a success, and Thompson discouraged press interest in the project. After sustaining collision damage in 1952 the recently renumbered 62768 was withdrawn.

In the North Eastern Area, as in Scotland, the 1950s saw 'B1' 4-6-0s and then diesel multiple-units take over much of the local-service work performed hitherto by the 'D49s'. Withdrawal of the latter began in 1957, the last example, No 62712 *Morayshire*, being condemned in July 1961 after 15 months' use as a stationary boiler at Slateford Laundry. Fortunately further use at Slateford (until January 1962) saw the locomotive survive long enough for preservation plans to take shape, these finally bearing fruit in July 1964, when it was purchased by Ian Fraser, an overhaul at Inverurie Works, which included restoration to apple-green livery as LNER No 246 being completed in January 1965. Donated to the Royal Scottish Museum in Edinburgh, the locomotive was stored at Dawsholm shed for many years until eventually loaned to the Scottish Railway Preservation Society at Bo'ness, which facilitated a full return to working order. One highlight was an appearance at the Stockton & Darlington 150 celebrations at Shildon in 1975, another being a brief main-line career in Scotland in 1980/1. Following an overhaul completed in 2005 it has strayed far from its traditional haunts, visiting the Llangollen Railway as well as more familiar 'D49' territory at Shildon and the Great Central Railway.

The 'A3' Pacifics

With the reconstruction of the valve gear of 'A1' No 2555 *Centenary* in March 1927 the scene was set for the final enhancement of the 'A1' design when, in May, No 4480 *Enterprise* received a new 220lb boiler, becoming the prototype 'A3'. In August Doncaster received an order for 10 Pacifics of the new design, further orders being placed in December 1928 for eight locomotives and finally in November 1933 for a final nine. The first of these 27 locomotives was No 2743 *Felstead*, placed in traffic in August 1928, the last being No 2508 *Brown Jack*, delivered in February 1935. Reconstruction of the 'A1s' was undertaken in typically economical LNER fashion, proceeding only as their 180lb boilers (and the spares) required replacement and thus taking more than 20 years, finally being completed with the rebuilding of *Sir Visto* (by now BR No 60068) in December 1948.

The economy of the new locomotives now facilitated a significant change in train working which in the summer timetable of 1928 saw the principal daytime Anglo-Scottish express, the 'Flying Scotsman', altered to run non-stop the 392 miles from King's Cross to Edinburgh – the longest non-stop journey in railway history. In part this was a response to the initiative of the LMS, which, with its 1927/8 winter timetable, had begun running the newly named 'Royal Scot' non-stop over the 299 miles between Euston and Carlisle. The winter working of the 'Royal Scot' included a six-coach portion with its own dining and kitchen car for Edinburgh, so this was in direct competition with the LNER service from King's Cross. The old 'gentlemen's agreement' on minimum times to Edinburgh still applied, but the publicity value of the 'non-stop' claim could not be ignored. It was felt that the limit of the powers of a single crew had been reached in the Newcastle non-stop running of the 1927 summer service and that it was undesirable on grounds of safety to carry two crews on one locomotive, so the idea of the corridor tender was conceived. Along with the order placed in August 1927 for 10 new 'A3' Pacifics (which emerged as Nos 2743-52), was placed an associated tender order (No 50). The tenders in question were to materialise as Nos 5323-32, built to a revised design incorporating a side corridor to permit the exchange of crews without stopping and thus facilitate the safe operation of the new non-stop service planned for the 1928 summer timetable. Indeed the original intention had been that both the daytime 'Flying Scotsman' and overnight 'Night Scotsman' services should run non-stop, (which would explain why as many as 10 corridor tenders were constructed), but in the case of the latter service this was never implemented. Gresley, in an exercise to determine the optimum dimensions of the side corridor, apparently undertook trials with his family at home, using dining chairs to confirm the required minimum width. In addition to the side-corridor feature, the tender was redesigned to carry an extra ton of coal.

ABOVE No 4472 *Flying Scotsman* (Doncaster, February 1923) on shed at Doncaster Carr on 27 November 1934, fresh from a brief visit to 'The Plant' for a special examination prior to being used for a King's Cross–Leeds high-speed test run on the 30th; it was on the return trip that the first fully authenticated speed of 100mph would be achieved. Driver Sparshatt and Fireman Webster pose in the cab, having travelled to Doncaster to collect their own allocated locomotive. *Ian Allan Library*

Having received new long-travel valves and had its cab and boiler mountings reduced in height (to fit the less generous loading gauge north of York) during a visit to Doncaster Works in February and March 1928, No 4472 *Flying Scotsman* was selected as one of three Southern Area locomotives nominated for use on the new service (the others being Nos 4476 *Royal Lancer* and 2547 *Doncaster*). As such it acquired brand-new corridor tender (No 5323) before leaving Doncaster Works, being reallocated to King's Cross shed as of 11 April 1928.

Thus it was that at 10am on 1 May 1928 the world's longest-ever scheduled non-stop service was inaugurated by Driver Pibworth with No 4472 *Flying Scotsman* from King's Cross and Driver Henderson with No 2580 *Shotover* from Edinburgh Waverley. On the down run some anxious moments were caused north of Newcastle when a tender axlebox showed signs of overheating, but the journey was still completed 12 minutes early! Indeed No 4472 was well enough to return to London with the up train on the following day. The publicity to be derived from this service was so important that on 27 April, four days before the LNER's new service began operation, the LMS split the 'Royal Scot' into two portions, running non-stop the 401 miles to Glasgow and the 399 miles to Edinburgh. This exercise was clearly designed solely to steal the LNER's thunder and was not repeated, particularly as the through working was well beyond the regular limits of one locomotive crew. It is worth noting that during the summer of 1928 the Pacifics used on the non-stop 'Flying Scotsman' service covered 125 round-trips (a total of 98,165 miles) with only one late arrival and one locomotive failure, which itself did not result in a late arrival!

High-speed trials and the first 100mph run

Gresley had taken a keen interest in the German high-speed 'Flying Hamburger' diesel train, reporting on its performance to the LNER Board in the spring of 1934, and in September of that year he led a party visiting Germany in order to ride on the train. A decision of the LNER Board on 29 June to pursue investigations led to details of the King's Cross–Newcastle route being supplied to the train's builder, Maybach Motorenbau, with a view to an experimental service for the LNER. The results of this evaluation were, however, disappointing, the best overall journey times on offer being 4hr 15min in the down direction and 4hr 17min in the up. The projected average speed of just 62.5mph (compared with the 77.8 achieved in Germany) reflected the much more demanding nature of the East Coast route, with heavy gradients and severe speed restrictions not found between Berlin and Hamburg. Equally the diesel unit's spartan passenger accommodation for just 140 Third-class passengers, offering only a cold buffet for refreshment, was felt to be unacceptable.

Encouraged by Wedgwood, Gresley set out to demonstrate what could be achieved by his latest Pacifics. Firstly, on Friday 30 November 1934, a high-speed test run was arranged between King's Cross and Leeds. Surprisingly, modified 'A1' Pacific No 4472 *Flying Scotsman* was chosen in preference to one of the new 'A3s'. It is possible that it was the choice of driver that selected the locomotive, for No 4472 was the regular steed of Bill Sparshatt, who had recently been making a name for himself on the Pullman trains as a 'hard runner' and come to the attention of the Southern Division Locomotive Running Superintendent, I. S. W. Groom, who apparently made the selection of locomotive and crew. Gresley held thinly disguised ambitions to make the LNER pre-eminent in locomotive speed and performance, and the return run from Leeds would give the opportunity to try for a record down Stoke Bank. It was known that, once the idea had been mooted, Sparshatt would need little encouragement to rise to the challenge!

To mirror the accommodation offered by its German diesel competitor the special was loaded to only four carriages on the outward journey, the outstanding achievements on the down run being an average speed of 90.2mph over the 24.1 miles from Hitchin to Offord, with a maximum of 94.75mph, an average speed of 82.2mph on the ascent from Helpston to Stoke and a journey time to Leeds of 2hr 31min – a record that was destined to stand for more than 30 years, until well into the diesel era. For the return (up) journey two more coaches were attached to the train, so an overall time of 2hr 37min was still a great achievement. A 'world first' was claimed, for a fully authenticated maximum speed of 100mph was recorded in the dynamometer car at a location between Little Bytham and Essendine that was to become more famous less than four years later. The complete round-trip was made at an average speed of 72.2mph. Credit should also be paid to Bill Sparshatt's regular mate, Fireman Webster. That a British steam train could equal its German diesel rival had been conclusively demonstrated.

On 4 January 1935 Wedgwood presented to the LNER Board a paper summarising the investigations to date, the results of the previous November's high-speed test and the scope for

further service accelerations. His proposals were approved, and the scene was set for the second test run on 5 March 1935 – a much harder task than that set previously for Sparshatt and No 4472. This time Class A3 Pacific No 2750 *Papyrus* was to be given the job of hauling six coaches from King's Cross to Newcastle and back on a four-hour schedule in both directions. The outward journey, with Driver Gutteridge in charge, was completed three minutes inside schedule, in a net time of just 3hr 50min, despite a severe delay due to a freight-train derailment at Shaftholme. On the return journey Driver Sparshatt managed to wind No 2750 up to a new world-record maximum speed of 108mph. In fact no fewer than *four* new world records had been established – 12.3 miles at an average speed of 100.6mph, 500 miles at a 72.7mph average speed by one locomotive in a single day with a 217-ton train, 300 miles of one round-trip at an average speed of 80mph, and the new maximum of 108mph. The return journey was accomplished in just under 3hr 52min gross (3hr 48min net).

Subsequent development of the 'A3' design

In 1937 No 2751 *Humorist* had been fitted with a Kylchap double chimney in an attempt to solve the problem of drifting exhaust obscuring the driver's forward view. At this stage the benefits of the Kylchap arrangement in terms of reduced back-pressure and better combustion had not been fully appreciated. Since 1932 *Humorist* had been the subject of a variety of trial fittings, concluded only in January 1938, when a rimless chimney and side vanes were fitted, with acceptable results, but these were insufficient to justify alterations to the rest of the class until May 1958, when authorisation was received for the fitting of the Kylchap double chimney to all the surviving 'A3s'.

Despite their clear preference for the Kylchap double-chimney 'A4s' for use during the 1948 Locomotive Exchanges the ER authorities were surprisingly slow to seek any conversions beyond the four 'A4s' delivered with this equipment in 1938 and the solitary 1937 conversion of 'A3' No 2751. Gresley had previously indicated that he would seek further conversions once the patent – and thus the need to pay significant royalties – had expired in 1941, but obviously the exigencies of wartime and his death early that year (coupled with the antipathy of his successor, Thompson, towards much of his legacy) had prevented any further developments in this direction. Indeed, from the completion of the trials it would be almost 10 years before the persistence of the King's Cross Shedmaster, Peter Townend, eventually overcame this resistance, and on 15 May 1958 the conversion of all of the 'A3s' was finally authorised. It would be no exaggeration to state that this modification completely rejuvenated all of the Gresley Pacifics.

The fitting of the Kylchap exhaust and double chimney to the 'A3s', with its much softer exhaust, brought a return of the problems experienced previously with No 2751. Ever the

ABOVE King's Cross-allocated 'A3' No 60103 *Flying Scotsman* (Doncaster, February 1923) rests on shed at Doncaster on 20 April 1958. The former 'A1'/'A10' No 1472/4472 had been rebuilt as an 'A3' in 1946/7 but would not acquire a Kylchap exhaust and double chimney until late 1958, German-style smoke-deflectors being added in December 1961. The locomotive would be withdrawn for preservation in January 1963. *W. Potter/Kidderminster Railway Museum*

innovator, Townend submitted photographs of a DB (German Railways) '01' Pacific fitted with the 'trough' type of deflector that had been widely adopted in Germany. A further four 'A3s' were authorised for fitting with this type of deflector, and the first, No 60049 *Galtee More*, was loaned to King's Cross by its home shed, Grantham, for a full week's testing. The locomotive was put on the (by now) regular diesel diagram on the 10am King's Cross–Newcastle service, returning with the 10.10pm. During the week running of over 3,000 miles the total time vision was obscured was 25 seconds! Accordingly in early 1961 authority was granted for the fitting of all but four 'A3s' with this type of deflector, and some 55 'A3s' were quickly equipped, many at running sheds using kits containing the necessary parts, supplied by Doncaster.

The scene was now set for what many regard as the 'Indian Summer' of the 'A3s'. The arrival in 1958 of the first five English Electric 2,000hp diesels at King's Cross shed had marked the beginning of the end for steam, but perversely their introduction presented the rejuvenated Pacifics with the opportunity to show just what they could achieve, the Kylchap 'A3s' now being used turn and turn about with the 'A4s' – and delivering similar performance. The diagrams for the new diesels were designed to maximise the high availability of the new traction, with none of the layover times traditionally required for adequate servicing of their steam predecessors; return trips to Newcastle within 12 hours became commonplace, and if necessary the locomotive would head back to Newcastle within a few hours. However, the early

ABOVE Preserved 'A3' No 4472 *Flying Scotsman* stabled at St Margarets shed in Edinburgh on 25 June 1967, having arrived from Doncaster with the 'Scunthorpe Forum Flyer'. Note the second tender, used since 1966 to provide additional water capacity, replenished from the few surviving water troughs. The train returned to Doncaster later the same day. *W. Potter/Kidderminster Railway Museum*

unreliability of the diesels ensured frequent steam substitution, and in many cases the substitutes fulfilled the diesel diagram with distinction; as late as 1961 the four-weekly mileage returns showed the highest mileage of any King's Cross-allocated locomotive was not one of the diesels but a 36-year-old 'A3'. But despite such performances it was clear – from the increasing numbers of diesels and their improving reliability – that steam was living on borrowed time, and with the introduction of the 'Deltics' in 1961 the Pacifics were gradually ousted from the East Coast main line, leading to the use of 'A3s' between Leeds and Glasgow via Carlisle and the Glasgow & South Western route. Withdrawal had commenced in December 1959 with No 60104 *Solario*; of the remainder all survived 1960, but six were condemned in 1961, 12 in 1962 and no fewer than 33 in 1963. December 1964 saw the withdrawal of the last three English representatives, leaving only three survivors at St Margarets. Nos 60041 *Salmon Trout* and 60100 *Spearmint* succumbed in June and December 1965 respectively, leaving just No 60052 *Prince Palatine* to be withdrawn in January 1966.

The preservation of No 4472/60103 *Flying Scotsman*

Alan Pegler was a businessman with family interests in Doncaster and with the Northern Rubber Co at Retford. He was also a prominent railway enthusiast, President of the Gainsborough Model Railway Club and had organised a number of special trains during the 1950s, including the 'Centenaries Express' of 1952 and the 'Plant Centenarian' in 1953. In 1954 he was invited to join the Eastern Area Board of the British Transport Commission. This gave him privileged access to key personnel at BTC headquarters, notably the officer responsible for drawing up the list of steam locomotives to be preserved, Terry Miller. Of the LNER Gresley Pacifics only *Mallard* was listed, as

ABOVE On 16 May 1992 No 4472 *Flying Scotsman* storms past Milepost 260 with a returning Carlisle to Preston 'Preston Guild 92 Special' close to Ais Gill summit on the Settle to Carlisle line. *Gresley Society collection*

an example of the ultimate design as well as holder of the world speed record. Alan failed to get *Flying Scotsman* (by now BR No 60103) included on the list, but from his discussions with Terry Miller emerged an agreement in principle at the end of 1962 to undertake a complete overhaul of the locomotive, prior to sale for the then not inconsiderable sum of £3,000. Already actively raising funds for its acquisition was the Gresley A3 Preservation Society, which, after being pipped at the post by Alan Pegler, became the Gresley Society and instead acquired the only preserved Gresley tank engine, 'N2' No 69523 at the time of writing restored as GNR No 1744, of which your author is currently the caretaker.

No 60103 worked its last BR train, the 1.15pm King's Cross–Leeds, as far as Doncaster on 14 January 1963. After a well-attended high-profile media event at King's Cross the journey north proceeded without incident – apart from passing 'A4' No 60007 *Sir Nigel Gresley* on the 12.45 Hull–King's Cross service at Claypole. Arrival at Doncaster was six minutes early, just as the up 'White Rose' passed, enabling an exchange of whistles with its locomotive, world-record-holder

ABOVE In its last season of operation, No 4472 *Flying Scotsman* is ready to depart from York for Scarborough in the summer of 2004. By this stage, No 4472 has acquired a double chimney, Kylchap exhaust and German-type smoke deflectors, mirroring its final BR condition. *Gresley Society collection*

No 60022 *Mallard*. After retiring to the place of its birth almost 40 years earlier at Doncaster No 60103 was quietly withdrawn from BR service on 15 January – not to follow the ultimate fate of all the other 'A3s' and be scrapped but to pass into the ownership of Alan Pegler, who had ridden on the footplate on its last BR journey.

The task of restoration began almost immediately after the locomotive's formal withdrawal. By 7 February the Kylchap exhaust, double chimney and German-style smoke-deflectors had all been removed, restoring the locomotive to close to its original appearance, and the 1936-built streamlined non-corridor tender, No 5640, to which it had been coupled since July 1938, swapped for a corridor tender from the original, 1928 batch – No 5325, ex No 60034 *Lord Faringdon*. By 29 March

work had progressed sufficiently for a test run to be undertaken over the classic LNER testing route from Doncaster to Barkston Junction and back. Having resumed its old identity as LNER No 4472 and with a new coat of apple-green paint, the locomotive looked very smart.

Signed on 16 April 1963, the formal sale agreement included a far-sighted (as subsequent events would prove) three-year running and maintenance arrangement (later extended to 1968 and then 1971) and permitted contractually guaranteed access to the BR network, *Flying Scotsman* being the only steam locomotive granted this right. Also included in the agreement was provision for a new home for the locomotive with the lease, at a rate of £65 per annum, of the old engine weigh-house just beyond the southern end of Platform 8 at Doncaster. George Hinchcliffe, formerly Secretary of the Gainsborough Model Railway Club, was recruited as Locomotive Manager, ably supported by a small group of former railwaymen and other members of the club.

No 4472 began its career in preservation in appropriate style on 20 April 1963 with a Paddington–Ruabon Festiniog

Railway special, Alan Pegler being Chairman of the Festiniog Railway Co. The second was a trip sponsored by the Gainsborough Model Railway Club from Doncaster to Southampton. Subsequent outings in 1963/4 included trips over the Great Central main line from Marylebone to Manchester and visits to the Eastleigh Works Open Day, Cardiff, Darlington, the Forth Bridge, the Farnborough Air Show and Ilfracombe. Early in 1965 the locomotive visited Darlington Works for a boiler change before further undertaking trips throughout Britain, including most notably on 1 May 1968 a successful reprise, 40 years on, of its original King's Cross–Edinburgh non-stop run. From 11 August 1968, following the cessation of regular BR steam-hauled services, No 4472 was the only steam locomotive operating on the national network until the lifting, with effect from 2 October 1971, of the infamous 'steam ban'. However, wider events were to curtail its British operations when a promotional tour of North America was agreed. In preparation the locomotive visited the Leeds works of the Hunslet Engine Co between November 1968 and January 1969, resuming charter work in February until withdrawn for tour preparations at the end of August, after a brief July visit to Doncaster for the fitting of US-style fittings including cowcatchers, headlight, whistle and bell.

In September 1969 No 4472 left the UK for a tour of North America hauling an exhibition train to promote British goods, initially partly backed by the Board of Trade. During 1970 and 1971 No 4472 toured more than 15,450 miles of eastern Canada and the USA from New York, Washington, Houston, Dallas and Montreal. Despite huge crowds there were problems with the finances of the tour, as individual sponsors had conflicting aspirations for maximum visitor numbers and exclusive access for invited guests only. After some reconsideration of the layout of the train an invitation to British Week in San Francisco in March 1972 brought a move from Toronto to San Francisco in August and September 1971. After some refurbishment of the train, operations along Fisherman's Wharf commenced on 18 March 1972. After initial success complaints from competing attractions and the loss of car-park spaces caused a reduced scale of operation which was not a financial success, leading to termination of the operation and an August move to storage at the safe sanctuary of a local US Army base. The eventual conclusion of these unhappy events was the appearance of Alan Pegler in the London bankruptcy court in October 1972. Plans were already being hatched in several quarters for the rescue of the locomotive; eventually Sir William McAlpine emerged as its saviour, and after payment of some of the outstanding debts No 4472 was repatriated in February 1973.

After a visit to Derby Works No 4472 moved for a summer season on the Paignton & Dartmouth Steam Railway in Devon. Main-line charter work was resumed in September 1973 with a train which No 4472 double-headed with another previous

visitor to the USA, ex-GWR 'King' No 6000 *King George V*. After briefly being based at Market Overton in Lincolnshire No 4472 made its home at Steamtown, Carnforth, in late 1974. Further periods of main-line work followed, including an appearance at the Stockton & Darlington Centenary celebrations at Shildon in 1975, before another overhaul was required, this time at Vickers Armstrong in Barrow-in-Furness, in 1978. During this overhaul No 4472 acquired a boiler previously carried by 'A4' *Bittern*, for which there are several precedents. In 1980 the locomotive featured in a special set of stamps to celebrate 'Mail 150', but the high-point was the 'Rocket 150' celebration at Rainhill, in which No 4472 played a prominent role. Thereafter it continued to work on the main line, perhaps most notably in 1983, when it returned to its old East Coast stamping-ground for a sold-out series of Peterborough–York specials. The highlight of 1984 was a Royal Train working at North Woolwich for HM The Queen Mother, this being followed by the commencement of a highly successful period of operation out of Marylebone on Sunday Lunch specials to Stratford-upon-Avon. In 1986 came a move of home to Sir William McAlpine's new operating base at Southall, while the summer of 1987 saw a return to Carnforth for a series of 'Sellafield Sightseer' trains along the Cumbrian coast before a return to Southall in February 1988.

Work now concentrated on a further overhaul and preparatory work for the visit to the Australian Bicentennial Celebrations in 1988/9. During the 55 weeks between October 1988 and October 1989 No 4472 visited Sydney, Melbourne, Brisbane, Alice Springs and Perth, covering more than 28,000 miles. *En route* from Melbourne to Alice Springs on 8 August 1989 the locomotive established a new world-record non-stop run of 422 miles between Parkes and Broken Hill.

Returning from Australia via the Pacific and Panama, No 4472 completed a circumnavigation of the globe which is probably unique for any locomotive – steam, diesel or electric. After a full examination at Southall it was back on the main line by May 1990. Further work continued through to the expiry of the seven-year main-line boiler certificate in November 1992, the intention being to use the remainder of the 10-year boiler insurance by running on heritage railways, although this came to a premature end with a boiler-tube failure at the Llangollen Railway in March 1993. A return to Southall for a re-tube allowed the locomotive to resume its tour of heritage lines by November, this continuing until a further failure at Llangollen in April 1995, by which it had covered some 30,000 miles in the space of two years. Unfortunately the mileage accrued over the previous seven years, including the Australian visit, had generated insufficient funds for the required overhaul, and *Flying Scotsman*'s future was again in doubt.

Bio-tech multi-millionaire Dr Tony Marchington was also a railway enthusiast who had long harboured the ambition of owning a Gresley Pacific, and discussions with Sir William McAlpine led to a transfer in March 1986 to No 4472's third owner in preservation, the sale including the Southall base that had been its home since 1986. The overhaul took until June 1999, when the locomotive resumed its main-line career, passengers paying premium prices for a consciously limited number of trips including haulage of the prestige 'English Pullman' service of the Venice Simplon Orient Express business. The next five years, to March 2004, would see a sorry saga of increasing unreliability and financial failure such that the parent organisation eventually ran out of credit, and *Flying Scotsman*, as the main asset, was put up for sale. The media stoked fears that it might be sold abroad, and a national appeal was launched, including a contribution from Richard Branson, which eventually saw the locomotive transferred to the owner-ship of the National Railway Museum, for £2.3 million.

Flying Scotsman duly arrived at the NRM in May 2004, pushed by a diesel after a failure – one of several that had dogged its last season of operation. The required overhaul commenced at York in early 2005, but it soon became clear that a more extensive General Overhaul, including major boiler repairs, would be required, and an early decision was taken in 2005 to refurbish the now spare 'A3' boiler that had been replaced in 1978. Work continued throughout the years 2006-12, yielding a seemingly endless discovery of new problems that have seen the boiler replaced in the frames only to be subsequently removed on no fewer than three occasions. Work ceased in 2012 as the NRM commissioned an inquest into the problems and a consultation on the way forward. An initial report in March 2013 suggesting completion would be delayed until 2015 at the earliest. In July 2014 the NRM announced yet a further setback as a detailed examination of the locomotive's frames have revealed the necessity of replacing the front 12ft of both main frames because of severe elongation of over 100 of the bolt holes by which the cylinders are attached. Early in 2015 the NRM finally admitted that the completion of the work would not be achieved before 'early 2016'.

The 52 years of preservation to date have been a varied mixture of triumph and disaster for *Flying Scotsman*. Two of its three private owners have been brought to bankruptcy wholly or in part by the costs of operation and maintenance – a saga that continues to this day, its latest owner, the National Railway Museum, struggling with an overhaul years behind schedule and millions of pounds over budget.

The rebuilt 'B12' 6ft 6in express passenger 4-6-0s

By the late 1920s the increased weight of passenger trains and the generally poor quality of coal supplies in the wake of the General Strike of 1926 had brought GE Section locomotive provision to crisis point. There were no suitable LNER or constituent designs available, although temporary relief had been afforded by the allocation of 20 'K2' 2-6-0s in a

pre-planned move facilitated by the arrival of new 'K3s'. Work was in hand on a new design of three-cylinder 4-6-0 (which duly emerged in February 1928 as Class B17), but work on a new 2-6-4 tank intended for Southend-line services had been suspended in January 1928 as a result of press criticism over the use of tank engines on fast passenger trains, following the derailment in August 1927 of SECR 'River' No A800 near Sevenoaks. In place of the aborted 2-6-4 tanks Gresley ordered, from Beyer Peacock, 10 additional 'B12' 4-6-0s with detailed differences from the original Holden design of 1911, the most significant being the incorporation of Lentz poppet valves, resulting in the classification 'B12/2'.

By 1931 improvements to the GE permanent way made it possible to increase the permitted locomotive weights. This at last allowed a more extensive rebuilding of the 'B12' class, the design work being carried out at Stratford under the Assistant Mechanical Engineer (Stratford), Edward Thompson. Between 1932 and 1944 some 54 examples, including all 10 'B12/2s', were rebuilt with a completely redesigned front end incorporating long-travel piston valves and larger-diameter boilers with round-topped fireboxes, the locomotives in question being reclassified 'B12/3'. The modifications proved highly successful, and after initial trials with No 8579 rebuilds followed rapidly until ultimately all the examples of the class remaining permanently in England (save No 8534, withdrawn in 1945) had been reconstructed.

In 1931/2 the first five 'B12s' had been despatched to an unlikely new home on the former Great North of Scotland Section, followed by a further six in 1933, a single engine in 1937 and seven in 1939, four in 1940 and two in 1942. The Scottish-allocated examples were excluded from rebuilding on account of the continuing limitations on maximum axle loading on the Great North of Scotland Section, which precluded the additional 1ton 7cwt axle weight of the rebuilt locomotives.

The initial rebuild, No 8579, was transferred from Colchester to Stratford, but subsequent rebuilds remained at their existing home sheds, although their enhanced performance saw them work turn-and-turn-about with the new 'B17s'; the only real difference was that the 'B17s' were preferred for the longer London–Norwich out-and-back jobs, which did not present much opportunity for remaking the fire, whereas the 'B12s' were preferred for jobs requiring shorter bursts of hard running, such as to Ipswich and Southend. During World War 2 some of the 'B12s' found themselves running well away from home territory, 11 examples being selected for their power, wide route availability and dual braking to haul ambulance trains for the use of American forces. These heavy trains used US-built air-braked vehicles and required assistance over heavy grades, for which a special proportional valve was fitted to facilitate assistance by a vacuum-braked locomotive. The trains were based at Westbury, Newbury and Templecombe, and their GE Section crews and

ABOVE 'B12/3' 4-6-0 No 8577 emerges from Audley End tunnel with a Liverpool Street to Cambridge local service in the late 1930s. This Beyer Peacock-built locomotive was delivered as a Holden-design 'B12/2' in September 1928, being rebuilt to Gresley 'B12/3' in 1934. The locomotive was renumbered to No 7491 in October 1942, to No 1577 in October 1946 and finally as No 61577 in March 1949. The locomotive was withdrawn from Cambridge shed in September 1959. *Gresley Society collection*

a fitter lived with the train for long periods, visiting some (for LNER locomotives) unusual locations as they transported their casualties to hospitals across England.

The Scottish-allocated examples were largely confined to the ex-GNoS Section and only rarely ventured south of Dundee. The sole exception was that each summer between 1931 and 1939 Eastfield borrowed a 'B12' in order to resource a regular excursion to Oban via the Crianlarich chord, double-headed with the sole surviving 'D36'. When not employed on such work Eastfield used the locomotive on local work to Polmont or Edinburgh and on at least one occasion to Fort William. In Scotland the 'B12s' acquired the nick-name 'Hikers', thought to refer to the ACFI feedwater heaters seemingly being likened to rucksacks! The last Scottish 'B12', No 61539 (8539), was withdrawn from Keith in November 1954.

By 1948 the surviving 50 English 'B12/3s' were largely concentrated at Stratford, which had 37 examples, the remainder being at Colchester (four), Ipswich (seven), Norwich (one) and Yarmouth (one). Also in 1948 a new area of operation was established and commenced with the allocation of seven locomotives to Yarmouth Beach and South Lynn sheds for passenger services over the Midland & Great Northern route east of Spalding, this continuing until wholesale closure of the M&GN network in 1959. In 1955/6 five were based at Peterborough Spital Bridge, to work services over the ex-LNWR routes to Rugby and Northampton.

From December 1959 Norwich's No 61572 (turned out by Beyer Peacock in 1928 as LNER No 8572) was the last survivor. Norwich Shedmaster Bill Harvey, later to feature in the restoration of No 4771 *Green Arrow*, saw to it that the locomotive was well looked after and kept out of the eye of higher authority until its withdrawal in September 1961. Because of the celebrity status it had gained during the last two years a successful appeal was launched by the M&GN Preservation Society, and following a period in store at Norwich it was moved to the North Norfolk Railway at Weybourne. The most recent overhaul has been undertaken by Ian Riley Engineering at Bury from which the locomotive returned to service in March 2012, restored to full LNER livery as No 8572.

In March 2012 preserved 'B12/3' No 8572 (Beyer Peacock, August 1928) returned to service on the North Norfolk Railway following an extensive overhaul. Here the locomotive poses at Sheringham station on its first day back in service, ready to depart with a complete Gresley train formed of the preserved 'Quad Art' set of carriages. *Gresley Society Trust*

BOTTOM LEFT Later in 2012 No 8572 visited the Severn Valley Railway, permitting this re creation of the 'Day Continental' boat train using the SVR's beautiful rake of eight preserved Gresley teak-bodied carriages. Here the train approaches Highley *en route* for Bridgnorth. *Steve Allen*

The 'B17' passenger 4-6-0s

In the early years of the LNER the Great Eastern Section, hampered as it was by cheaply constructed structures which restricted locomotive axle weights and by some very tight layby sidings and small turntables at Liverpool Street and other key locations, had been well served by the excellent fleet of Class D15 and D16 'Claud Hamilton' 4-4-0s and the Class B12 ('1500') 4-6-0s. By the late 1920s, however, increasing train weights and traffic growth were demanding something more powerful. Initially some of the ex-GNR 'K2' 2-6-0s were reallocated to Stratford, March and Cambridge, 25 having arrived by 1928, but although useful these could be only a stop-gap solution, and a specification emerged for a three-cylinder 4-6-0 with a tractive effort of at least 25,000lb but a maximum axle weight of just 17 tons and an overall length of no more than 50ft. Although the King's Cross office produced some designs all failed to gain the approval of either the Civil Engineer or the Operating and Locomotive Running departments, so Doncaster was asked to assist. By October 1927, however, the

ABOVE An official North British photograph of the prototype 'B17' 4-6-0, No 2800 *Sandringham* (NBL, December 1928). Destined to be renumbered 1600 in 1946, it was allocated new to Stratford shed, where, aside from a spell (1947-51) at Ipswich, it would remain until withdrawn as BR No 61600 in July 1958. *Express Photos*

Locomotive Committee had still not received any satisfactory proposals, and the decision was taken at a very senior level to involve the North British Locomotive Co.

In view of the close friendship between some of the LNER's senior officers and NBL Chairman Sir Hugh Reid, coupled with the known shortage of work for private locomotive builders and NBL's proven expertise in meeting challenging specifications worldwide, it is not surprising that the company was thought likely to offer a solution. NBL had also recently designed and constructed a new design of express passenger locomotive for the LMS, the 'Royal Scot', and the eventual 'B17' design is said to exhibit some features reflecting the same design parentage.

By 1928 an improved understanding of vehicle dynamics resulting from the deliberations of the Bridge Stress Committee had prompted a relaxation of the 17-ton maximum-axle-weight stipulation for a three-cylinder design, and the 18-ton axle weight of the NBL design was accepted for a locomotive capable of running 'over certain GE main lines' (rather than more widely, as originally proposed), an initial order for 10 locomotives placed with NBL in February 1928 being followed by orders for a further 27 placed with Darlington in December 1928 (12) and December 1929 (15). Numerous features of the design were adopted from the drawings for the batch of 'A1' Pacifics built by NBL in 1924, while the boiler owed much to that used for the 'K3' 2-6-0s and 'O2' 2-8-0s; indeed this

ABOVE On 27 September 1937 a new high-speed service was introduced between Norwich and Liverpool Street, the 'East Anglian'. A new six-carriage set was constructed for the service, and two 'B17s' were rebuilt with 'A4'-style streamlined casing. Here Norwich-based No 2859 *East Anglian* (Darlington, June 1936) poses with the new stock before the introduction of the service. No 2859 had originally been named *Norwich City*, this being transferred in January 1938 to No 2839, hitherto *Rendlesham Hall*. By now renumbered No 61659, *East Anglian* lost its streamlining in April 1951 and was transferred to Yarmouth shed, ultimately being condemned from Lowestoft in March 1960. *Gresley Society collection*

BELOW The second streamlined 'B17' was No 2870 *City of London* (Robert Stephenson & Hawthorn, May 1937), originally to have been *Manchester City* but in the event named *Tottenham Hotspur* until September 1937, the latter name being transferred to No 2830 (hitherto *Thoresby Park*) in January 1938. Here No 2870 poses at Norwich Thorpe station in May 1939. The locomotive would be renumbered 1670 in 1946 and again as 61670 by BR in August 1948 prior to removal of the streamlining in April 1951. Originally a Norwich locomotive, upon removal of the streamlining in April 1951 it would be transferred to Yarmouth, whence it would be withdrawn in April 1960. *J. P. Wilson*

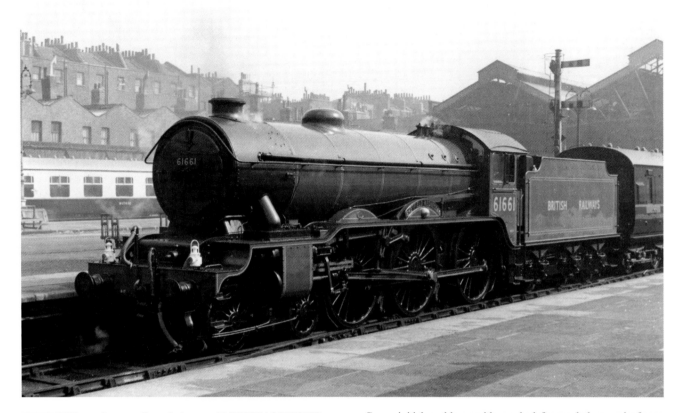

ABOVE Still in apple-green livery but now with 'BRITISH RAILWAYS' on the tender, 'B17' No 61661 *Sheffield Wednesday* (Darlington, September 1936) poses at Marylebone in 1948. As LNER No 2861 it was initially allocated to Leicester (GC) shed, later moving to March and Stratford before withdrawal from Cambridge in July 1959. The appearance of a March-allocated 'B17' at Marylebone suggests a special visit for inspection of the livery. *B. Granby*

Diagram 100 design would, with only minor modifications, become the widely used Diagram 100A, which was to continue in production under Thompson and subsequently under Arthur Peppercorn. The length problem, meanwhile, was addressed by the provision of short, GE-pattern tenders, although this would not be necessary for a later batch of 25 locomotives, delivered between 1933 and 1936 for the Great Central Section, which received larger LNER Group Standard tenders. The final batch of 11 was ordered from Robert Stephenson & Co in late 1936, the last example being delivered in July 1937.

The new 4-6-0s were classified 'B17' by the LNER, class leader No 2800 *Sandringham* setting the theme for naming the early examples after country houses – initially those located in East Anglia, although the scope was subsequently broadened to encompass other parts of England served by the LNER. Later locomotives, for GC-line services, were named after football clubs based within the LNER's English Areas.

Some initial problems with cracked frames led to early frame renewals, but after strengthening the 'B17s' settled down to hard work on the GE Section, where their economy and increased power over the 'B12s' soon came to be appreciated, and although they soon gained a reputation for rough riding this trait was tolerated by most crews because of their significant advantages over their predecessors. In 1939 plans were developed for a strengthening of the boiler plates to permit a raising of boiler pressure to 220/225lb. Gresley signed the drawings for this Diagram 100A boiler, but wartime economies saw the scheme cancelled, only to be resurrected by Thompson in 1943, when two 'B17s' received this design of boiler; ultimately 57 examples would be so fitted.

Although they did displace 'B12s' to Scotland as intended, at many East Anglian sheds the 'B17s' were used turn-and-turn-about with the 'B12s', particularly from 1932, as the 'B12/3' rebuilds entered service. The first 10 'B17s' were shared between Stratford (four), Parkeston (three), Ipswich (two) and Gorton (one). The Ipswich and Gorton locomotives were used to work the Harwich–Liverpool boat train between Ipswich and Manchester; the 215-mile route via Lincoln and Sheffield was a severe challenge for a locomotive, and it is a reflection of their qualities that the 'B17s' maintained this service almost exclusively from 1929 until the arrival of the 'Britannias' in 1951. Whilst on layover in Manchester the 'B17' that had arrived from Ipswich would be used by Gorton shed

LEFT Cambridge-based 'B17' No 61657 *Doncaster Rovers* (Darlington, May 1936) awaits departure from Doncaster with a specially decorated fourth-round FA Cup-tie special to Middlesbrough on 6 February 1952. New as LNER No 2857 and previously allocated to Neasden and Colwick, the locomotive would be withdrawn from March depot in June 1960. *G. Oates*

on an overnight GC-line service to and from Leicester, anticipating the extensive use of the later locomotives on the Great Central route from 1934, these being allocated to Neasden and Leicester as well as strengthening the stud at Gorton. By 1939 changes in East Anglia permitted the use of the later locomotives ('B17/4s') with larger tenders, leading to a concentration there of the entire class that would be complete by 1951.

In September 1937 the LNER's list of high-speed services was expanded to include one between Liverpool Street and Norwich, the 'East Anglian'. To provide suitably prestigious motive power two 'B17s', Nos 2859 and 2870, were rebuilt at Doncaster with streamlining in similar style to the 'A4s', the pair losing their *Norwich City* and *Tottenham Hotspur* names in favour of the more appropriate *East Anglian* and *City of London* (the football-team names being transferred to former 'Halls' Nos 2839 and 2830 respectively). The side valances were removed, as on the 'A4s', during 1941, and the locomotives resumed their former appearance when rebuilt in 1951, although they retained their names.

Having implemented the re-boilering of two 'B17s' in 1943 with Gresley-designed 100A boilers, Thompson had already begun the design of a new 6ft 2in 4-6-0, to be designated 'B1', the first of which appeared in 1942. Despite this he decided upon rebuilding

ABOVE Having been rebuilt by Thompson as a two-cylinder 'B2' in August 1945, No 61671 *Royal Sovereign* — originally 'B17' No 2871 *Manchester City* (Robert Stephenson & Hawthorn, June 1937) – is seen near Elsenham with the ex-LNER Royal Train conveying HM The Queen from Wolferton to Liverpool Street on 30 May 1953. This locomotive had been new to Gorton shed, arriving at Cambridge in 1945; one of 10 'B17s' rebuilt as 'B2s', it had been renamed in April 1946 when selected to be the regular 'Royal' engine at Cambridge. Upon its withdrawal (from Cambridge, in September 1958) the *Royal Sovereign* nameplates would be transferred to sister No 61632, destined to spend its last five months as a Royal engine. *BR*

the re-boilered 'B17s' with two cylinders, the first such rebuild, No 2816 *Fallodon*, emerging in November 1945, reclassified 'B2'. Although 20 conversions had been authorised the realisation that the 'B2' offered little advantage over the new 'B1' caused the work to be curtailed after only 10 locomotives had been rebuilt.

The first 'B17' to be withdrawn was No 61628, in September 1952, two more following in 1953. Thereafter there were no further withdrawals until 1958, when a rapid programme of scrapping was implemented, and the last survivor, No 61668 *Bradford City*, was withdrawn from March depot in August 1960.

ABOVE The old order and the new at Stratford shed on 25 March 1956 as 'B17' No 61661 *Sheffield Wednesday* (Darlington, June 1936) stands ahead of 'Britannia' No 70001 *Lord Hurcomb* (Crewe, February 1951). The former No 2861 was allocated to Leicester, March and Stratford before being withdrawn from Cambridge in July 1959. *G. Clarke*

BELOW March-allocated No 61627 *Aske Hall* (Darlington, March 1931) rests on shed at its home depot on 26 June 1958. Originally numbered 2827, the 'B17' was allocated to Parkeston and Cambridge before being withdrawn from March in July 1959. *P. Groom/Gresley Society collection*

The 'W1' ('Hush-Hush') 4-6-4 experimental high-pressure locomotive

Ever the innovator, in September 1924 Gresley held a meeting with marine-boiler designer Harold Yarrow, following which design work began on a joint project to build a locomotive of comparable power to an 'A1' Pacific but with a water-tube boiler of high pressure, the objective being more-efficient steam generation and hence fuel economies. To gain maximum benefit and efficient use of high-pressure steam it was necessary to incorporate a further complication in the form of compound working. A joint patent for a high-pressure water-tube boiler was issued in January 1928, along with one in Gresley's name for the arrangement of independent operation of the valves of the high- and low-pressure cylinders. The locomotive was conceived as a three-cylinder design, with an inside high-pressure cylinder located high above the rear bogie axle and driving the second coupled axle. Presumably to gain operating experience, it was decided that two of the three-cylinder 'D49' 4-4-0s on order from Darlington should be completed as compounds. Drawings had also been obtained from the LMS for its standard Class 4 compound locomotives before a decision was made that the new locomotive should be a four-cylinder compound, whereupon the plan for compound 'D49s' was dropped. Further work was undertaken to refine the relative dimensions of the high- and low-pressure cylinders and the planned working pressure of the

boiler, the latter eventually being settled at 450lb. The sheer size of this boiler dictated a 4-6-4 wheel arrangement, one not previously employed on a British tender engine (and, indeed, destined to remain unique in the UK). Although the locomotive's original design envisaged the use of Lentz poppet valves, the decision was taken later to reduce the degree of innovation and employ traditional Walschaerts valve gear.

The boiler was constructed by Yarrow & Co in Glasgow, where it was fitted to the Darlington-built chassis in March 1929, the part-assembled locomotive returning to Darlington amid some secrecy in November. Wind-tunnel tests had been conducted in order to ascertain the optimum front-end design for driver vision and resulted in a highly unconventional appearance. Numbered 10000 and classified 'W1', it finally emerged from Darlington on 12 December 1929 attached to a new corridor tender, No 5484. (This tender has survived and is now attached to preserved 'A4' No 60009 *Union of South Africa*.) *British Enterprise* nameplates were cast but never carried.

In order that it should remain close to Darlington the 'W1' was allocated to Gateshead, so it was this shed's top-link drivers

BELOW In original condition, 'W1' 4-6-4 No 10000 (Darlington, June 1930) arrives at King's Cross in July 1931 with the up 'Junior Scotsman', which it had worked from Newcastle. *G. R. Griggs/John Adams collection/ Kidderminster Railway Museum*

who were charged with handling the locomotive in a series of dynamometer-car test runs – initially south to York, then to King's Cross, Edinburgh and Perth. During the assault on Glenfarg Bank on the return journey from Perth to Edinburgh on 23 February, with the redoubtable Gateshead driver Tom Blades in charge and with a St Margarets driver as conductor, there were reported to be no fewer than 17 people on the footplate, among them not only Gresley himself but also his two daughters! After three months' trial running No 10000 returned to Darlington for adjustments before being officially placed in traffic on 20 June 1930.

After two months' running on a variety of typical Gateshead turns to Leeds and Edinburgh – including on 31 July and 1 August successfully working non-stop the up and down 'Flying Scotsman' – the locomotive returned to Darlington for further adjustments. These took until January 1931, although a September visit to the Liverpool & Manchester Centenary celebrations was permitted. Further spells in traffic, including further appearances on the 'Flying Scotsman', interspersed with periods back at Darlington for further adjustments continued until May 1933, when, having completed 70,000 miles from new, No 10000 entered Darlington Works for its first General Repair. This took more than a year, the locomotive finally re-emerging in June 1934. May 1934, meanwhile, had seen the first LNER installation of the Kylchap double blastpipe and chimney, on 'P2' 2-8-2 No 2001 *Cock o' the North*, and early in 1935 No 10000 returned to Darlington for the fitting of a similar Kylchap exhaust arrangement, returning to traffic in May 1935, now allocated to Leeds Neville Hill. In between regular work it undertook further dynamometer-car tests between Leeds and Hull, with controlled testing on this level route at a constant 60mph; the highest recorded power output was 1,702hp at 56.7mph, although there were lengthy periods developing 1,520hp at 60mph.

Having covered 20,823 miles since the 1934 overhaul and approximately 90,000 miles from new, No 10000 returned to Darlington on 21 August 1935 for further repairs. No more work was authorised, however, and it remained at Darlington until 13 October 1936, when under its own steam it travelled light-engine to Doncaster for reconstruction as a conventional three-cylinder single-expansion locomotive with a Diagram 108 boiler similar to that attached to 'P2' No 2006 *Wolf of Badenoch*.

The 'W1' was the result of brave experiment which eventually produced a capable machine, particularly after the restricted steam supply to auxiliaries was improved, greatly enhancing its reliability. All in all, much was learned, but the significant costs incurred in workshop time undertaking frequent modifications eventually told. When the locomotive was rebuilt the high-pressure boiler was returned to Darlington, where it was put into use for pressure testing and space heating, only being finally cut up in April 1965. The subsequent career of the 'W1' in rebuilt form is described later in this chapter.

The 'V1' and 'V3' 2-6-2 three-cylinder passenger tank engines

The genesis of the 'V1' 2-6-2 tank engine lasted more than two years, the first proposal emerging at a meeting in April 1928 of Joint Traffic & Locomotive Committee with a reference to 28 locomotives for use over the Metropolitan Widened Lines, complete with condensing apparatus and short chimneys. By November any mention of these features had disappeared, the proposed locomotives being now destined for use in Scotland and reduced in number to 26. Design changes were still being made up to August 1929, when Gresley indicated that the narrow water space above the foundation ring, whilst adequate for the soft water in Scotland, would be insufficient in the London area, where the indifferent water supplies would cause an unacceptable build-up of sludge, indicating a further change of thinking with regard to the deployment of the locomotives.

Twenty-eight 'V1s' finally appeared between September 1930 and December 1931, delivery being delayed by adverse economic conditions which affected the LNER's ability to fund new locomotive construction. Allocated to the Scottish sheds at Eastfield, Haymarket, St Margarets, Parkhead and Kipps, they quickly took over many suburban services in the Edinburgh and Glasgow areas. Further orders were also delayed by the Depression, such that it would be 1935 before the next six locomotives were delivered to the Scottish Area, joining earlier examples at the same sheds in Glasgow (four) and Edinburgh (two). Another 10, intended for the North Eastern Area, were ordered in 1933, 18 more being added in the 1935 programme of which three were for Scotland and 15 for the North East (reduced from 25 as a result of the Tyneside electrification scheme). The Scottish locomotives were based at Dunfermline, while those for the North East were allocated to Heaton,

TOP RIGHT St Margarets 'V1' No 2908 (Doncaster, December 1930) stands on the turntable at its home shed before heading to Waverley to haul the 'Lothian Coast Express' to North Berwick. Nos 2907 and 2908 were outstationed at North Berwick for some years and were immaculately maintained by their dedicated crews. This locomotive would be renumbered 7608 in 1946 and (as BR No 67608) would in 1959 be transferred to Glasgow Parkhead, duly becoming the last 'V1' to be converted to a 'V3', in February 1961 (see right). *Gresley Society collection*

BOTTOM RIGHT Prior to allocation to Gateshead the first new-build 'V3', No 390 (Doncaster, September 1939), is seen in ex-works condition at Doncaster in September 1939. Renumbered 7682 in 1946, the locomotive would remain at Gateshead (latterly as BR No 67682) until transferred to Hexham in January 1955, moving thence to Hull Botanic Gardens in January 1959 and then Dairycoates in June, a final allocation to Darlington, from November 1961 culminating in its withdrawal in September 1963. LNER

ABOVE Middlesbrough-allocated 'V3' No 7684 (Doncaster, October 1939) was the only 'V1' or 'V3' painted apple green after World War 2, at Darlington in 1946, being seen here posing 'at home' in 1949, still in full LNER livery. Originally numbered 392, it had been new to Middlesbrough, where it would remain until a May 1956 transfer to Hull Botanic Gardens and then Dairycoates, surviving to become one of the last 11 survivors withdrawn in November 1964 from Gateshead. *Ian Allan Library*

BELOW Kipps-allocated 'V3' No 67674 (Doncaster, November 1938) heads a Hyndland–Airdrie local near Bellgrove on 1 May 1958. Originally LNER No 480, the locomotive had been new to Glasgow's Eastfield shed, later being transferred to Parkhead and thence Kipps before conversion as a 'V3' in August 1957; it moved to St Margarets in October 1961 following the reintroduction of the 'Blue Trains', it would be withdrawn in December 1962. *G. H. Robin*

ABOVE Newly converted from a 'V1', 'V3' No 67608 poses outside Darlington Works on 5 March 1961. Transferred to Parkhead in 1959, it was the last to be converted, temporary withdrawal of Glasgow's 'Blue Train' electric units shortly after their introduction in late 1960 granting the local 'V1s' and 'V3s' a 14-month reprieve. This locomotive was formally condemned at Eastfield on 29 December 1962.
G. W. Morrison

Blaydon and Gateshead, being supplemented by another 20 locomotives from the 1936 programme. This programme, fulfilled in 1938/9, envisaged 15 locomotives for the Great Eastern Section and a further 5 for Scotland, the former comprising 12 dual-braked examples for Stratford and three vacuum-only engines for Norwich. The 'V1' fleet thus stood at 82 before experiments were undertaken with raised boiler pressure on the Newcastle–Middlesbrough service. These were sufficiently encouraging for the final batch of 10 'V1s', ordered in December 1938, to be amended to include Diagram 102HP boilers pressed to 200lb, designated 'V3'. Between 1940 and 1961 some 63 'V1s' received higher-pressure boilers and were reclassified 'V3', resulting in an eventual fleet of 73 'V3s' and 19 'V1s'.

The Great Eastern 'V1s' and 'V3s', tight for water and coal capacity on many turns, were displaced by new 'L1' 2-6-4 tanks in 1948/9, being then reallocated to the Scottish and North Eastern Regions. Here the 'V1s and 'V3s' were popular with crews and fully masters of their allotted tasks, particularly on the North Clyde suburban services and the tightly timed 48-mile Newcastle–Middlesbrough service, on which they were the mainstay for many years. The Edinburgh-based examples monopolised services to North Berwick, Musselburgh and Galashiels (via Peebles) until displaced by diesels, and several, with dedicated crews, were kept in immaculate condition.

The first locomotive to be withdrawn was 'V1' No 67671, in July 1960, but many of the Scottish 'V1s' and 'V3s', rendered surplus as a result of electrification in the Glasgow area, were successfully resurrected in 1961 when the newly introduced 'Blue Train' electric units had to be withdrawn for almost a year (after suffering a series of explosions in their 6.25/25kV changeover equipment), the last three 'V1s', all at Eastfield shed, finally being condemned when electric services were reintroduced in December 1962; the 'V3' became extinct when the last 11 examples were withdrawn by the North Eastern Region in November 1964. The Gresley Society tried to save a 'V3' from the scrapyard in 1964, but the £1,400 asking price exceeded the funding available at the time.

ABOVE Dunfermline-allocated 'V3' No 67672 (Doncaster, November 1938) was condemned in December 1962, being seen here in store at Thornton early in 1963. This locomotive was converted from a 'V1' in March 1943; originally numbered 472, it had been new to Stratford shed, remaining there until transferred to Dunfermline in 1949. Behind is 'J88' No 68353, based locally and by now also withdrawn.
G. Jones/Kidderminster Railway Museum

The 'A8' 5ft 9in 4-6-2 passenger tanks

The 45 Raven Class D (LNER 'H1') 4-4-4Ts had been the largest passenger tank engines on the NER, but following the Grouping Gresley had decided that the urgent needs of the North East Area would be best met by construction of more Robinson 'A5' 4-6-2 tanks, and the operation of these locomotives alongside the 'H1s' soon demonstrated the advantages of their six-coupled wheel arrangement. In 1931, therefore, No 2162 was rebuilt at Darlington as a 4-6-2T, designated 'A8', with satisfactory results, and consequently reconstruction of the remaining 44 locomotives was undertaken between 1933 and 1936. From 1929 a new design of superheated boiler (Diagram 63A) had been constructed by NBL (five) and Darlington (14) for use primarily on the 'H1s' and 'A8s' (although one was fitted to a 'T1' 4-8-0). From 1935 further such boilers were built to an enhanced specification, a final variant (Diagram 63B), which ran to 70 examples, being constructed from 1937 for use on Classes A6, A7, A8 and T1.

ABOVE Pictured on 27 May 1950, Scarborough-allocated 'A8' No 69885 (rebuilt from 'H1' at Darlington, May 1936) has just emerged from a General Overhaul at Darlington Works. New as No 1526 and renumbered 9885 in October 1946, this locomotive would spend the winter of 1951/2 at Selby and the winters of 1956/7 and 1957/8 at Neville Hill, returning to Scarborough each summer until condemned on 20 June 1960, being broken up at Darlington later that year.
L. W. Perkins/Kidderminster Railway Museum

LEFT Whitby-allocated 'A8' No 69890 (rebuilt from 'H1' at Darlington, October 1935) pulls away from Pickering station with a Whitby–York local on 29 June 1951. The former No 1521 had been renumbered 9890 in October 1946 and would spend four months in the spring of 1956 at York before leaving Whitby for Malton shed in June 1957, finally being condemned on 13 January 1958, to be cut up at Darlington. Pickering station would later lose its typical NER overall roof, only to see it restored in 2012 by the North Yorkshire Moors Railway. *P. J. Lynch/Kidderminster Railway Museum*

The 'A8s' put in good work on the heavy suburban traffic on Tyneside and Teesside as well as on the steeply graded coastal routes north from Hull to Scarborough, Whitby and Saltburn. Although from 1933 they had been replaced on the more demanding turns by 'V1s', the 'A8s' continued to give good service in these areas until displaced by DMUs in the 1950s. The first withdrawal was of No 69876 in October 1957, and a period during which locomotives were stored at Scarborough, Thornaby and Sunderland culminated in a rush of condemnations early in 1960, the last five survivors being withdrawn in June.

ABOVE Whitby-allocated 'A8' No 69861 (rebuilt from 'H1' at Darlington, August 1935) climbs the 1 in 49 gradient near Goathland with a local Whitby–Malton train in April 1954. The locomotive would be withdrawn from Malton shed in June 1960 and cut up at Darlington, but the route survives as part of the North Yorkshire Moors Railway. *J. M. Jarvis/Kidderminster Railway Museum*

The 'S1' 4ft 8in 0-8-4 heavy-shunting tanks

The opening of the new 'hump' marshalling yard at Whitemoor created a requirement for more heavy-shunting locomotives, and again Gresley turned to a successful pre-Grouping design, the '8H' (LNER 'S1') 0-8-4T designed by Robinson for the GCR in 1907. The four locomotives of this class had demonstrated complete mastery of their task at Wath Yard for almost 25 years, so it was hardly surprising that when the need for more locomotives was identified two further examples were constructed at Gorton; fitted with boosters to the rear bogie (one of the original quartet having been similarly rebuilt) and classified 'S1/3', they were delivered in May and June 1932 and put to work from March shed. Two further locomotives were ordered from Doncaster in February 1932, but these were cancelled in June.

The March locomotives were displaced by diesel shunters from December 1949, which led to a brief spell at Frodingham, but from December 1950 all six 'S1s' were concentrated at

Mexborough (for use at Wath) until the arrival there of diesel shunters in the summer of 1953. Trials conducted with the 'S1s' at Immingham proved unsuccessful, so all were transferred to Doncaster before being withdrawn between 1954 and 1957.

Rebuilding of the 'D15' and 'D16' 4-4-0s

In February 1933 No 8900, the first of the famous Holden/ Hill 'Claud Hamilton' 4-4-0s (LNER Classes D15 and D16), was rebuilt at Stratford Works with a new Diagram 28A boiler (similar to that supplied for the reconstruction of the 'B12' 4-6-0s), along with new cylinders fitted with piston valves, which showed immediate advantages over the earlier slide-valve locomotives. A further 19 'D16/3' conversions were authorised, but it soon became apparent that the increased power of the rebuilt locomotives was causing the frames to crack, so subsequent rebuilds retained the slide valves as a means of minimising the problem. In total some 104 of the 121 'Clauds' were rebuilt as 'D16/3s', the work being carried out while Edward Thompson was in charge at Stratford; although Gresley was in overall control the Assistant Mechanical Engineers were given a degree of latitude as long as higher authority was consulted, so to what extent these rebuilds were Gresley's responsibility rather than Thompson's remains a matter of conjecture. The first to be withdrawn was No 8866, in September 1945, the last, as BR No 62613, surviving until October 1960.

ABOVE Looking very smart, King's Lynn-allocated Class D16/3 'Claud Hamilton' No 62614 (Stratford, July 1923) draws into Cambridge station with a London train in 1951. Rebuilt from a 'D16/2' in December 1939, this locomotive, previously numbered 8783, would be withdrawn from King's Lynn in August 1958. *M. Roberts/Kidderminster Railway Museum*

The 'P2' express passenger 2-8-2s

The 131-mile route between Edinburgh and Aberdeen abounds in short, stiff gradients and tight curves, many beginning at the end of station platforms and thus presenting a demanding specification for the locomotive designer. After the displacement of the ex-NBR Atlantics by Gresley Pacifics in the early 1920s bridge weight restrictions continued to prevent double-heading by the largest locomotives, requiring the use of pairs of smaller engines on the heaviest of trains. By the late 1920s trains exceeding the maximum loadings (480 tons in the down direction, 420 up) permitted for an 'A3' Pacific were becoming more common, and the expensive and unsatisfactory alternative of double-heading with pairs of smaller locomotives was being adopted more frequently. Gresley therefore sought to provide a powerful locomotive with sufficient adhesive weight to be able to cope with getting trains of up to 530 tons safely underway up gradients as steep as 1 in 70. This meant an eight-coupled driving-wheel arrangement, notwithstanding the

severe curvature on parts of the route, length restrictions dictating provision of only a leading pony truck rather than a bogie. Against this difficult specification Gresley produced six spectacular machines of such striking appearance as to leave a lasting impression on all who saw them.

Construction of two locomotives was authorised in March 1933 after 12 months' deliberation over the details – which nevertheless continued, as in June a revision incorporating ACFI feed-water-heating equipment was issued, and in July drawings for a Kylchap double blastpipe and Lentz rotary-cam poppet valve gear were provided by the Associated Locomotive Equipment Co; meanwhile the order was reduced to one locomotive in April, reverting to two in November 1933. Classified 'P2', the 6ft 2in 2-8-2 design, with an adhesive weight of just over 80 tons, was capable of producing a tractive effort of 43,462lb and over the critical Edinburgh–Aberdeen route would be able to take two carriages (50 tons) more than could the 'A3s' northbound and almost four carriages (110 tons) more southbound. (There is some evidence that the type was also intended for use over the 98-mile Waverley route between Edinburgh and Carlisle, which had long stretches of 1-in-70/75 grade, but no loading has ever been found, and no instances of use over this route were ever recorded.)

ABOVE On 12 May 1934 the original 'P2', No 2001 *Cock o' the North*, poses for an official photograph of the proud team involved in its construction at Doncaster Works, from left to right R. A. Thom (Mechanical Engineer, Doncaster), E. Windle (Chief Locomotive Draughtsman), J. S. Jones, (Assistant Works Manager), J. Eggleshaw (Works Manager), three charge-hand fitters, the Erecting Shop foreman and the Paint Shop foreman. *LNER*

Delivered on 22 May 1934, the first locomotive, No 2001 *Cock o' the North*, was shown to the press at King's Cross on 1 June 1934 and to the public at Ilford on the 2nd; interestingly it was fitted with a chime whistle that had been presented to Gresley in April 1934 by Captain Howey, of the Romney, Hythe & Dymchurch Railway, this being the first such installation on a Gresley locomotive. On the 3rd it travelled light-engine to Edinburgh, thence to work a test train the following day to Aberdeen; exhibited there and again at Edinburgh Waverley on the 6th, it then returned to London for initial three-week period of dynamometer-car and normal-service running to and from Peterborough, ahead of a transfer to Doncaster on the 21st and further dynamometer-car and in-service running to and from King's Cross. During this early testing No 2001 demonstrated a great free-running capacity, speeds of up to 87mph being recorded on trains of up to 649 tons, suggesting a drawbar horsepower in excess of 2,100. After some adjustments to the blastpipe – required on account of the fact that the locomotive represented the LNER's first experience of the Kylchap double chimney – No 2001 arrived at Haymarket shed on 30 July and on 1 August began two days of test running with a 586-ton train to and from Aberdeen before entering ordinary service, daily making two round-trips to Dundee. Reports of heavy coal consumption required further tests including a special Dundee trip on 1 October, when a miscalculation led to the locomotive's running out of coal at Dalmeny on the return journey. After changes to blastpipe dimensions a further test was undertaken to Dundee on 5 October which saw coal being consumed at the rate of almost 92lb per mile – an exceptionally high figure, even allowing for the hard work being undertaken, and one in which the Lentz poppet valves were subsequently proven to be a major contributory factor.

The second locomotive, No 2002 *Earl Marischal*, was delivered in October 1934 and differed from No 2001 in lacking a feed-water heater and having conventional Walschaerts-Gresley valve gear. The piston valves produced a much softer exhaust than the poppet valves and did not give the required degree of clearance of smoke and steam, despite the Kylchap chimney,

ABOVE Fitted with an indicator shelter, *Cock o' the North* stands at Peterborough on 19 June 1934, having arrived from King's Cross with a test train. *Ian Allan Library*

BELOW The second 'P2', No 2002 *Earl Marischal*, as recorded in an official Doncaster Works photograph taken on 15 December 1934. Fitted from new with Gresley/Walschaerts valve gear, this locomotive would be withdrawn April 1944 for rebuilding as an 'A2/2'. *LNER*

requiring the fitting of additional deflector-plates outside the originals. In November 1934 a four more 'P2s' were ordered, also with conventional valve gear.

Gresley's friendship with André Chapelon now facilitated a visit by No 2001 to the SNCF testing station at Vitry-sur-Seine, south of Paris, the locomotive and its train of bogie coal wagons being transported via the Harwich train ferry on 4 December 1934. Testing took place on the rollers at the test plant, plus some road testing between Vitry and Étampes as well as over the ex-Paris–Orléans main line between St Pierre des Corps and Orléans. The tests were dogged by persistent 'hot boxes', which developed when operating on the rollers at the testing

ABOVE Shortly after arrival in Scotland No 2001 *Cock o' the North* takes water in the yard at Haymarket shed in June 1935. Note the tablet-catcher on the tender front. *Ian Allan Library*

TOP LEFT Newly arrived in France, No 2001 is steamed at SNCF's Dunkerque shed on 7 December 1934 prior to hauling its train south to the testing station at Vitry. *O. V. S. Bulleid*

BOTTOM LEFT Bound for Vitry, south of Paris, No 2001 passes through Amiens station with its train of British vehicles, including bogie coal wagons. *O. V. S. Bulleid*

station but, surprisingly, not when out on the line. The tests were supervised by Gresley's technical assistant, Oliver Bulleid, and Doncaster draughtsman E. Windle. After display at Gare du Nord in Paris on 17 February 1935 the locomotive and train returned under their own power to Dunkirk for the train ferry to Harwich. The tests did not lead to any clear conclusions other than to vindicate the decision not to equip the four additional 'P2s' with Lentz poppet valves.

Following its return from France No 2001 initially spent four months at Doncaster before it settled down from mid-June to regular work from Haymarket shed. No 2002, allocated initially to Doncaster, usually worked a daily round-trip to King's Cross until May 1935, when, following attention at

Doncaster Works, it spent two weeks working from Haymarket before being transferred to Dundee, moving on thence to Aberdeen in September 1936.

The last four 'P2s', Nos 2003-6, delivered between June and September 1936, looked radically different from the first two, being fitted with the streamlined front end introduced on Gresley's new 'A4' Pacifics, this having already demonstrated its effectiveness in clearing drifting smoke from the driver's line of sight. No 2003, named *Lord President*, was allocated to Dundee in September after running-in at Haymarket, to which it returned in October 1942 before a curious loan to the North Eastern Area from the end of November 1942 for 14 months before returning once more to Haymarket; no details of its use during this period have survived. No 2004 *Mons Meg* was always a Haymarket engine, while No 2005 *Thane of Fife* was only ever allocated to Dundee; this differed from the others in having a single Kylchap blastpipe and chimney and was always regarded as the poorest steamer. No 2006 *Wolf of Badenoch* was based at Aberdeen until October 1942, when it joined Nos 2003 and 2004 at Haymarket.

After the adoption of the 'A4'-style front end for Nos 2003-6 it was not long before the opportunity was taken to standardise on this front-end design and remove the troublesome Lentz poppet valves and ACFI feed-water heater from No 2001. Doncaster took No 2002 in hand during its first General Overhaul in August

ABOVE An official works photograph of No 2001 *Cock o' the North* as rebuilt at Doncaster in April 1938 with Walschaerts valve gear and an A4 style front end similar to that fitted from new to Nos 2003-6. Note the hole in the tender front, for the tablet-catcher apparatus. The locomotive was destined for a short life in this form, being withdrawn in June 1944 for rebuilding as an 'A2/2' Pacific. *LNER*

LEFT Three generations of Doncaster express locomotive are lined up in this staged February 1935 shot of 'P2' No 2002 *Earl Marischal* (December 1934), bearing the 'Flying Scotsman' headboard, overtaking 'A1' Pacific No 2552 *Sansovino* (November 1924) and GNR 'C1' Atlantic No 3288 (June 1904). *LNER*

1936, reconstruction of No 2001 following during its second General, between September 1937 and April 1938.

Initially through workings between Edinburgh and Aberdeen were undertaken, but worries over coal consumption saw these through workings substituted by locomotive changes at Dundee from early 1937, only to be resumed during World War 2. Until 1939 workings were largely confined to the Aberdeen route, which entailed some use of these puissant machines on lighter trains which did not require their power, scarcely assisting the drive for coal economies. From 1939 there were regular workings to Glasgow and to Perth, as well as occasional appearances as far south as Newcastle. The locomotives' frequent visits to Doncaster for overhaul were usually made light-engine, although there was at least one recorded instance of a 'P2' returning on a service train between Newcastle and Edinburgh. Cowlairs Works in Glasgow also participated in the

overhaul of the 'P2s', usually only when light repairs were required, although No 2001 alone received heavy repairs at Cowlairs in 1935 and 1943.

The locomotives' rigid wheelbase of 37ft 11in (against the 35ft 9in of the 'A3s') gave some problems with wear on the leading driving wheelset and side-rod bearings, which led to some redesign of the suspension of the leading pony truck;[1] they also gained a reputation for minor derailments in sidings, although not on running lines. During a visit to Edinburgh in 1942, a year after Gresley's death, Thompson reportedly informed local officials of his intention to 'get the "P2s" off the Aberdeen road', which gave rise to speculation that the locomotives were to be moved south, where they could be usefully employed working the heavily loaded East Coast wartime services out of King's Cross. That this sensible redeployment was never implemented is still a matter of great speculation with regard to Thompson's real motives. It is clear that his intentions were far more radical, and much in the way of scarce design resources and materials would be expended in turning six graceful, powerful and capable machines into ugly locomotives of dubious value. Between October 1942 and September 1944 the six 'P2s' returned to Doncaster for complete reconstruction as Class A2/2 Pacifics.

---

1 Scrutiny of the A1 Trust's plans for a new 'P2' confirms that this is still an issue in 2015, albeit one easily resolvable by means of minor changes to the side control of the pony truck already successfully implemented with the bogie of *Tornado*.

The 'A4' streamlined Pacifics

At 10am on 30 September 1935 locomotive No 2509 Silver Link departed Newcastle Central station with the 'Silver Jubilee' train for King's Cross, beginning a new era in high-speed rail transport which would lead ultimately to the InterCity 125 and Eurostar. However, the explanation of how that train was designed and built in only five months requires some explanation. To begin we can use no better source than the Address to the Institution of Mechanical Engineers by its President, and the designer of both locomotive and train, Sir Nigel Gresley, given on 23 October 1936.

'I visited Germany in the latter part of 1934 and travelled on the "Flying Hamburger" from Berlin to Hamburg and back; I was so much impressed by the smooth running of this train at a speed of 100mph, which was maintained for long distances, that I thought it advisable to explore the possibilities of extra high-speed travel by having such a train for experimental purposes on the London & North Eastern Railway.

'I accordingly approached the makers of that train and furnished them with full particulars as to the gradients, curves and speed restrictions on the line between King's Cross and Newcastle. With the thoroughness characteristic of the German engineers they made a very exhaustive investigation and prepared a complete schedule showing the shortest possible running times under favourable conditions and then added 10%, which they regarded

ABOVE The first 'A4', No 2509 *Silver Link* (Doncaster, September 1935), poses brand new at Doncaster Plant. Note the initially fitted short buffers and painted name, not replaced until July 1936 and December 1937 respectively. No 2509 exclusively worked the first 13 days of the 'Silver Jubilee' until the second locomotive, No 2510, was available. The later No 14/60014 was always a King's Cross locomotive apart from two spells at Grantham between August 1944 and May 1948, then June 1948 to May 1950. Condemned in December 1962, No 60014 was cut up with undue haste at Doncaster in January 1963. *LNER*

as adequate to meet varying weather conditions and to have sufficient time in reserve to make up for such decelerations or delays as might normally be expected

'The train, weighing 115 tons, was to consist of three articulated coaches and to be generally similar to the German train. The timings for the complete journey were given as 4 hours 15½ minutes in the down direction and 4 hours 17 minutes in the up. The train provided seating for 140 passengers. The accommodation was much more cramped than that provided in this country for ordinary Third-class passengers, and it did not appear likely to prove attractive for a journey occupying four hours. My Chief General Manager [Sir Ralph Wedgwood] suggested that with an ordinary "Pacific" engine faster overall speeds could be maintained with a train of much greater weight, capacity, and comfort. A trial with a train of seven bogie coaches demonstrated that the run could be accomplished with reliability in less than four hours under normal conditions.

'I felt that to secure a sufficient margin of power it would be essential to streamline the engine and train as effectively as possible, and at the same time to make sundry alterations to the design of cylinders and boiler which would conduce to freer running and to securing an ample reserve of power for fast uphill running. The designs for the engine and carriages were prepared and the complete train built in the company's works at Doncaster in the remarkably short time of five months, and I am pleased to place on record this achievement of my staff. The train was completed early in September of last year and, after a few runs on which exceptionally high speeds were reached, went into service on 30th September. It completed twelve months' service of five days weekly on 30th September last, and had run 133,464 miles during that period and carried about 68,000 passengers. There has only once been an engine failure when the train had to be stopped and another engine substituted.'

Displaying the modesty with which he was typically associated, Gresley acknowledged the contribution of Ralph Wedgwood to the decision to opt for a steam-hauled solution to the problem. Indeed Gresley was fortunate that the LNER, unlike its larger LMS rival, enjoyed a long period of stability in the senior-management team, which led to the ability to make the rapid decisions and firm implementation typified by the 'Silver Jubilee' project. Chairman William Whitelaw, Chief General Manager (Chief Executive in modern parlance) Ralph Wedgwood and Chief Mechanical Engineer Nigel Gresley had all been in post and therefore working closely together for 11 years, since the formation of the LNER in 1923. They all knew and trusted each other intimately through many years of close collaboration, and this gave the LNER a firmness of purpose which held it in good stead through the often difficult times of the 1930s. Wedgwood often displayed a strong commercial flair, which manifested itself in a number of strikingly successful initiatives, of which the ultimate trio of high-speed passenger services was but one example.

At the company's Annual General Meeting on 8 March, Wedgwood announced the proposed new high-speed service, to be called the 'Silver Jubilee'. On 28 March his paper to the Traffic Committee was accepted and authority given for the design and construction of the new high-speed train and locomotives, of which the former emerged only five months later as the 'Silver Jubilee'. Four more 'A3' Pacifics had been included in the locomotive-building programme for 1935; this allowed Gresley to anticipate the motive-power requirements for regular high-speed operations by modifying the design of the 'A3' in several important areas, and thus was born the 'A4'. Gresley had considered use of the Kylchap double

blastpipe as used on the 'P2' 2-8-2s but instead decided to use the single blastpipe with a jumper top, as used by the GWR. One consideration must have been that use of the Kylchap system would have required the payment of royalties, which would have amounted to 5% of the overall cost of the 'A4'; indeed Gresley reportedly confirmed not long before his death that all 'A4s' were to be so fitted when the patent expired!

External streamlining

The two 'P2s' of 1934 and the solitary experimental high-pressure 'W1' of 1929 had experimented with limited external streamlining. Although energy and thus fuel saving was the initial motivation, there was also concern regarding a problem common to large-boilered locomotives designed to be worked at short cut-off, namely drifting smoke obscuring the driver's view of signals and the line ahead. Initially Gresley was sceptical with regard to the potential benefits of external streamlining, but when calculations demonstrated that at above 75mph the reduction in air resistance offered the real advantage of power savings of up to 40% he gave authority for his assistant, Oliver Bulleid, to develop the detailed designs. Gresley himself had commented at the Institution of Railway Engineers in the autumn of 1934 that 'Experiments with models of existing types of coaches carried out by NPL show that air resistance of trains of average length, say, 12 coaches, at 100mph is approximately double that of similar trains at 70mph,' adding that 'Streamlining is essential at extra high speed because the air resistance increases approximately with the square of the speed.' Gresley had noted the wedge-shaped front end of the Bugatti high-speed railcar on which he had travelled between Paris and Deauville, and this shape was incorporated in a series of wind-tunnel tests undertaken on models at both the National Physics Laboratory (NPL) and the City & Guilds Institute (CGI). Initially the top of the boiler casing behind the chimney was flat, but prior to one test an unknown finger made an indentation in the Plasticine mould immediately behind the chimney, and Professor Dalby (of the CGI) noted that this accidental modification resulted in much-improved smoke-lifting. Indeed this highly distinctive feature of the 'A4' is a prime example of effective design in terms of its ability to lift smoke clear of the boiler side at even moderate speeds.

The streamliner era and the 'Silver Jubilee'

It is probable that no debut of a new British locomotive had ever caused such a sensation as did that of No 2509 *Silver Link*. That there was to be a four-hour 'flyer' to Newcastle was widely known, and that the locomotive would be streamlined was generally anticipated, but most observers expected something like a Pacific version of 'P2' *Cock o' the North* painted in the usual LNER green, with the usual rake of teak coaches. Hence when No 2509 first appeared at King's Cross in its silver-and-grey colour scheme, having been

The third 'A4', No 2511 *Silver King* (Doncaster, November 1935), hauls the Up 'Silver Jubilee' just south of Peterborough in 1937. After an initial 13-day allocation to King's Cross, No 2511 was moved Gateshead as a standby locomotive for the 'Silver Jubilee' service and was subsequently never allocated south of Newcastle, spending her last 17 months service in Scotland then two weeks at St Margaret's before moving to Aberdeen in November 1963. Withdrawn in March 1965, No 16/60016 was broken up at Wishaw. *Ian Allan Library*

worked up from Doncaster, on 13 September 1935, the effect on the media was immediate and dramatic. On the following day the locomotive made its first revenue-earning journeys, a return trip to Cambridge, followed on 22 September by some unpublicised high-speed braking tests with the 'Jubilee' stock between King's Cross and Doncaster; these tests confirmed that from high speed a train was unable to stop within normal braking distance and could potentially overrun signals, which led to a decision to introduce 'double-block' working (hitherto used only for the Royal Train) for the streamliners.

The impact became even greater when, on Friday 27 September, the complete train was presented to the media, a special from King's Cross to Barkston and back being organised to demonstrate it to the world's press, who were accompanied by representatives of the LNER and many of the manufacturers that had supplied equipment. The privilege of handling the locomotive fell to King's Cross driver A. J. Taylor, and he and No 2509 maintained the honour of the LNER in spectacular fashion with a demonstration of the fastest sustained running ever seen on rails, setting no fewer than three new world records for railway traction. It would appear that the Flaman speed-recorder that would be fitted to all the 'A4s' was inoperative or had yet to be installed, for after the speed record had been broken Gresley reportedly walked up to the driver's cab and exclaimed: 'Steady on, old chap! Do you know you have just done 112mph? Go a bit easier; we have an old director in the back, and he is getting a bit touchy!' Driver Taylor

was subsequently interviewed by the press and is reported to have described the 'A4' as 'the finest engine we have ever had,' adding: 'There is no vibration whatever. We could have gone faster if we had wanted to – we were not all-out by any means. Quite frankly I didn't think we'd been going much above 90mph, and apparently it was smoother on the engine than in the train.' The distance of 25 miles between Hitchin and Offord was covered at speeds of at least 100mph – and twice reaching 112.5mph – at an *average* of 107.5mph; the average speed over the 41 miles between Hatfield and Huntingdon was 100.6mph, and the entire distance covered at an average speed of 100mph was 43 miles. The advance in performance made possible by the 'A4' over that achieved by 'A3' No 2750 *Papyrus* on its record run some six months earlier was demonstrated for all to see, and in a most decisive fashion.

The 'Silver Jubilee' was so named, following a suggestion by Wedgwood, in celebration of the 25th anniversary of the accession of King George V, and four 'A4s' specially designed to haul the train were given names derived from this title – Nos 2509 *Silver Link*, 2510 *Quicksilver*, 2511 *Silver King* and 2512 *Silver Fox*. The service began on Monday 30 September 1935, departing Newcastle at 10.0am and (after one stop, at Darlington) arriving at King's Cross at 2.0pm. The return journey departed King's Cross at 5.30pm, arriving at Newcastle (again, stopping at Darlington) at 9.30pm. Surprisingly, in view of the overnight stabling of the train on Tyneside, the service was worked exclusively by King's Cross locomotives and crews, No 2511 *Silver King* being based at Gateshead merely as a back-up in case of failure of any of the other three locomotives. However, for the first 13 days (until 17 October, when the second locomotive, No 2510 *Quicksilver*, was used) only No 2509 was available, covering 537 miles each day at a scheduled average speed of 70.4mph start to stop, five days a week (a total of almost 7,000 miles), with absolute regularity and without any mechanical troubles – a magnificent performance.

Locomotive reliability notwithstanding, operation of the 'Silver Jubilee' was not without incident, for on 27 August 1936 the dynamometer car was attached to the train for the purposes of testing coal and water consumption prior to the introduction of the proposed new Aberdeen to London streamliner. There was also apparently a conscious decision to attempt to break No 2509's 11-month-old record of 112mph. This was achieved by a margin of 1mph, but with potentially disastrous consequences. On the up run the middle big-end of No 2512 *Silver Fox* virtually disintegrated and the train limped in to Kings Cross 7 minutes late.

The 'Silver Jubilee' was an immediate commercial success, and a cost/benefit review of the first year results presented by Wedgwood to the Joint Locomotive & Traffic Committee in October 1936 revealed that the service had carried an average of 130 passengers on the up service and 143 on the down – a load factor of 86%. The income from the supplementary fares alone repaid the complete investment in the train, and the gross revenue was as much as six times the operating cost. Overall Newcastle–London business had grown by 12% since the train had started running and had acted as 'a stimulus to traffic'. Initially formed of seven vehicles demand was such that in 1938 a further corridor third was added to the trailing articulated twin to form a second triple and increase the train to eight carriages. The train ran for almost four years, from 30 September 1935 until 31 August 1939, being withdrawn on the eve of World War 2, in common with the LNER's other streamliners.

Some 1,952 journeys were made by the 'Silver Jubilee', of which 564 were worked by No 2509, 456 by No 2510, 409 by No 2512 and just 80 by No 2511. Other 'A4s' were responsible for the other 440 runs, and there were with three workings by 'A3s'. There were only 16 recorded instances of locomotive failures (nine of them involving No 2510 and five No 2509), which translates to a miles-per-casualty figure of almost 33,000.

Sir Nigel

Aside from the setting of a new British speed record by one of his locomotives, 1936 proved to be a memorable year for Gresley personally, for on 21 February he became President of the Institution of Mechanical Engineers. He was also made an honorary Doctor of Science (DSc) by the University of Manchester, but this would be topped later in the summer by the announcement in the King's Birthday Honours List that he was to receive the honour of a knighthood, for his services (as *The Times* felicitously expressed it) 'as engineer and speeder-up to the LNER'.

The 'Coronation'

When the 'Silver Jubilee' started running the LNER had announced that, depending upon public reaction, further high-speed trains would be introduced. Following the operational and commercial success of the 'Silver Jubilee', Wedgwood's memo of October 1936 proposed two new services – one between London and Edinburgh in six hours, with one stop at Newcastle, to be called the 'Coronation' and to start with the 1937 summer timetable, the other between Bradford, Leeds and London, to start in the autumn of 1937. In fact there had been planning from the spring of 1936 for a high-speed King's Cross–Edinburgh–Aberdeen train running to a nine-hour overall schedule, but the idea of an extension to/ from Aberdeen was abandoned that October.

At the end of December 1936 the first two of a new batch of 10 'A4s' were delivered from Doncaster Works, these being Nos 4482 *Golden Eagle* and 4483 *Kingfisher*. In recognition of their intended use on general express services rather than exclusively on the streamliners they were finished in the standard LNER livery of apple green and had their names on cast plates affixed to the side of the smokebox, as had been originally intended for the 'Silver Jubilee' quartet. Four more green 'A4s' were turned out between February and April 1937, Nos 4484-7, respectively *Falcon*, *Kestrel*, *Merlin* and *Sea Eagle*. The next to appear, No 4489 *Woodcock*, in the same month as the coronation of King George VI, was lined out like the other green locomotives but painted grey for photographic purposes. This gave the first indication that the new streamliner, named the 'Coronation', would not perpetuate the grey and silver of the 'Silver Jubilee'; instead its coaches wore a striking two-tone colour scheme of 'garter blue' below the waist and Cambridge blue above. Clearly a green locomotive would have looked out of place at the head of this train, so the five new 'A4s' earmarked for the service were painted also in garter blue. In a burst of patriotic fervour the locomotives were to be named after the major countries of the British Empire, and thus No 4489 was repainted and renamed *Dominion of Canada* at a ceremony at King's Cross on 15 June. The other four locomotives were numbered 4488/90-2 and named respectively *Union of South Africa*, *Empire of India*, *Commonwealth of Australia* and *Dominion of New*

Zealand. Construction of green 'A4s' resumed thereafter, No 4493 taking the displaced name *Woodcock*, and No 4494 *Osprey* this latter having been intended originally for No 4488. Thus the 18 'A4s' delivered by the end of August were running in three different liveries – four in silver/grey, five in garter blue and nine in apple green. No 4495 was initially green and not repainted blue and renamed until 25 September.

For a locomotive the 'Coronation' represented a far harder proposition than did the 'Silver Jubilee'. With nine coaches (instead of seven, later eight) and a tare weight of 312 tons (as against 220), it required a proportionate increase in power output, but far more of an issue was the prospect of a single locomotive working throughout between London and Edinburgh, trains being scheduled to depart King's Cross at 4.0pm and Waverley at 4.30pm and to arrive at their respective destinations exactly six hours later. Although there was a change of crew *en route*, the 9 tons of coal had to last throughout for 392 miles of hard, high-speed running, and on the up journey 2 December 1937 No 4490 was so short of coal as to require assistance from Hitchin, No 4492 similarly seven days later; as a result minor modifications were made to the locomotives' tenders to increase their capacity.

Locomotive failures were very few. On 1,084 runs between 3 July 1937 and 31 August 1939 there were only 13 failures in 1937, 21 in 1938 and 12 in 1939. This equates to just over 9,000 miles per failure, this figure reflecting the fact that the 'Coronation' was a much tougher proposition than the other streamlined trains (yet still much higher than that typically achieved by today's InterCity 125 power cars). Some of the 'A4s' achieved great feats of reliability, No 4491 being used on 48 of the first 51 days of the service and No 4489 covering 18,327 miles in the course of 34 days' continuous working, while in the spring of 1939 No 4497 *Golden Plover* made 39 consecutive round-trips on the 'Coronation', running 2,358 miles weekly on the high-speed service and achieved a total of 15,327 miles in just over six weeks. Demonstrating the superiority of the 'A4s', on 18 May 1938 the up train was worked by 'A1' No 4473 *Solario*, arriving at King's Cross 16 minutes late.

The 'Coronation' was formed of two nine-coach sets, Nos 102 and 103 (the 'Silver Jubilee' set being numbered 101), each comprising four articulated twins and, at the rear, a 'beaver-tail' observation car; in the winter months, because much of the running was in the dark and to give an additional performance margin, the observation car was deleted from the formation. Originally the 'Coronation' sets were to have followed the 'Silver Jubilee' in terms of internal design, but in January 1937 it was

BELOW The third of the batch of 'A4s' ordered for service hauling the 'Coronation', No 4491 *Commonwealth of Australia* (Doncaster, June 1937) brings the Up service near Burnmouth in 1937. No 4491 was always a Scottish-based locomotive and as No 60012 was withdrawn from Aberdeen in August 1964, being broken up in March 1965 at Wishaw. *Ian Allan Library*

ABOVE The 20th 'A4', No 4497 *Golden Plover*, appears at King's Cross shed yard in spring 1939, during the period of 39 consecutive days it worked the 'Coronation'. Delivered new in garter blue livery, No 4497 was always a Scottish-allocated locomotive, its home being Haymarket until allocation to St Rollox in February 1962. Withdrawal took place in October 1965. *Gresley Society collection*

decided that all the coaches should be of open layout, with all seats (save in the observation cars) reservable, the provision of two kitchen cars in each set thus making it possible to serve all passengers with meals at their seats. Seating followed the 'Silver Jubilee' pattern of 2+1 in Third class and 1+1 (with swivelling armchairs) in First. The 'Coronation' was a lucrative venture for the LNER, in July 1938 reportedly returning a profit of 13s 8d (69p) per mile – slightly more than the 'Silver Jubilee'.

The 'West Riding Limited'

On 27 September 1937 the third streamlined train entered service between Bradford, Leeds and King's Cross. Departing Bradford Exchange at 11.10am and Leeds Central (after reversal) at 11.31, it was scheduled to arrive at King's Cross at 2.15pm. The return journey left King's Cross at 7.10pm, reaching Leeds at 9.53 and Bradford at 10.15. This train employed a set (No 104) similar to those used for the 'Coronation', comprising four articulated twins but lacking an observation car. Livery was the same as for the other streamlined trains, although the coaches were lettered 'West Riding Limited' and numbered within the GN Section series rather than the East Coast series. (A fifth eight-car set, No 105, was constructed at Doncaster to act as a spare for the other four.) Two new 'A4s', Nos 4495 and 4496, were allocated to the service, being painted garter blue and given names appropriate to the Yorkshire woollen trade – *Golden Fleece* and *Golden Shuttle*.

From 27 September 1937 to 31 August 1939 the 'West Riding Limited' made 968 runs, 258 of them behind No 4495 and 277 with No 4496. In 1939 No 4495 was used for 14 consecutive weeks, with only three days' break, while No 4496 managed 15 weeks with just two days' break. There are only two recorded instances of locomotive failure (giving a miles-per-casualty figure of 90,000), reflecting the fact that the 'West Riding' was the least arduous of the three streamlined services, and 10 substitutions (eight by an 'A1', one by an 'A3' and one by a 'V2'), the latest recorded arrival being 11 minutes after schedule.

By the autumn of 1937 the operating department was experiencing some difficulty in ensuring that the streamlined trains were allocated 'A4s' of the appropriate colour, especially as some of the latter were green and therefore not suitable for use on any of them. Thus the decision was taken hereafter to paint all the 'A4s' in garter blue, the last to be repainted being green No 4493 in July 1938 and silver No 2511 in August. A blue locomotive would, of course, look just as good heading a rake of standard East Coast stock, in traditional varnished teak, as at the head of the 'Silver Jubilee'.

Altogether the three streamlined trains made 4,004 runs, locomotive No 2509 being the most prolific performer, making 608 runs (15% of the total) , including 32 on the 'Coronation' and 12 on the 'West Riding'. The total mileage run was 1,128,112, giving an aggregate miles-per-casualty figure for the three high-speed trains of 17,626 (of which modern fleet engineers would be most envious). Curiously one 'A4' never featured on any of the streamliners, this being the final example, No 4903 *Peregrine*, built in July 1938.

The 100th Gresley Pacific

After the 'West Riding' pair the next 'A4' to be turned out was No 4497 *Golden Plover*. It was noticed that this was the 99th Gresley Pacific, prompting a suggestion to the LNER by Mr K. Risdon Prentice, of the Railway Correspondence & Travel Society, that the next 'A4', as the 100th locomotive of an illustrious line, be named after its designer. So it was that No 4498, completed at Doncaster on 30 October 1937, was worked over to Marylebone on 26 November to be named by the LNER's Chairman, William Whitelaw, as *Sir Nigel Gresley* – arguably the greatest tribute to be paid to a British locomotive engineer while still in office.

Build-up to the world speed record

On 3 March 1938 the 28th 'A4' Pacific entered traffic. No 4468 *Mallard* differed from its predecessors in being fitted from new with a Kylchap double blastpipe and chimney. Together with the wedge-shaped front of the 'A4' this installation completely solved the problem of drifting steam, although it was not immediately repeated on the next four 'A4s' placed in traffic, in March (No 4469), April (4499 and 4500) and May (4900). By June the installation on No 4468 was delivering sufficiently good results for the final three 'A4s', Nos 4901-3, to be delivered with the full Kylchap installation. Like most LNER locomotives involving experimental installations No 4468 was kept close to Doncaster Works for observation and was allocated to Doncaster shed.

In their search for continual improvements, particularly in the wake of the high-speed braking trials of 22 September 1935, the Gresley team appreciated that the existing vacuum-braking system had significant practical limitations in that the application of the brakes at the rear of the train was slow and, in the case of a sudden brake application, could be violent and cause snatching. Double-blocking south of York was no more than an interim expedient, and from 1935 experiments had been conducted with suburban 'Quad-Art' sets to which Westinghouse quick-service application (QSA) valves had been fitted; whilst they do not increase the *power* of the application these get the brakes at the rear of the train on

much more quickly than would otherwise be the case and considerably shorten the stopping distance. The results were encouraging, although, somewhat surprisingly, it was the six-coach set produced in 1937 for the 'East Anglian' that was the first to be fitted from new with the QSA valves. In due course 'Coronation' set 103 was similarly equipped, being also fitted with automatic slack-adjusters, and this was the set selected for a series of brake trials conducted on alternate Sundays during the spring and early summer of 1938.

Towards the end of June 1938 Gresley was apparently discussing some of the results of the trials with a member of his technical staff, Norman Newsome. What transpired during that conversation has been reported by George Dow, at that time working for the publicity department of the LNER. Leaning back in his chair, Gresley enquired when the next test was to be, and, on being told that it would be on the following Sunday, asked: 'Do you think we could go faster than the LMS?' Newsome reportedly replied: 'I think so, if we could go to Barkston and if we put the dynamometer car on and take one twin off,' to which Gresley rejoined: 'Will you fix it up then, for next Sunday?' So was set the scene for 3 July 1938. Plans were made with the utmost secrecy and were known only to a handful of higher officials. The locomotive was carefully selected, being the four-month-old Kylchap-double-chimney-fitted 'A4' No 4468 *Mallard*, with its regular driver, Doncaster-based Joe Duddington, and his fireman, Tommy Bray, accompanied by Inspector Jenkins. Noted train-performance recorder Cecil J. Allen was invited to ride on the 'brake test' but, unaware of the real purpose of the run and having an aversion to working on a Sunday, he declined the invitation!

3 July 1938

The usual Westinghouse testing team were apparently surprised and curious to note that on Sunday 3 July the usual 'Coronation' set provided for the test train was reduced to just three pairs of articulated coaches, supplemented by the ex-NER dynamometer car and headed by an 'A4' which they had not had previously seen and which was manned by a crew with broad Yorkshire accents rather than the more usual Cockney. They were also surprised to learn that the run was to be extended from its usual Peterborough terminus to Grantham and Barkston.

The usual tests were conducted between King's Cross and Peterborough, and only after the extended run to Barkston was the true nature of the day's events revealed. The Westinghouse staff were offered taxis back to Peterborough if they did not wish to participate in the record attempt – an offer they all declined. At Barkston the triangle was used to reverse the train and run-round the locomotive and dynamometer car. Shortly after 4pm Driver Duddington opened the regulator of No 4468, and they began the run that was to make history. Driver

Duddington became something of a celebrity, and I can do no better than repeat his own account of the day's events, as given to the BBC following his retirement in April 1944.

'It was one Sunday in July 1938. That was the day that the grand streamlined engine *Mallard*, that I had driven ever since it came new from the Shops in March that year and looked upon as almost my own property, made, with me driving her and Tommy Bray as my fireman, the world's record for high-speed steam-locomotive running. The record has not been equalled to this day. [Of course it still stands, a further 70 years later.] We made it between Grantham and Peterborough on the LNER main line. I'd taken expresses along at, well, 60, 70 or 80mph, but this day we were really going out to see just what we could do.

'When we drew away from Grantham we had besides the train a dynamometer car containing a speed-recorder and other instruments. I accelerated up the bank to Stoke Summit and passed Stoke 'box at 85. Once over the top I gave *Mallard* her head, and she just jumped to it like a live thing. After three miles the speedometer in my cab showed 107 miles per hour, then 108, 109, 110 – getting near 'Silver Jubilee's' record of 113. I thought "I wonder if I can get past that ... well, we'll try", and before I knew it the needle was at 116 and we'd got the record. They told me afterwards that there was a deal of excitement in the dynamometer car, and when the recorder showed 122mph for a mile and a half it was at fever heat. "Go on, old girl," I thought, "we can do better than this." So I nursed her and shot through Little Bytham at 123, and in the next one and a quarter miles the needle crept up further – 123.5, 124, 125 and then for a quarter of a mile, while (they tell me) the folks in the car held their breaths, 126 miles per hour. That was the fastest a steam locomotive had ever been driven in the world – and good enough for me, though I believe if I'd tried her a bit more we could have got even 130.'

After the locomotive had been eased for the bend at Essendine a strong smell of aniseed was noticed, indicating overheating of the middle big-end, so the run came to a somewhat premature end at Peterborough. (In fact the damage sustained was no more than overheating sufficient for the white metal to have run out of the big-end brasses, and *Mallard* would soon be repaired and returned to traffic.) An Ivatt GN Atlantic worked the train forward from Peterborough to King's Cross, and the press, who had been alerted to the record speed, had to content themselves with photographs inside the dynamometer car of the paper speed-trace made by the recording equipment. So the world record speed for steam propulsion was wrested from Germany,

which had claimed 124.5mph, and the British record from the LMS, which in June 1937 had managed 114. Although in 1938 the LNER claimed to have achieved only 125mph, it will be noted that in his 1944 account Driver Duddington spoke of 126mph, and indeed this is the speed recorded on the plaques that were affixed to the locomotive in 1948. Cecil J. Allen having declined the invitation to ride on the train, there was no experienced train-timer aboard, so we have only the dynamometer-car rolls as evidence. Apparently, despite the rolls' showing a peak of 126mph, Gresley refused to use this as the basis for a record claim because it was only a peak and, in his view, a claim should be for a sustained speed over a distance. In the immediate aftermath of the record-breaking run he received a number of congratulatory telegrams, notably one from his rival on the LMS, Sir William Stanier. Lady Wedgwood, wife of the LNER Chairman, also sent a brief telegram, reported by Geoffrey Hughes in his biography of Gresley: 'Three cheers for the Mallard. LMS out for a duck.'

Echoing the views of Driver Duddington, Gresley himself believed that a speed of 130mph was feasible for a Kylchap-equipped 'A4'; indeed there is some evidence that a further attempt was being planned for September 1939, but this would be frustrated by the outbreak of World War 2 and ultimately by Gresley's untimely death in April 1941.

General 'A4' work in the 1930s and '40s

By the end of July 1938 all 35 'A4s' were in service, allocated to King's Cross (11), Grantham (two), Doncaster (three), Gateshead (eight), Heaton (one) and Haymarket (10). Apart from the four locomotives rostered to the three daily high-speed services they were utilised on ordinary express services. From the summer of 1937 the non-stop 'Flying Scotsman' had been rostered to 'A4s', these replacing 'A1s' and 'A3s' after nine years of successful summer workings. The 'A4s' soon demonstrated a level of reliability similar to that established on the high-speed services. Particularly notable was King's Cross-based No 4492 *Dominion of New Zealand*, which worked the 'Flying Scotsman' for 10 consecutive days from 18 July 1937, before having two days off as pilot to the 'Coronation', working to Peterborough and back; then the non-stop working was resumed for no fewer than 44 consecutive days (including the usual Sunday workings on ordinary expresses), to be followed by a further eight days on which the 'Flying Scotsman' made a stop at Newcastle, so that, within a period of 64 days, the locomotive worked a total of 62 trips (more than 24,000 miles) between London and Edinburgh, 52 of them on consecutive days! Not to be outdone, during the summer of 1939 No 4489 *Dominion of Canada* covered 18,327 miles in seven weeks (including 34 days of continuous use), spending one week on the 'Coronation', four weeks on the non-stop 'Flying Scotsman', one week on the 'West Riding Limited' and finally another week on the 'Coronation'.

To one or the other of Grantham's two 'A4s', Nos 4466 *Herring Gull* and 4494 *Osprey*, fell the task of working the down 'Aberdonian' sleeping-car express north from Grantham to Edinburgh (the locomotive returning the following day on the up 'Night Scotsman' sleeper), while Doncaster's allocation were used principally on 'West Riding Pullman'. The sole Heaton locomotive, No 4464 *Bittern*, was diagrammed to the 8.15am Newcastle–King's Cross service on Mondays, Wednesdays and Fridays, returning the following day on the down 'Flying Scotsman', Gateshead's allocation being charged with working three weekly turns to King's Cross (increased to four each summer), in addition to standing pilot to the King's Cross locomotive working the 'Silver Jubilee', after which the standby locomotive, if not required, would work the 11.8am Newcastle–Edinburgh, returning with the Edinburgh–Newcastle leg (5.12pm from Waverley) of the afternoon Glasgow–Leeds express.

The 'A4s' during World War 2

Upon the outbreak of World War 2 on 3 September 1939 Britain's railways were placed under Government control for the second time in the 20th century, overall direction being exercised by a Railway Executive under the control of the Ministry of War Transport. For the public the most obvious sign of change was the implementation of a new Emergency Timetable consequent on a blanket 60mph maximum speed limit, which saw many passenger trains cancelled and long-distance expresses consolidated, with greatly extended journey times.

The three streamliner services made their last runs on Thursday 31 August 1939, whereupon the King's Cross stud of 14 'A4s' was placed in store until in December, when two were moved to Grantham. Other sheds kept their 'A4s' at work, Haymarket retaining seven locomotives, Gateshead eight, Heaton one, Doncaster four and Grantham one. As early as July 1939 the Ministry of Transport had consulted the railways over an estimate, prepared by the War Office, indicating a potential military requirement for 800 locomotives (subsequently reduced to 100). Although most of this requirement was for freight and shunting locomotives, the impact was felt immediately throughout the locomotive fleets of the 'Big Four', recently withdrawn locomotives being reinstated and the journey times of many services being extended so that smaller locomotives could be used than hitherto. Long-distance expresses, meanwhile, had extra coaches added but, being less frequent, were often packed to capacity, such that it was not uncommon to see trains of 20 or more coaches departing King's Cross, with hundreds of standing passengers. In view of the pressure on resources it is not surprising that the King's Cross 'A4s' soon found themselves back in traffic, albeit on services that were very different from their former speciality. On 4 December 1939 a new, augmented East Coast timetable was introduced, whereupon the 'Top Shed' allocation were all once more gainfully employed.

Although wartime reports of train running were of necessity much curtailed, some details did emerge. On 5 April 1940, for example, No 2509 *Silver Link* was put in charge of 25 coaches (850 tons gross) on the 1.0pm King's Cross–Newcastle, only 15 minutes being booked against the locomotive on its journey. Shortly afterwards, wartime speed limits notwithstanding, No 4901 *Capercaillie* was recorded taking a train of 21 coaches (730 tons gross) south from Newcastle at an average speed of almost 76mph over 25 miles, posting a maximum of 78.5mph, while in contrast none other than No 4468 *Mallard* was noted in January 1940 passing Darlington at the head of a down goods train! Clearly none the worse for this indignity, the same locomotive was recorded in 1942 working the up 'Flying Scotsman' and, having left Newcastle 14 minutes late, had regained 8 minutes by Grantham with a train loaded to well over 700 tons gross.

On 29 April 1942 No 4469 *Sir Ralph Wedgwood* (formerly *Gadwall*) was unlucky to find itself in the wrong place at the wrong time. Ex-works after a general overhaul completed only 12 days earlier, it was being run-in on local trains, stabling overnight at York's north shed. Unfortunately this was the date chosen by Hitler's Luftwaffe for the so-called 'Baedeker' raid on York, the 'A4' taking the full blast of a high-explosive bomb on its right-hand side. The remains arrived at Doncaster on 18 May, and the locomotive was condemned on 20 June. Only the tender survived, to be attached in 1945 to Thompson 'A2/1' No 3696 (later No 507 *Highland Chieftain*).

Inevitably, given the demands of wartime service, intense utilisation, 'common-user' deployment and reduced standards of maintenance, the Gresley Pacifics – the 'A4s' in particular – became progressively run down as the war continued. The Gresley conjugated valve gear did not take kindly to a lack of maintenance, and severely 'off-beat' locomotives became commonplace. However, Haymarket depot somehow managed to keep its seven 'A4s' on regular 'out-and-home' workings with top-link crews, and despite shortages of staff and materials its locomotives were maintained in a condition that allowed their levels of performance to be sustained at a very high level, with very few failures; O. S. Nock recorded a Newcastle–Edinburgh run behind Haymarket's No 4483 *Kingfisher* in the summer of 1945, when a 17-coach, 610-ton train was worked up to no less than 84mph.

The LNER's renumbering of the 'A4s'

In 1943 Thompson announced a scheme for renumbering the LNER's entire locomotive fleet, the 34 surviving 'A4s' being allocated the numbers 580-613, to be applied in order of construction. However, the priorities of wartime operation meant that it was not practicable to implement the general renumbering until 1946, and only five of the class (Nos 585-8 and 605, between 26 January and 19 April) had assumed their intended new identities by May of that year, when the scheme was revised, the 'A4s' now being allotted the numbers 1-34, but not in order

ABOVE 'A4' No 6 *Sir Ralph Wedgwood* (Doncaster, January 1938) stands at Belle Isle on 7 June 1947, waiting to drop on to Top Shed. The original No 4466 *Herring Gull* until 1 December 1943, renamed on 6 January 1944, regained her garter blue livery in April 1947, one of six different livery variations carried during a 27-year career. No 60006 was based at King's Cross apart from a period between April 1938 and August 1944 at Grantham. With the closure of Top Shed in June 1963 the locomotive moved to New England for for months before spells at St Margaret's (October 1963 to April 1964) and Aberdeen (June 1964 to September 1965). Condemned on 3/09/65, the locomotive met its end like many Scottish 'A4s' at Wishaw. *Ian Allan Library*

of construction. In deference to the LNER's senior officers, past and present, the locomotives after whom they had been renamed in the period 1939-44 were renumbered 1-6; 7 was allocated to *Sir Nigel Gresley*, the remaining 'celebrity' locomotive, *Dwight D. Eisenhower* (the erstwhile *Golden Shuttle*, renamed in September 1945 to honour the Allied Forces' Supreme Commander in Europe during World War 2), being given 8. The five locomotives that had been selected in 1937 for hauling the 'Coronation' adopted 9-13, the remainder being renumbered 14-34 in ascending order of original running number – which, of course, differed from the construction sequence and gave some of the later-built examples lower numbers (18-22) than they would otherwise have received. Although most renumbering was undertaken at running sheds, locomotives that displayed their original numbers in metal cut-out figures posed more of a problem and were generally left until their next works visit.

Nationalisation and the Locomotive Exchanges

On 1 January 1948 the railways were nationalised, and the LNER ceased to exist. At nationalisation the 34 'A4s' were more-or-less evenly spread between four sheds, King's Cross and Grantham (both on BR's new Eastern Region) having respectively nine and 10 locomotives, Gateshead (North Eastern Region) eight and Haymarket (Scottish Region) seven. Early in the year five 'A4s' moved from King's Cross to Grantham and five others, significantly including the three ER-allocated Kylchap-double-chimney examples, all with corridor tenders, moved south in return. Nationalisation also meant further renumbering. With one exception those ex-LNER locomotives that survived long enough would have their 1946 numbers increased by 60,000, but until this was finalised many ran with their existing number prefixed with the letter 'E'.

Shortly after nationalisation it was announced that, in order to produce, in as short a time as possible, indications as to the most desirable features to incorporate in future standard designs, a series of locomotive exchanges were to be undertaken between Regions. These were not intended to be a contest between locomotives of similar types, which, it was acknowledged, had been designed to fulfil the specific requirements of their respective railways. It was also acknowledged that the trials would be of a broad nature, as the tests were to be conducted under normal operating conditions and without any special preparation of the locomotives. It was arranged to take straight from traffic locomotives which had run between 15,000 and 25,000 miles since their last general repair, and this

was the only stipulation laid down as far as actual locomotive selection was concerned. There were to be three designated categories of locomotive – Express Passenger, General Purpose and Freight. In each category it was intended that one class of locomotive should be selected from each of the 'big four' pre-nationalisation companies, save that in the Express Passenger category the LMS would be represented by both the 'Princess Coronation' and the rebuilt 'Royal Scot'; moreover, as the SR had no modern heavy-freight locomotives it was decided that the 'WD' 2-8-0 and 2-10-0 types should both be assessed in the Freight category. A further anomaly was that in the General Purpose category the three Class 5 locomotive types drawn from GWR, LMS and LNER would be joined by the SR 'West Country' design of Class 7 Light Pacific. The routes chosen for the Express Passenger trials were to be, in order of operation, ER King's Cross–Leeds in April, WR Paddington–Plymouth in early May, LMR Euston–Carlisle in late May and SR Waterloo–Exeter in June.

ABOVE No 60033 *Seagull* (Doncaster, June 1938) was the third 'A4' to be fitted from new with Kylchap exhaust and double chimney. The original No 4902 was always a King's Cross engine apart from the usual spell at Grantham between April 1944 and March 1948. Here later in 1948 she heads the up Flying Scotsman at an unidentified location. Condemned in December 1962, the locomotive was cut up at Doncaster in January 1963. *W. J. Reynolds*

By the spring of 1948 the Eastern Region had 26 Thompson Pacifics, of Classes A1/1, A2/1, A2/2 and A2/3, plus a handful of brand-new Peppercorn 'A2s'. Given the indifferent performance of the Thompson Pacifics it is not surprising that the choice of ER Express Passenger type fell to the 'A4'. Initially Nos E21 *Wild Swan*, 25 *Falcon* and 26 *Miles Beevor* were chosen, but Doncaster succeeded in substituting the entire ER fleet of Kylchap 'A4s', so that Nos E22 *Mallard*, 60033 *Seagull* and 60034 *Lord Faringdon* (all of which, fortunately, satisfied the mileage criteria) were selected, having been transferred to

King's Cross shed from Grantham in March and April; the fourth Kylchap 'A4', No 60005 *Sir Charles Newton*, was a North Eastern Region locomotive, based at Gateshead.

In each series of tests four days of running were to be preceded by four days of familiarisation trips on the designated routes and trains for the 'foreign' locomotives and their crews. For the ER tests *Lord Faringdon* was selected and ran without problems. For all of the 'away' trips the ER management deliberately chose *Mallard*, newly adorned with boiler-side plaques proclaiming it as the holder of the world speed record for steam traction. The running staff at King's Cross shed had protested that *Mallard* was not their best 'A4' at that time and strongly advocated the use of another example, but higher authority insisted, with unfortunate results. *Mallard* had been moved to Old Oak Common for the preliminary WR familiarisation trips, which began on 27 April, but did not even complete its first round-trip, being failed with a hot middle big end at Savernake on the way back to London on the 28th. *Seagull* was quickly worked over to Old Oak Common and successfully completed all of the WR runs. For the two weeks of the LMR trials the third 'A4', *Lord Faringdon*, was used and again ran without any problems.

The SR familiarisation trips commenced on 1 June with the 'Atlantic Coast Express' to Exeter, worked by *Seagull*. Unfortunately the 'A4' weak-point was again apparent, and No 60033 was failed just short of Exeter. By now repaired, *Mallard* was worked over to Nine Elms and put up a splendid performance with the first dynamometer-car run on 8 June, but the jinx struck again on its way back to London on the 9th, the locomotive being failed at Salisbury. The final two test runs on the SR were undertaken by a newly repaired *Seagull*, without any further problems.

When the test results were published the 'A4' emerged as the most economical in both coal and water consumption of any express passenger locomotive tested. Although there were wide variations in the way individual drivers interpreted the test conditions and train schedules the handling of the 'A4s' must inevitably have reflected the apprehension felt by their drivers after the series of public failures of the inside big-end, to which their charges seemed all too prone. Despite this they were the only locomotives whose drivers drove consistently at full regulator with short cut-off, the results being a vindication of the efficiency of the Gresley front-end arrangement.

Despite their clear preference for the Kylchap locomotives for use during the Locomotive Exchanges the ER authorities were surprisingly slow to seek any conversions to add to the four locomotives delivered with this equipment in 1938. Gresley had previously indicated that he would seek further conversions once the patent (and thus the need to pay significant royalties) had expired in 1941, but the exigencies of

wartime and the antipathy of his successor Thompson towards anything associated with Gresley had put paid to any further developments in this direction. Moreover the Running Department had long held the view that the Kylchap cowl restricted access to the tubes for cleaning and had resisted any further conversions. Indeed, in order to minimise the risk of problems caused by a shortage of steam, it became standard practice at King's Cross for every single-chimney 'A4' that had worked beyond Doncaster to have the fire thrown out on its return, the tubes rodded and the tube-plate scraped to remove any accumulation of 'bird's nests'. That this was unnecessary on its three Kylchap 'A4s' – because the blast kept the tubes clear – does not appear to have percolated through to 'official' thinking on the subject, and it would be a further nine years before the persistence of the King's Cross Shedmaster, Peter Townend, finally overcame this resistance to the extent that conversion of the surviving 30 single-chimney 'A4s' was authorised.

The return of the non-stop

The first sign of a return to prewar conditions came with the reinstatement from 31 May 1948 of the summer-only non-stop working of the 'Flying Scotsman' service, the first runs being made by Nos 60034 *Lord Faringdon* (northbound) and 60009 *Union of South Africa* (southbound). However, on 12 August disastrous flooding affected eastern Britain, the East Coast main line suffering washouts at 12 locations between Berwick and Dunbar. Trains from Edinburgh were diverted over the Waverley route as far as St Bosells and thence via Kelso to Tweedmouth – which, besides being almost 16 miles longer, included a 1-in-70 climb southbound to Falahill (for which banking was usual for loads in excess of 400 tons) and a line speed of just 25mph over the single-track section between St Boswells and Kelso, this rising only to 45mph onward to Tweedmouth. A water stop at Galashiels was also required, the first troughs being otherwise some 91 miles away, at Lucker. After 12 days the Haymarket crews responded to the challenge: on 24 August Driver Stevenson, in charge of the up train, succeeded in making the run unassisted to Lucker troughs without stopping for water, and the challenge of maintaining the non-stop run over the 408 miles of the amended route had been established; thereafter until resumption of the normal route on 22 September Haymarket crews managed a non-stop run on no fewer than 17 occasions, including one on 15 September with No E22 *Mallard*.

By the end of 1948 the principal East Coast locomotive workings had been reorganised to facilitate 'single-home' workings (out and back in a day), with locomotive changes at Grantham and Newcastle (locomotives being based at King's Cross, Grantham, Gateshead and Haymarket sheds). This facilitated the allocation of regular crews to locomotives and, despite often indifferent coal supplies, led to a general improvement in locomotive appearance, morale and thus performance. In May 1949 a test run from King's Cross to Edinburgh and back was undertaken in order to assess the feasibility of enhanced schedules, and on the return journey No 60017 *Silver Fox* attained a maximum speed of 102mph descending Stoke Bank. However, whilst the 'A4s' were obviously ready and able, the same could not be said of the track, and it would be a further two years before 90mph was authorised over certain sections of the main line.

By the summer of 1951 things had begun to slip back, and in an effort to restore matters the Eastern Region's redoubtable Motive Power Superintendent, L. P. Parker, had its locomotive allocations and workings further reorganised, its entire allocation of 'A4s' being concentrated at King's Cross, and the 'A3s' and the new 'A1s' moved out to Grantham, Doncaster and Leeds Copley Hill. Thus began a regular association of King's Cross

'A4s' with specific drivers that was to continue almost until the end of East Coast steam in the early 1960s. There was some competition for the most famous locomotives, like *Silver Link*, which went to Ted Hailstone, newly arrived at King's Cross from the West Riding. Ted was possibly the most dedicated to 'his' No 14 and had special pins made for the middle big-end oil feed, to give it a little more than the standard, along with specially polished buffers, which 'Top Shed' made sure to retain whenever the locomotive was required to visit Doncaster. *Mallard* was shared by J. Burgess and A. Smith; Burgess soon retired, J. Howard transferring from No 60028 *Walter K. Whigham* to replace him, and the trio of Howard, Smith and *Mallard* established a fine reputation for performance, possibly overshadowed only by Bill Hoole and No 60007 *Sir Nigel Gresley*.

1951 was the year of the Festival of Britain, and, in an attempt to raise standards generally, the non-stop service was accelerated to a 7hr 20min schedule and transferred to the advance portion of the 'Flying Scotsman', which was named the 'Capitals Limited'. By May 1952 a further series of three trial runs was being undertaken between King's Cross and Doncaster. No 60003 *Andrew K. McCosh* was the locomotive used, with Ted Hailstone in charge, accompanied by *Mallard*'s famous record-breaking Inspector Jenkins, the runs establishing new records for the 156 miles of 154.5min with 350 tons, 163.5min with 400 tons and 168min with 500 tons.

BELOW During the 26 April 1948 preliminary run for the Locomotive Exchanges No 22 *Mallard* (Doncaster 3/38) departs from Paddington with the 1 30pm Plymouth express. Note the absence of the dynamometer car added for the actual test runs and the newly fitted World Speed Record Holder plaque on the boiler side. The original No 4468 was another long-term Top Shed locomotive with a Grantham spell between October 1943 and April 1948. No 60022 was withdrawn for preservation in April 1963. *C. C. Herbert*

Rejuvenation of the 'A4s' – the work of K. C. Cook

The other change in 1951 was a general change-around in the mechanical-engineering management within the BR Regions, and to Doncaster as Mechanical & Electrical Engineer of both the ER and NER came K. C. Cook, hitherto at Swindon. Cook was an expert in workshop practice and was fortunate in having on his staff at Doncaster Bert Spencer, who had played such a prominent part in the revitalisation of the original 'A1' Pacifics in the 1930s. It would be some time before Cook's influence became apparent, but let it be said at once that his arrival at Doncaster was a great day for the Gresley Pacifics. Cook set about a systematic programme of rehabilitation by eliminating those features of detailed design that had proved sources of weakness. A supplier was found to provide the type of optical-alignment equipment that had been used for many years at Swindon to achieve a high degree of accuracy when setting up frames and motion. This permitted pins and bearings to be machined to much finer tolerances, and the Gresley conjugated valve gear in particular was now assembled with such precision that the wildly syncopated exhaust beats that had become so characteristic of Gresley's three-cylinder locomotives became a thing of the past. Locomotives overhauled at Doncaster now ran with the silence and precision of well-oiled sewing machines. The inside big-end bearings, for so long the Achilles heel of the

ABOVE No 60003 *Andrew K. McCosh* (Doncaster 8/37) heads the Up 'Capitals Limited' down Stoke Bank in 1949. Newly introduced in the summer of 1949, the 'Capitals Limited' was the precursor of the 1953 'Elizabethan' summer non-stop Anglo Scottish service. The former No 4494 carried the name *Osprey* until July 1942 when renamed to honour the Chairman of the LNER Locomotive Committee and long-standing Director. Although mainly a Top Shed locomotive, No 60003 had early spells at Heaton, Doncaster and Grantham (twice) before arriving at King's Cross in May 1939. As usual there were brief spells at Grantham in 1941 and 1957 before withdrawal from King's Cross in December 1962 and being cut-up at Doncaster in January 1963. *E. R. Wethersett*

Gresley Pacifics, were also adressed by Cook, the Gresley marine big end being modified with the Swindon form of white-metal bearing, with the same very high standards of surface finish and methods of lubrication. This proved to be wholly effective, the problems of wear in the conjugated valve gear and overheating of the middle big end being entirely overcome, and the Gresley Pacifics embarked upon a glorious Indian Summer.

The final enhancement to the 'A4s' came as the result not of Cook's work at Doncaster but of the persistence of the King's Cross Shedmaster, Peter Townend. Throughout the 1950s the sheds maintaining the single-chimney 'A4s' had fought a not always wholly effective battle against the tendency, particularly when supplied with less-than-ideal coal supplies, for the locomotives to be reported by their crews as 'short of steam'. The modifications concentrated on variations in the size of the blastpipe orifice, which by 1957 had been progressively reduced to a diameter of $5^{1}/_{8}$in. This had led inevitably to significantly increased blastpipe pressure and showed that the lesson of the double chimney was being missed, inasmuch as the considerable improvement in steaming was being obtained by a *reduction* in exhaust pressure. At Swindon, meanwhile, S. O. Ell was rejuvenating the ex-GWR 'King' and 'Castle' classes by equipping them with double chimneys and higher degree of superheating, with excellent results, but despite this the BR Board and ER CME resisted requests for double-chimney conversion of the 'A4s'.

Finally, after four years of fruitless requests from King's Cross and as a result of a local initiative, comparative tests were carried out between single-chimney and Kylchap 'A4s' working round-trips for five days each between King's Cross and Doncaster; this was done to demonstrate the known economy of the Kylchap

system in a form which would convince the General Manager that the costs of conversion (at just over £200 per locomotive) could quickly be recovered, the saving in coal being in the order of 6-7lb per mile. Before the patent expired in 1941 the licence costs for the Kylchap design had been in the order of £400-500 per locomotive, so Gresley's reluctance to authorise such significant expenditure was understandable; the subsequent 16-year wait for the authorisation of such an obvious enhancement was less explicable. However, the tests proved conclusive, and the remaining 'A4s' were finally converted between 1957 and 1958, the last to emerge from Doncaster, on 27 November 1958, being No 60032 *Gannet*.

BELOW Still with single chimney, 'A4' No 60007 *Sir Nigel Gresley* (Doncaster, October 1937) pulls out of Edinburgh Waverley station on Saturday 1 September 1956 with the return working of the previous day's non-stop 'Elizabethan', the reversed headboard of which is carried on the locomotive's centre lamp bracket. 'No 7' worked five single journeys on this service in 1956. *E. Treacy/Gresley Society collection*

ABOVE No 60009 *Union of South Africa* roars down Stoke Bank, near Little Ponton, with the up 'Elizabethan' non-stop express from Edinburgh to King's Cross on 23 August 1961. 'No 9' was always a Scottish locomotive, being based at Haymarket until a final move to Ferryhill in May 1962. In this, the train's final season, No 9 would work the 'Elizabethan' for an unbroken period of 29 days, from 23 August until 8 September, when it powered the final up journey; it had also worked the first up train, in 1953. *H. S. E. Appleton/Kidderminster Railway Museum*

The 'Elizabethan' and other regular 'A4' work

In 1953 the summer non-stop service was renamed the 'Elizabethan' in honour of the new queen, the first down run being made by No 60028 *Walter K. Whigham*, the up train having Haymarket's favourite 'A4', No 60009 *Union of South Africa*. By 1954 the schedule for this prestigious service had been reduced to 390 minutes, representing an average speed of just over 60mph. Haymarket shed tended to reserve its best 'A4s' for the 'Elizabethan', and some of its locomotives saw long periods of continuous working, among them No 60027 *Merlin*, which in 1960 made 74 runs, including 46 consecutively from 22 June to 6 August and a further 21 likewise from 21 August to 10 September. Despite the introduction of the Type 4 diesels from 1958 and the 'Deltics' in 1961 there were insufficient available to cover all the work, and the 'Elizabethan' continued to be 'A4'-hauled until the end of the 1961 season, the last such runs being made on 9 September. The honour of working the last steam-hauled northbound 'Elizabethan' fell to No 60022 *Mallard*, Haymarket's choice for the last southbound service being yet again No 60009 *Union of South Africa*.

Other regular 'A4' turns worked throughout the 1950s were to Leeds and back with the 'Yorkshire Pullman', to Newcastle on the 'Tees–Tyne Pullman' and to Edinburgh and Glasgow on the 'Queen of Scots' and the 'Talisman'. The East Coast Pullman services maintained a tradition going back to 1923, when the newly formed LNER had inherited contracts with the Pullman Car Co entered into by the GER in 1920; boat trains aside, the GER Pullman services were unprofitable, so the LNER redeployed the cars to new 'Queen of Scots' and 'West Riding' Pullman services, the latter being renamed as the 'Yorkshire Pullman' upon the addition of a Hull portion in 1935.

From 1956 the greater reliability demonstrated by the Gresley Pacifics was reflected in a greater reliance on through locomotive workings to Newcastle. One of the hardest workings was not even a passenger train but No 266 Down, the afternoon King's Cross–Niddrie fast fully fitted goods, worked by a King's Cross top-link crew with their own regular 'A4' to Newcastle. Punctuality was thought to be enhanced by the fact that an on-schedule arrival in Newcastle permitted a well-earned pint or two to be consumed before closing time!

From the winter of 1958/9 2,000hp Type 4 diesels were rostered to East Coast expresses on diagrams of some intensity. The new diesels proved troublesome, in many cases due to staff unfamiliarity and the less-than-ideal facilities provided initially for maintenance of this relatively 'high-tech' form of motive power. Because trains were still heated by steam the diesels were provided with oil-fired steam generators (and even water scoops for replenishing their water supplies on the move!), which proved troublesome and were a frequent source of failures. The only available replacements were steam locomotives, and there are numerous recorded instances of steam locomotives successfully replacing non-available diesels on diagrams of much greater intensity than had ever been contemplated in earlier times. On 13 days between 30 November and 20 December 1958, for example, No 60030 *Golden Fleece* worked the 'Flying Scotsman' from King's Cross to Newcastle before returning south on the 5.0pm up working and, with other services included, covered some 9,018 miles during a 21-day period, while in the week ending 2 April 1960 No 60022 *Mallard* worked this same turn on six consecutive days before making another return trip to Newcastle on the seventh day, covering 3,752 miles in the process.

Special 'A4' occasions

Over the years the 'A4s' were employed on many special trains, but none could equal the feat achieved on 23 May 1959. With the imminent retirement of the locomotive's regular driver (and SLS member) Bill Hoole and the Golden Jubilee of the Stephenson Locomotive Society its other members arranged a 'Golden Jubilee' special from King's Cross to Doncaster and return, to be hauled by No 60007 *Sir Nigel Gresley* and driven by Bill himself. During the course of the day a speed in excess of 100mph was achieved on three separate occasions, one of them, on the descent of Stoke Bank, producing a postwar maximum of 112mph. Some years later Bill confided to me that he had carefully studied *Mallard*'s record run and had intended to go for the record, but higher authority intervened once the Civil Engineer's specially increased line speed of 110mph had been exceeded, and the record attempt came to a frustrating end. So ended another epic performance by an 'A4', almost a quarter of a century after *Silver Link*'s stunning debut in 1935.

Another auspicious occasion in the annals of 'A4' running on the East Coast was the wedding of HRH the Duke of Kent and Katharine Worsley at York Minster on 8 June 1961, the number of guests travelling from London requiring two First-class specials in addition to the ex-LNER Royal Train; after the reception at Castle Howard all three returned to King's Cross from Malton.

Although diesels, including some 'Deltics', were now covering the majority of East Coast expresses the ER management had insufficient confidence in the reliability of these new machines for such high-profile workings, and 'A4s' were chosen for all three. King's Cross shed turned out three immaculate locomotives, plus a standby, with white cab roofs on Nos 60028 and 60014 and on all four locomotives all unpainted metal parts burnished to a very high standard, no silver paint being permitted! The day passed without a hitch, the trains all arriving back in London ahead of time, despite late starts, and including in one instance a maximum speed of 100mph down Stoke Bank. 'Top Shed' selected No 60028 *Walter K. Whigham* to work the Royal Train, Nos 60003 *Andrew K. McCosh* and 60015 *Quicksilver* working the other two specials and No 60014 *Silver Link* acting as standby.

Among the last special 'A4' workings from King's Cross was the RCTS 'Aberdeen Flyer' of Saturday 2 March 1962. The train was billed as 'the last non-stop steam run of all' between London and Edinburgh, an ambition sadly frustrated by a signal stop at Chathill, as a result of a 'hot box' on a preceding freight train. For the London–Edinburgh leg the locomotive selected was the record-breaking No 60022 *Mallard*, the train being worked forward to Aberdeen by No 60004 *William Whitelaw*. To celebrate the 25th anniversary of *Mallard*'s record run on 7 July 1963 the Locomotive Club of Great Britain sponsored a special to Doncaster; *Mallard* itself having by now been withdrawn, the train was hauled by No 60007 *Sir Nigel Gresley*, which achieved a maximum speed of 103.5mph descending Stoke Bank.

The beginning of the end for the 'A4s'

On 29 December 1962 came the first five 'A4' withdrawals (excepting the untimely demise of No 4469 in 1942), class pioneer No 60014 *Silver Link* being joined by Nos 60028 *Walter K. Whigham*, 60003 *Andrew K. McCosh*, 60033 *Seagull* and 60030 *Golden Fleece*, all of them ending their days at 'Top Shed'. *Silver Link* had run a little over 1.5 million miles during its 27 years' service, and its ignominious fate at Doncaster was an unfitting end for a magnificent machine which, for many, represented the very pinnacle in terms of the development of the British express passenger steam locomotive; although six 'A4s' have been preserved, among them the world-record-breaking *Mallard*, the loss of *Silver Link* is mourned to this day by many Gresley enthusiasts. April 1963 saw a further three withdrawals from King's Cross, these being Nos 60015 *Quicksilver*, 60013 *Dominion of New Zealand* and 60022 *Mallard* – the last, fortunately, being spared *Silver Link*'s fate and instead becoming the first 'A4' to pass into preservation. A few weeks before withdrawal, incidentally, it was still sprightly enough to be entrusted with the 11-coach 2.0pm 'Tees–Thames' from King's Cross to Grantham, recovering 14 minutes of delays and climbing from Essendine to Stoke at an average speed of 80.6mph before arriving on time at Grantham.

ABOVE No 60007 *Sir Nigel Gresley* (now with double chimney) awaits departure from King's Cross on 29 June 1961 with the 5.35pm service to Newcastle. The locomotive displays the very smart turnout achieved by 'Top Shed' with its 'A4s', right up until closure in June 1963.
L. Nicolson

With the run-down of steam on the East Coast and the improved reliability of the diesels the inevitable end for 'Top Shed' at King's Cross came on 16 June 1963, its 11 surviving 'A4s' being moved to Peterborough New England. The distribution of 'A4s' was now New England (11), Gateshead (nine), Haymarket (two), St Rollox (two) and Aberdeen (three). The withdrawal of Gateshead's No 60018 *Sparrow Hawk* on 19 June was swiftly followed by the second withdrawal for preservation, No 60008 *Dwight D. Eisenhower* being formally taken out of service at New England on 20 July.

With the end of the 1963 summer services there was little work left for the 'A4s'. The last recorded normal working of an 'A4' from King's Cross was of New England's No 60017 *Silver Fox*, which hauled the 6.40pm Leeds express on 19 October; shortly afterwards this locomotive and four others – Nos 60021 *Wild Swan*, 60025 *Falcon*, 60029 *Woodcock* and 60032 *Gannet* – were all withdrawn from New England. The shed's five survivors (Nos 60006/7/10/26/34) were then transferred to

Scotland, along with four (60005/16/19/23) from Gateshead. The finale at King's Cross came on 24 October 1964, when the RCTS/SLS 'Jubilee Requiem' special was worked to Newcastle and back by No 60009 *Union of South Africa*, now based at Ferryhill. On the return journey the maximum speed down Stoke Bank was 96mph, arrival back at King's Cross being 26 minutes early, the train having kept well ahead of the following diesel-hauled express from Leeds. The three 'A4s' remaining at Gateshead survived only until 20 March (60020), 5 April (60002) and 12 October (60001). No 60001 *Sir Ronald Matthews* was unusual in having only ever been allocated to Gateshead shed throughout the course of its 26 years of service.

Scottish 'A4' finale

The deployment of 'A4s' within Scotland had been traditionally confined to services on former LNER routes between Edinburgh and Aberdeen, Perth (via Glenfarg) and Glasgow Queen Street, and since the allocation of brand-new No 4483 *Kingfisher* in December 1936 Haymarket shed had housed the entire Scottish allocation. True, in 1949 No 60012 *Commonwealth of Australia* had spent some months on loan to Polmadie, working on the West Coast main line to and from Carlisle, but it was the reallocation in February and May 1962 respectively of Nos 60031 *Golden Plover* and 60027 *Merlin* to the former Caledonian shed at St Rollox that marked the beginning of the class's deployment on internal services between Glasgow Buchanan Street and Dundee and Aberdeen. On 22 February, still allocated to Haymarket, No 60027 had been used to work a return test run between Buchanan Street and Aberdeen in order to validate the accelerated timings required to achieve overall three-hour timings on this route. In May and June respectively Nos 60009 *Union of South Africa* and 60004 *William Whitelaw* moved from Haymarket to Ferryhill shed at Aberdeen – again, the first 'A4s' to be allocated to this shed, although visits by Haymarket locomotives on workings from Edinburgh had been commonplace since 1937.

The Glasgow–Aberdeen service had been improved progressively by the LMS during the 1930s, culminating in 1937 in the first three-hour trains, hauled by 'Jubilee' 4-6-0s, and in 1938 the eight-coach 'St Mungo' and 'Bon Accord' services which supplemented the longstanding ex-Caledonian 'Granite City' and 'Grampian Corridor'. In the summer of 1956 the majority of intermediate stations on the route between Perth and Aberdeen via Forfar were closed to passenger traffic, and the entire express service between Glasgow, Dundee and Aberdeen was put on an even-interval basis, with accelerated overall schedules of 3hr 30min, the service being worked reasonably successfully by both ex-LMS and BR Standard Class 5 4-6-0s. From 1959 some of the new 2,000hp Type 4 diesels were used on filling-in duties between use on both the East and West Coast routes, but the first classes of diesel to be allocated to the Scottish Region were the BRCW/Sulzer 1,160hp Type 2s, later to be joined at Inverness by an allocation of BR Derby/Sulzer 1,160hp Type 2s.

The Scottish Region's aspiration to make full use of its new locomotives was quickly frustrated by their unreliability, and the acceleration of services, if not to be postponed, had of necessity to be achieved by steam; the policy of eliminating steam area by area had by 1962 seen the almost complete 'dieselisation' of the Highland and West Highland lines, Glasgow–Aberdeen being a lower priority. The Region was fortunate to be blessed with a visionary General Manager, James Ness, and it was apparently he who suggested the use of 'A4s' to work the Glasgow–Aberdeen services, which, from the 1962 summer timetable,

were to be accelerated to restore the prewar three-hour schedules. Initially the 'A4s' were welcomed by the Aberdeen and Perth crews, who were familiar with the class; at St Rollox the ex-LMS crews were more reluctant, but, faced with a threat to transfer their work to other sheds, they fell into line, and the 'A4s' settled down to almost four years' solid work.

Typically the locomotives soon demonstrated that the 19min allowance over the 16 hilly miles from Aberdeen to Stonehaven, which even the 2,000hp Type 4 diesels struggled to achieve and which was impossible with the Type 2s, was habitually reduced to 17½ minutes by the 'A4s'. In addition to the Glasgow–Aberdeen expresses the 'A4s' found regular work between Aberdeen and Carstairs hauling the famous 'West Coast Postal' service, which actually ran as a passenger train as far south as Perth, and they continued to be used between Aberdeen and Edinburgh, particularly on reliefs, specials and at weekends, when the regular diesels were frequently unavailable, undergoing much-needed servicing and repairs!

By January 1963 Ferryhill had swapped No 60004 for Haymarket's No 60011 *Empire of India*, leaving the same two 'A4s' (60027/31) at St Rollox, three at Haymarket (60004/12/24) and two at Ferryhill (60009/11). Of the nine 'A4s' transferred to the Scottish Region in October 1963 seven, nominally all allocated to St Margarets shed, were initially placed into store – Nos 60006/7 at Dalry Road, 60016/19 at Ferryhill, 60023 at Bathgate and 60026/34 at Galashiels for a month before joining No 60023 at Bathgate. No 60005 *Sir Charles Newton* stayed at St Margarets for two weeks before moving to Ferryhill, whilst No 60010 *Dominion of Canada* went straight to Ferryhill. The Scottish Region had already stored No 60012 and No 60024 at Dalry Road upon the closure of Haymarket shed on 9 September 1963 and at the start of October had only five active 'A4s' – Nos 60004/9/11 at Ferryhill and 60027/31 at St Rollox. The Region took a while to assess the condition of its newly acquired assets, but by the 1964 summer timetable all were back in active service save Nos 60005 (withdrawn 12 March) and 60011 (withdrawn 11 May), giving a total in June of 14 active 'A4s', shared between Ferryhill (10), St Rollox (two) and St Margarets (two). Further 1964 withdrawals, both from Ferryhill, were of Nos 60012 *Commonwealth of Australia* on 20 August and 60023 *Golden Eagle* on 30 October. By January 1965 just 11 remained active – eight (Nos 60004/6/7/9/10/19/26/34) at Ferryhill, two (60024/27) at St Margarets and one (60031) at St Rollox (No 60027 having moved to St Margarets upon the cessation of the summer timetable in September 1964).

A further six withdrawals took effect in 1965, all bar No 60027 from Ferryhill shed. No 60016 was withdrawn in March, No 60010 in May and Nos 60006 and 60027 (the latter from St Margarets) at the end of the summer timetable in September, to be followed by No 60031 in October and No 60026 in

ABOVE Ferryhill-allocated No 60019 *Bittern* (Doncaster, December 1937) departs Forfar with an Aberdeen–Glasgow express in 1966. The former No 4464 would pass into private ownership in September of that year, one week after the withdrawal of the last two 'A4s' in service, Nos 60019 and 60024. *W. Potter/Kidderminster Railway Museum*

December, leaving a final six locomotives, all based at Ferryhill, in service at the close of 1965. The next two withdrawals were much more fortunate, No 60007 *Sir Nigel Gresley* being withdrawn for preservation on 1 February and No 60009 *Union of South Africa* similarly on 1 June. For the 1966 summer timetable this left four active locomotives to cover three diagrams. The next locomotives to expire were No 60004 *William Whitelaw* on 17 July and the last-built (and 1948 Locomotive Exchange celebrity) No 60034 *Lord Faringdon* on 24 August, and on Saturday 3 September the Scottish Region took the opportunity to run a special final steam-hauled three-hour express from Glasgow to Aberdeen and back, worked by No 60019 *Bittern*.

Following the termination of the 1966 summer timetable the last two 'A4s', Nos 60019 and 60024 *Kingfisher*, were formally withdrawn on Monday 5 September, apparently bringing to an close 29 years of illustrious service. This was not

quite the end, however, for a week later, on Tuesday 13 September, No 60024 was resurrected by Ferryhill to work the 5.15pm Aberdeen–Glasgow 'Granite City', returning on the morning of the 14th with the 8.25am Buchanan Street–Aberdeen. The final fling for the class in BR service was a Perth–Aberdeen–Edinburgh special on Easter Saturday (25 March) 1967, when No 60009 *Union of South Africa*, assisted by 'Black Five' No 44997, hauled an 18-coach, 640-ton special throughout, following which the 'A4' took the empty carriage stock unassisted from Waverley to Craigentinny.

'A4' preservation
No 4468/60022 Mallard

No 60022 *Mallard* had been earmarked for preservation in 1960 and, on a visit to Doncaster for classified repairs in April 1963, was found to be in need of work that would exceed the limit by then set for repair costs. Withdrawal came on 25 April, and thus it was that *Mallard* became the first 'A4' to be preserved. Doncaster undertook what was supposed to be a cosmetic restoration, although when the locomotive was being considered for restoration to working order in 1986 it was discovered that 'The Plant' had in fact done a very thorough job, without which its return to steam would have been prohibitively expensive. Upon withdrawal No 60022 was coupled to corridor tender No 5651, whereas on 3 July 1938 it had run with non-corridor tender No 5642. By 1963, however, this tender was attached to No 60026 *Miles Beevor*, still very much in active service from King's Cross, so non-corridor tender No 5670 from recently scrapped No 60003 *Andrew K. McCosh* was used, being accordingly renumbered 5642; as the original No 5642 survived beyond the withdrawal of No 60026 in 1965 (eventually being scrapped in Leeds in 1973), for at least 10 years there were two 'A4' tenders so numbered! *Mallard* was earmarked for display in the new British Transport Museum, located in a non-rail-connected former bus garage at Clapham, in South London. Restoration having been completed by February 1964, the locomotive was hauled by rail from Doncaster to Nine Elms goods yard via the Great Central main line through Nottingham Victoria on 26 February, then, on 29 February, with locomotive and tender separated, by road low-loader to the museum. Following the decision to create a National Railway Museum at York, the Clapham museum closed in 1975, *Mallard* moving north from Stewarts Lane on 12 April.

With the impending 50th anniversary of *Mallard*'s world-record run on 3 July 1938 attention focused on the possibility of the locomotive's returning to steam. As the NRM was operating on a strictly limited budget, Scarborough Borough Council generously agreed to sponsor the overhaul, and this was advanced to 1986 in order to earn as much income as possible from operation of the locomotive. Because the restoration budget covered only a partial overhaul the main-line 'ticket' was issued on a restricted basis, limited to a maximum of 26 runs over five years. *Mallard* was first steamed for 22 years on the occasion of the NRM's 10th-anniversary celebrations, on 27 September 1985.

By 25 March 1986 the locomotive was ready to move under its own steam on a single-coach test train via Scarborough and Hull to Doncaster Works, where final adjustments were made and a new coat of garter-blue paint was applied. The first passenger run was on the inaugural 'Scarborough Spa Express' on 9 July 1986. Other 'Scarborough Spa Express' workings were hauled by LMS 'Black Five' No 5305 and GWR No

3440 *City of Truro*, *Mallard* making a second appearance on 25 August, when the train had to be strengthened to 13 coaches, such was the demand. A further one-way trip from York–Scarborough was undertaken on 4 September as part of a cricket festival sponsored by ASDA. An invitation to visit the French National Railway Museum at Mulhouse for its 10th-anniversary celebrations on 27/28 September 1986 had been accepted and, in return for free shipment to France, it was agreed that *Mallard* should work a number of the BR sponsored 'Shakespeare Limited' trains between Marylebone and Stratford-upon-Avon. The visit to Mulhouse did not take place, but the locomotive worked south to Marylebone on 4 October with the 'South Yorkshire Pullman', thereafter working three 'Shakespeare Limited' trips to Stratford, on 12 and 26 October and 2 November, before returning to York on 8 November at the head of the 'Peter Allen Pullman' and retiring to the NRM for a well-earned rest.

The 10th anniversary of the Friends of the National Railway Museum was celebrated on 25 April 1987, and to mark the occasion *Mallard* reappeared on a 'Scarborough Spa' itinerary, this being repeated on the 26th owing to popular demand. An RSBP-sponsored special from York to Carnforth and back on 16 May was followed on the 25th by a York–Manchester return trip, while for the Doncaster Works open day on 3 October 1987 the 'A4', along with '9F' No 92220 *Evening Star*, worked from York to Doncaster and back. Thus in 1987 it was used for four trains and two light-engine movements.

Marked by the Post Office on a set of commemorative stamps, 1988 was the year of the Big Event. The celebration beginning with *Mallard* attending a press launch and making a York–Harrogate–Leeds–York test run with Travelling Post Office (TPO) vehicles on 6 May in advance of working the Post Office exhibition train to Marylebone for two days of display on 8/9 May; on the 9th it worked a 'Postal Pullman' special to Banbury, this being followed on the 10th by the 'Pennine Postal Pullman' from Manchester to Scarborough. On the day of the anniversary, 3 July, *Mallard* took over a London–Scarborough special at Doncaster. The next task comprised a series of 10 'Scarborough Spa Express' workings (all of which were sold out), interspersed with trips to Carlisle on 16 July and to Grange-over-Sands on the 23rd. On 30 July the locomotive worked the RCTS 'Transpennine' to Manchester, while 13 and 27 August saw further trips to Carlisle, the second of these, its last main-line working, being marred by a stop for a 'blow-up', the locomotive being short of steam on account of a blocked spark-arrestor, on the return climb to Ais Gill Summit on the Settle & Carlisle line. It then retired to the NRM, its boiler ticket expired, and subsequently has only appeared 'dead' at other events such as the Doncaster Works open days in 1988, 1998 and 2003 and the 'NRM on Tour' exhibition at Swindon in 1990. Given the current financial situation and the huge expenditure lavished on

ABOVE Preserved 'A4' No 4468 *Mallard* (Doncaster, March 1938) accelerates away from a Giggleswick photo stop with the 'Birdwatch Europe Express' from York to Carnforth on 16 May 1987. *D. S. Lindsey/ Gresley Society collection*

Flying Scotsman, *Mallard* appears to be somewhat overshadowed at the NRM, and a future return to steam seems unlikely, although in 2012 the locomotive was repainted in preparation for its starring role in the 'Mallard 75' celebrations in 2013 (see separate section on the 'Great Gathering').

No 4496/60008 Golden Shuttle/Dwight D. Eisenhower

The second 'A4' to be preserved was the former No 4496 *Golden Shuttle*. Renamed *Dwight D. Eisenhower* on 25 September 1945 to honour the Allied Forces' Supreme Commander in Europe during World War 2, it was renumbered 8 on 23 November 1946 and finally 60008 by BR on 29 October 1948. Always an English-allocated locomotive, it was the 11th 'A4' to be withdrawn, on 20 July 1963. This time Doncaster gave only a cosmetic restoration in final BR condition, complete with electrification warning flashes (subsequently painted over), AWS

equipment and Smith-Stone speedometer, and at Southampton Docks on 27 April 1964 Doctor Beeching, Chairman of the BR Board, formally handed it over for shipment to the USA aboard the United States Lines vessel *American Planter*; in a nice touch the 'A4' had been hauled from Eastleigh by Bulleid 'Merchant Navy' Pacific No 35012 *United States Lines*. Having been unloaded at Chicago the locomotive was then moved by rail to the US National Railroad Museum at Green Bay, Wisconsin, where it would remain for almost 50 years.

In 2012 the NRM announced plans to reunite all six surviving 'A4s' at York for the 'Mallard 75' event, and agreement was soon reached for a two-year loan of No 60008, whereupon it was carefully extracted and moved by rail to Halifax, Nova Scotia, for shipping with No 60010 to Liverpool. Moved by road transfer to Shildon, No 60008 was cosmetically restored to its final BR condition with a new coat of BR Brunswick green, before moving back to York at the end of 2012, ready for display with the other surviving 'A4s' in July and October 2013. Despite some attempts to retain No 60008 in the UK, after the closing of the 'Great Farewell' exhibition at 'Locomotion', Shildon, in February 2014, No 60008 moved to Liverpool docks for shipment to Canada with No 60010. Arriving at Halifax on 11 May, both 'A4s' were again moved on rail flat cars via Quebec and Montreal so that by 6 June No 60008 was back home at Green Bay, Wisconsin.

No 4489/60010 Dominion of Canada

Early in May 1965 the Scottish Region sent No 60010 *Dominion of Canada* from Ferryhill shed to Darlington Works for an Intermediate Heavy repair. The poor condition of its boiler prompted the locomotive's withdrawal on the 29th, but instead of being offered for sale to scrap merchants it was towed to the running shed at Bank Top. Here it remained in a forlorn state for over a year until hauled in August 1966 to Crewe Works, where, at a cost of £1,600, it was given a cosmetic restoration to its final BR condition. On 10 April 1967 the locomotive was presented to the Canadian High Commissioner by BRB Member John Ratter aboard the Canadian Pacific freighter *Beaveroak*, moored in Royal Victoria Dock, London. Following shipment to Montreal it was moved to the Canadian Railroad Historical Association museum at Delson, near Montreal. The Canadian Pacific Railroad bell, which it had carried from 1938 to 1957 until the double-chimney conversion required its removal, was returned with the locomotive but not, for obvious reasons, fitted.

In 2012 the NRM extended an invitation for No 60010 to attend the 'Mallard 75' celebrations at York in 2013, on a two-year loan similar to that proposed for No 60008. The locomotive duly returned to the UK with No 60008 and on arrival in Liverpool was moved by road to Shildon for an extensive cosmetic restoration to its original 1937 LNER condition as garter-blue No 4489, complete with full side valances and single chimney. As with No 60008 after the closure of the 'Great Farewell' exhibition at 'Locomotion', Shildon, at the end of February 2014, No 4489 was moved by road to Liverpool docks for shipment, arriving at Halifax on 11 May. Both locomotives were then transferred to rail flat cars for the onward movement to Quebec and Montreal. No 4489 was back home on 3 June 2014. The full restoration to original condition has much improved the authenticity of the locomotive as an exhibit at Exporail and it is to be hoped that the Canadian authorities will look after the newly re-envigorated locomotive rather better than they had in the past!

No 4498/60007 Sir Nigel Gresley

The fourth 'A4' to pass into preservation was the famous 100th Gresley Pacific, *Sir Nigel Gresley*. The A4 Preservation Society had launched an appeal for funds in 1965, and this was so successful that it was able both to acquire the locomotive (withdrawn on 1 February 1966) in March 1966 and finance a General Overhaul and restoration to main-line running order at Crewe Works. This commenced in August, and in order to speed the restoration the most recently withdrawn 'A4', No 60026 *Miles Beevor*, which had been withdrawn on 21 December 1965 at Perth and sold for scrap, was recovered from the scrapyard and by 25 September 1966 was at Crewe Works in order to donate parts. In fact all of No 60026's driving wheels had better tyres and were transferred to *Sir Nigel Gresley*. By coincidence No 60026 was attached to the original non-corridor tender (No 5642) that had been attached to No 4468 *Mallard* on the occasion of its record-breaking run on 3 July 1938, and this also passed into the ownership of the A4 Society. However, after several years during which it donated parts for the restoration of *Flying Scotsman* at Hunslet in Leeds this tender was deemed surplus to requirements, being scrapped in 1973. The restoration of *Sir Nigel Gresley* was something of a compromise inasmuch as the locomotive had lost its side valances in 1942 and acquired a Kylchap double chimney in December 1957, neither of these highly visible modifications being reversed, although the livery chosen was the garter blue, with shaded numbers and lettering, in which it had been delivered in 1937. (The 1939 embellishments of stainless-steel cut-out letters and numerals would be restored in 1975 prior to display at the 'S&D 150' event at Shildon.)

After some running-in trips in March No 4498 (as it was once more) returned to main-line service on 1 April 1967 with a Crewe–Carlisle return trip – out via Shap and back via the S&C and Blackburn. Thereafter it proved immediately popular for a succession of enthusiast specials, including a return trip from Edinburgh to Aberdeen on 20 May. This required a positioning move to Scotland, so the locomotive was used to haul several parcels and mail services over the West Coast route from Crewe to Edinburgh. In June it headed south in order to work series of specials from Waterloo station, and before returning north (on 23 July) it made an emotional return to King's Cross in order to work a trip to Newcastle and back. By 28 October No 4498 was back on the West Coast racing-ground, hauling the 'Border Limited' from Crewe to Carlisle. By now nicely run in, it was given the opportunity to show the opposition what a real 'greyhound' could achieve, O. S. Nock, who recorded the run, commenting: 'The start out of Crewe was virtually up to electric standards, for in just 10 minutes from the dead start No 4498 was travelling at 96mph!' The 31.4 miles from Carnforth to Shap Summit were covered in three seconds under the half-hour – an average of all but 63mph over a stretch on which the

ABOVE The by now preserved No 4498 *Sir Nigel Gresley* prepares to leave Edinburgh Waverley with a return charter to York on 20 August 1967. *Rodney Wildsmith/Gresley Society collection.*

adverse gradient averages 1 in 187. In November the locomotive began losing work as BR's infamous 'steam ban' took effect; it also required a new home closer to the homes of the majority of the support crew, most of whom lived in the North East. The National Coal Board offered temporary refuge at its Philadelphia workshops, near Washington, the locomotive moving from Crewe via Shap, Carlisle and Newcastle on 31 July 1968. The steam ban having been lifted, No 4498 returned to the main line on 17 June 1972 with the 'Steam Safari' railtour from Newcastle to Carlisle and back. Further trips followed in 1973, 1974 and 1975, culminating in an appearance at the 'S&D 150' celebrations at Shildon on 31 August 1975.

With the expiry of its seven-year main-line boiler certificate looming No 4498 was withdrawn after the Shildon exhibition and did not reappear on the main line until 1977; on 30 April it worked an A4 Locomotive Society (now renamed from the A4 Preservation Society) special from York to its new home at

Carnforth; the previous night the society had held a dinner alongside the locomotive at the NRM to celebrate the 1976 centenary of Gresley's birth. There now followed a six-year period of operation which included an appearance in the 'Rocket 150' cavalcade at Rainhill over the bank-holiday weekend of 24-26 May 1980. In the autumn of 1982 No 4498 was again withdrawn for overhaul, including re-tubing, and this took until 9 June 1984, when the locomotive made a triumphant return to the main line with a private charter from Clitheroe to York via Manchester and Leeds. Thereafter it ran for a further six years, its 1987 itinerary including a series of four trains to celebrate both its 50th birthday and the 21st anniversary of its acquisition by the A4 Locomotive Society.

ABOVE In March 2009 preserved 'A4' No 60007 *Sir Nigel Gresley* (Doncaster, October 1937) visited the Severn Valley Railway, being seen hauling an eight-coach Gresley teak set between Bridgnorth and Hampton Loade en route for Kidderminster. The locomotive has worn early-BR blue livery since 1993. *Richard Hill*

On 27 March 1989 it suffered a bent left eccentric rod at High Wycombe whilst working the return 'Peaks Express' from Marylebone to Derby, and in late June, during a routine examination at Didcot, serious cracking was discovered around the throat-plate washout plug. The A4 Locomotive Society therefore took the difficult decision to bring forward by two years its next seven-year overhaul, the locomotive being towed back to Carnforth on 17 July 1989.

No 4498's third overhaul in preservation took until 1992, a test run around the circuit at Derby being completed on 27 August 1992. However, a planned return to service on 30 August was frustrated by a cracked bogie-axlebox horn cheek that had been detected on the 27th, the situation being compounded by a derailment at Carnforth on 4 September, immediately before the locomotive was due to work a Farington–Carlisle 'Gold and Silver Jubilee' special to celebrate both the 25th anniversary of the A4 Locomotive Society's ownership of the locomotive and the 50th anniversary of Ian Allan Ltd. After a brief visit to the Severn Valley Railway No 4498 finally returned to the main line at the head of a 'Cumbrian Mountain Limited' from Bradford Forster Square to Carlisle on 21 November. This time it managed to achieve a full seven years' operation, running until 1999, albeit not as No 4498; during an intermediate overhaul of the locomotive in 1994 the A4 Locomotive Society held a poll of members which resulted in a change of identity to No 60007 and the early BR livery dark blue with black and white lining which it had worn from September 1950 to April 1952. One of the highlights of this period of operation was its participation in the 1995 'Shap Time Trials', in which successive trains were operated from Crewe

to Carlisle via Shap, returning via the S&C and Blackburn; No 60007 worked the first run on 30 September, subsequent runs on 2 and 3 October being operated by No 71000 *Duke of Gloucester* and No 46229 *Duchess of Hamilton*.

After working a King's Cross–Scarborough–York special on 16 June 1999 No 60007 headed to the North Yorkshire Moors Railway, which had now become its home base and would be the location for its next overhaul, which turned out to be the most comprehensive (and expensive) undertaken since the locomotive passed into preservation in 1966. Besides attention to the usual items this entailed the installation of an air-braking control system, in addition to the Train Protection & Warning and Data Recording systems, both of which are now a requirement for operation on the main line. Fortunately financial support was obtained from the Heritage Lottery Fund, the locomotive returning to traffic on 31 March 2007 with an NYMR special for members of the Sir Nigel Gresley Locomotive Preservation Trust, although the tedious bureaucracy that nowadays attaches to main-line certification meant the 'Derogation from Group Standards' necessary for a main-line 'ticket' would not finally be obtained until 28 February 2008. Over the 49 years that *Sir Nigel Gresley* has been in private ownership the locomotive has covered in excess of 169,000 miles and has operated on the main line for 30 years, the remainder being accounted for by the four general overhauls that have been undertaken. A very special occasion for No 60007 came on 18 June 2012, when it was used to transport the Olympic Torch between Grosmont and Pickering, but the icing on the cake was the opportunity to see the six surviving 'A4s' reunited at the 'Great Gathering' celebrations in 2013/4. No 60007's main line ticket expires in September 2015 and the A4 Locomotive Society has decided that the required general overhaul will begin in October. The last main line run is planned for Tuesday 7 July between Edinburgh and York, following which the locomotive will retire to Grosmont for the summer season on the NYMR. The last operating day is Monday 21 September.

No 4488/60009 Union of South Africa

The fifth 'A4' to be preserved, No 60009 *Union of South Africa*, was had always been a Scottish-allocated locomotive and ended its BR career being withdrawn from Ferryhill shed on 1 June 1966. In July it was acquired by a group of four Scottish business associates led by John Cameron and after several months' storage at Ferryhill was moved to Thornton, in Fife, where it acquired a 62A (Thornton Junction) shed plate. Prior to the introduction of BR's steam ban No 60009 enjoyed one final run on the main line on 25 March 1967, when it was used to power a Scottish Region railtour between Perth and Aberdeen and again between Stirling and Edinburgh, after which it returned light to Thornton Junction shed. On 8 April 1967 it was moved to Crail and thence by road to the

specially constructed three-mile Lochty Private Railway, near Anstruther, Fife, where it made its first run on 14 June 1967.

Although BR lifted its steam ban in 1971 No 60009 was not initially among the locomotives listed for main-line use, presumably because of its isolated location. The lure of the main line proved irresistible, however, and 'No 9' (as it was commonly known) was used for the Scottish return to steam on 5 May 1973, which date saw it make the first of three round-trips that year from Inverkeithing to Dundee. These were followed over the ensuing decade by further main-line trips within Scotland, and a return to working south of the border was eventually achieved in 1984, when it was used for a series of workings over the Settle & Carlisle line and also to Scarborough. On 25 May 1985 a move to London was frustrated by a broken spring at York, the locomotive finally returning north on 30 November on a train from York to Carlisle, via Leeds and the S&C. On 5 July 1986, in connection with the Commonwealth Games then being held in Edinburgh, it worked a Perth–Edinburgh–Perth–Dundee special, but later in the year the need for a general overhaul prompted a move south to the Severn Valley Railway, which was to be its home for the next 21 years.

In 1990 the Forth Bridge celebrated its centenary, and 'No 9' was earmarked for a series of special trains on 4 March. The

ABOVE The preserved No 60009 *Union of South Africa* stands ready to depart Carlisle on 2 February 2013 with a southbound 'Cumbrian Mountain Express' to Farington Junction via the Settle & Carlisle line. In deference to the wishes of owner John Cameron 'No 9', as it is commonly known, has retained BR green livery. The former No 4488 bore the name *Osprey* briefly in 1937 before being renamed to fit in with the Empire theme applied to the five 'A4s' dedicated to the 'Coronation' streamliner, the original name was reinstated briefly in 1990 in order to forestall expected anti-apartheid protesters during the locomotive's use on a series of Forth Bridge Centenary specials. *Gresley Society Trust collection*

overhaul was a close-run thing, a successful test run being completed on 22 February before a trip (without nameplates) from Carlisle to Skipton on 24 February, after which the locomotive retired to Carnforth for more adjustments before heading to Edinburgh for the celebrations, although fears that its name might attract anti-apartheid demonstrations saw it adopt, as a temporary expedient, its originally intended *Osprey* (plates for which had actually been affixed when the locomotive was built in 1937 but removed before its release from Doncaster). Subsequently it was used by BR for a month of crew training around Fife to pass more crews for steam and, later in the year, had a number of outings on the 'Cumbrian Mountain Express' and 'North Wales Coast Express'. Regular employment in England, Wales and Scotland continued in 1991 and included a special between Edinburgh and Glasgow Queen Street on 16 February to celebrate 150 years of the NBR Edinburgh–Glasgow route, for which the locomotive was again disguised, this time as No 60004 *William Whitelaw* in honour of a man who, prior assuming the chairmanship of the LNER in 1923, had been Chairman of the NBR. A further period under repair followed before a return to the main line on 8 June 1993 with a ScotRail-sponsored Perth–Glasgow special; intended to operate five days a week for a month, this was terminated on the first day, after a failed steam joint in the cab caused the traction inspector to be severely scalded, although the service was reinstated in October and ran without problems. The highlight of 1994 came with the operation, on 29/30 October, of the first steam trains out of King's Cross for 25 years, to Peterborough and back. The following year saw the locomotive working from Waterloo to Southampton on 22 January and from Paddington to Exeter on 18 February, returning to London on the 19th and thereafter seeing extensive use culminating a return trip from Peterborough to York on 5 October 1996, after which it retired to the Severn Valley Railway for yet another overhaul.

Having reappeared on the main line in 2002, 'No 9' was used extensively for the next seven years, during which time, in April 2007, it was repatriated from the SVR to Scotland, owner John Cameron having acquired the former diesel depot at Thornton Junction in order to house his two main-line locomotives (the other being 'K4' Mogul No 61994). Following expiry of its boiler certificate the 'A4' was moved in 2010 to Crewe for its third overhaul in preservation, emerging in July 2012 to resume an active main-line career.

No 60009 played a key role in the 'Great Gathering' celebrations in 2014/5 and in October 2015 will become the sole 'A4' operational on the UK main line until the return of No 4464.

No 4464/60019 Bittern

Just a week after the withdrawal of the last operational 'A4s', on 5 September 1966, one of them, No 60019 *Bittern*, was bought by a consortium headed by York-based Geoff Drury, who had already made arrangements for the locomotive to be housed in the north roundhouse at York shed (today's Great Hall of the National Railway Museum). After its move south from Aberdeen some adjustments were made which required a test run, so arrangements were made for it to work a freight train from Skelton Yard to Healey Mills and back. After this the locomotive emerged from York on several occasions to work main-line specials (including a couple for the RCTS from Leeds to Scotland), the last of which ran on 4 November 1967. With the closure of York shed 'No 19' was moved to Neville

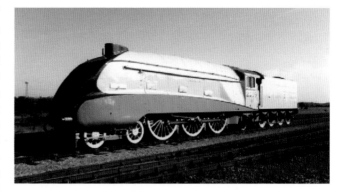

ABOVE Not what it seems. In 1988, as part of the celebrations marking the 50th anniversary of Mallard's record run, the North Eastern Locomotive Preservation Group, then custodians of No 60019 *Bittern*, arranged a cosmetic restoration of the unserviceable locomotive as the long-lost original 'A4' No 2509 *Silver Link*. This involved replacement of the double chimney it had carried since 1957 with an original-style single chimney and restoration of the side skirting removed during wartime. Restoration of the original recessed front coupling and short buffers (with which No 2509 had been fitted for only its first 10 months in service) was not considered worthwhile for this one-off exercise. *Maurice Burns*

Hill, Leeds, where it remained for several years before a spell at Dinting.

Upon the resumption of BR steam working in 1972 *Bittern* appeared on the 'approved' list and was used on a number of trains including on 16 September the 'Scarborough Flyer' from York to Scarborough and Hull. The locomotive had two outings in 1973 – the first on 22 April, when it relieved No 4498 *Sir Nigel Gresley* at Scarborough for a trip to Hull, the second, on 17 June, being a return trip from York to Scarborough – but thereafter the small group assisting Geoff Drury struggled to maintain it, and there began a long period of inactivity. In 1986, anticipating the 50th anniversary of *Mallard*'s record run, the North Eastern Locomotive Preservation Group offered to carry out a cosmetic restoration in exchange for custody of the locomotive, and an imaginative idea was enthusiastically taken up when it was cosmetically restored not as No 60019 but with single chimney and in silver/grey livery as LNER No 2509 *Silver Link*. However, the group had already huge restoration commitments with Geoff's other locomotive, Peppercorn 'A2' Pacific No 60532 *Blue Peter*, and no work was carried out subsequently on the 'A4'.

Following Geoff Drury's death in 1999 his family sold the locomotive to businessman Jeremy Hoskins, who arranged for movement from Teesside to the Mid-Hants Railway, where contract restoration to full main-line working order began in 2005. Duly restored to late-BR condition as No 60019 *Bittern*, it was first steamed in June 2007, performing its first main-line

passenger run on 1 December 2007 from King's Cross to York and returning to Finsbury Park on 15 December. Thus it was that, for the first time since 1986, there were three main-line-certified 'A4s'. Saturday 5 July 2008 was a particularly special day at York, all three operational 'A4s' being present along with No 4468 *Mallard*. In 2011 'No 19' assumed the identity of No 4492 *Dominion of New Zealand*, in garter blue and with side valances restored, but in March 2012 it finally resumed its true original identity as No 4464 *Bittern*.

The locomotive was to play a key role with the other two operational 'A4s' throughout the 'Great Gathering' events of 2013/14. However No 4464 was to fulfil one unique role as part of these celebrations. During the planning of what began as 'Mallard 75' the NRM approached the owners of the three operational 'A4s' with the idea of attempting to operate a high speed (100mph) run on the actual 75th anniversary of *Mallard's* record run 3 July 2013. None of the owners were prepared to risk the potential damage to their locomotives incurred by working what are now elderly pieces of machinery at such speed. The proposal was redefined for 90mph and, with an underwritten guarantee of repairs to any ensuing damage, Jeremy Hoskins and his team agreed to accept the challenge.

Two 90mph test runs were successfully completed in the early hours of 29 May 2013 with the required speed being achieved between Tilehurst and Didcot. Network Rail then approved the operation of three runs to operate over the East Coast main line later in 2013. The first run was on 29 June between King's Cross and York. 90mph was achieved on no less than three separate occasions with a maximum of 92.5 through Newark. Subsequent trips were planned for 19 and 27 July, with the 19 July trip steam-hauled between York and Newcastle, reverting to King's Cross for the 27 July trip.

Unfortunately the British climate then intervened with a period of hot dry weather which created sufficiently high risk of lineside fires to cause Network Rail to ban all unassisted steam operations so that these trips were twice postponed and only eventually rearranged for 5 and 7 December 2013. Both trips proved to be worth waiting for with the 5 December trip establishing a new Newcastle to York steam record time of 66 minutes, and an average of 72.5mph. Darlington was passed at 93mph and more than 15miles were run at above 90mph. Two days later it was to be a York to King's Cross run which proved

ABOVE Running as No 4492 *Dominion of New Zealand, Bittern* storms out of Milford Tunnel, between Belper and Duffield, with a special from York to Stratford-upon Avon on 12 May 2011. *Gresley Society Trust collection*

to be another triumph. It took only 23miles for the first 90mph to be achieved and held for five miles. After the Retford water stop a schedule for the 72 miles to the next water stop required an average of 69.8mph – which was beaten by 13 seconds with three separate stretches at 90mph and a peak of 92mph. Running after the Connington water stop was spoiled by poor regulation with no more fast running possible but again an 'A4' in good condition had demonstrated that it was still more than capable of the consistent high speed running for which the class was designed.

After a final King's Cross to Lincoln return trip on 30 December, *Bittern's* main line ticket expired on 20 January 2015 and so a move from Southall to Ropley took place on 19 January to enable the locomotive to use of some more of the boiler ticket at the Mid-Hants Railway through 2015. The plan is for No 4464 to move to Crewe for overhaul at the end of the year. The spare 'A4' boiler acquired from the NRM (off No 4472) is already at Crewe and restoration work has begun so that the overhaul will be enhanced by fitting this newly repaired item. Completion by the end of 2016 or early 2017 can be expected.

ABOVE In May 2012 preserved 'A4' No 4464 *Bittern* visited the Severn Valley Railway, being seen here drawing into Highley *en route* to Bridgnorth with a full rake of magnificently restored Gresley teak carriages. *J. Bryan*

The rebuilt 'D20' 4-4-0

Classified 'D20' by the LNER, the 60 Worsdell 'R'-class 4-4-0s were constructed by the NER between 1899 and 1907 and established a strong reputation for competent work on East Coast expresses until displaced on the hardest turns from 1911 by the Raven Atlantics. By 1936 the first batch were 37 years old, so it was a surprise when No 2020 emerged from Darlington reconstructed with new cylinders, long-travel valves and larger piston valves. Although Gresley, as CME, had overall respon-sibility for the work it was clear that Thompson, who in 1933 had become Mechanical Engineer at Darlington, was directly responsible for the redesign details. Indeed it is reported that Thompson, having released details of the reconstruction to the technical press without prior reference to Gresley, earned himself a public rebuke when they were both inspecting the rebuilt locomotive. During the next four and a half years of Gresley's tenure there were no further 'D20' rebuilds, these having to await Thompson's assumption of the CME role after Gresley's death, whereupon Darlington received instructions to convert the remaining 50 examples. However, the pressure of war work and other priorities meant that there was only a token implementation of this instruction, and just three further examples were rebuilt – two in 1942, and the last (No 62375) in October 1948.

The 'V2' mixed-traffic 2-6-2s

In August 1934 the first drawing appeared for a new mixed traffic 2-6-2 design as a smaller version of 'P2' No 2001, complete with ACFI feed-water heater, Lentz poppet valves and Kylchap double chimney and exhaust. By October 1935 the design had changed to an improved 'K3' with larger (6ft 2in) driving wheels, to facilitate higher speeds. Doncaster received an order for the first five locomotives in May 1935. Surprisingly in August 1935 a drawing was prepared showing a similar streamlined appearance to the new 'A4' class, but by October 1935 this had been superseded by a revised drawing showing a much simpler arrangement, lacking any of the 'P2' and 'A4' features save for the wedge-fronted cab. The first five locomotives, classified 'V2', appeared between June and November 1936. Further deliveries, now from Darlington, began in July 1937, continuing at the rate of three or four per month until January 1938, when deliveries slowed to a trickle, just six locomotives being turned out over the next seven months, but in September the previous rate was resumed, this continuing until June 1942, when deliveries one again slackened, the last example not emerging until July 1944. Doncaster, meanwhile, resumed construction with a batch of 10 locomotives delivered between April 1939 and October 1940, these being followed by a further 10 between June 1941 and March 1942. The class ultimately comprised 184 locomotives, all but 25 constructed at Darlington.

The original locomotive, No 4771 *Green Arrow*, was run in at Doncaster shed from 13 June 1936, arriving at its intended shed, King's Cross, on 3 July. The other four were widely distributed, to York, New England and Dundee, and quickly appeared on the premier express goods workings for which they had been designed. Indeed, as further examples were delivered the 'V2s'

were distributed along the length of the East Coast main line between London and Aberdeen, mainly because their designated Route Availability of 9 restricted their use to main routes. Depots particularly associated with the 'V2s' throughout their careers were King's Cross, New England, Doncaster, York, Gateshead, Heaton, Haymarket, St Margarets, Dundee and Aberdeen. The type arrived on the GC Section in October 1938 with the allocation of No 4798 to Gorton, where it worked to Marylebone turn and turn about with 'A1' Pacific No 2558 *Tracery*; subsequently it was joined by three further 'V2s', and then in 1939 Leicester gained two, although these later moved south to Neasden. Most of the GE Section routes were barred to 'V2s', although a number were allocated to March for work north to Doncaster and York, and these locomotives were also permitted south to Temple Mills via Cambridge.

The capabilities of the 'V2s' were amply demonstrated when, in cases of emergency, they were required to deputise for

BELOW Pictured on 9 June 1937, after less than a year in service, pioneer 'V2' No 4771 *Green Arrow* (Doncaster, June 1936) passes Marshmoor with its regular working, the heavy 3.40pm 'Scotsman' express goods, which it usually hauled as far as Peterborough Westwood before returning to London with a fast fish train from Hull. The first three wagons are 'flats' carrying containers. *E. R. Wethersett*

Pacifics, notably on the 'Coronation' on at least three occasions between York and Newcastle, as well as between Newark and King's Cross; in 1939 they were also employed on the 'West Riding Limited' and saw regular work hauling the 'Yorkshire Pullman'. During World War 2 there were numerous reports of lengthy trains being hauled by 'V2s', loads of up to 26 carriages being observed, which is how they earned their description as 'the engines that won the war'.

In the early days of the 'V2s' reallocations were rare, among the few of any significance prior to nationalisation being the transfer in 1945 of eight locomotives from Doncaster and Gateshead to Scotland. Perhaps more surprisingly, given the prominent role they had played in maintaining its services throughout World War 2, the GC Section's 'V2s' were displaced to other Southern Area sheds by an influx of 'B17s' and, later, 'B1s', such that by nationalisation there were no 'V2s' allocated to the GC Section. From November 1948, however, Woodford Halse shed regained 10, while from 1953 Leicester was once again responsible for a small stud of two or three locomotives. An unusual (albeit temporary) transfer in 1953 involved six examples which, between May and July, were loaned to Nine Elms to help cover for the temporary withdrawal of the Southern Region's Bulleid 'Merchant Navy' Pacifics following an axle failure, the 'V2s' being sent in lieu of the originally requested GE Section 'Britannia' Pacifics, which

ABOVE A late-1930s view of No 4771 *Green Arrow* awaiting departure from King's Cross Goods. Destined to be renumbered 800 in 1946 and then again as 60800 by BR, it would, excepting a five-week spell at Woodford Halse in 1953, remain a 'Top Shed' engine until withdrawn for preservation in August 1962. *C. C. B. Herbert*

TOP RIGHT King's Cross-allocated 'V2' No 60892 (Darlington, January 1940), passes Ganwick in 1950 with a 12-carriage down East Coast relief train — the sort of work on which the 'V2s' proved invaluable. New as LNER No 4863, this locomotive would remain allocated to King's Cross until transferred to St Margarets in February 1951, ultimately being condemned in November 1963 and broken up at Campbell's of Airdrie early in 1964. *E. R. Wethersett*

BOTTOM RIGHT King's Cross 'V2' No 60903 (Darlington, March 1940) gets the 3.15pm Leeds–King's Cross express underway from Leeds Central on 20 June 1950. New to Doncaster shed as LNER No 4874, this locomotive had moved to 'Top Shed' in 1943 but was destined to end its career at New England, being transferred there in January 1963 for a very brief spell ahead of withdrawal on 10 February and scrapping at Doncaster Works in May of the same year. *H. Weston/Gresley Society collection*

TOP LEFT The fireman on Doncaster-allocated 'V2' No 60896 (Darlington, February 1940) struggles to wind up the water-scoop as his locomotive heads a down relief over Wiske Moor troughs on 1 August 1951. New as LNER No 4867, the locomotive was to remain allocated to Doncaster barring three periods on loan to other sheds, most notably Nine Elms, on the Southern Region, for six weeks in May/June 1953 (helping to cover the temporary withdrawal of its Bulleid Pacifics); it would also spend three weeks at Ardsley in September 1953 and four months at Grantham in the summer of 1960. *E. R. Wethersett*

BOTTOM LEFT In October 1952 the staff at Doncaster Works sought to curry favour with their new, ex-Western Region chief and fitted a copper cap to New England 'V2' No 60854 (Darlington, April 1939), but when this came to the attention of higher authority instructions were issued for its removal, and the locomotive returned to Doncaster for four days at the beginning of December for the removal of the offending item. New as LNER No 4825, it had a somewhat nomadic career, being allocated successively to New England, Grantham, Leicester, King's Cross, Grantham and King's Cross, finally returning to New England just before withdrawal in June 1963. *T. Greaves*

ABOVE Another view of Doncaster's No 60896, this time whilst on loan to the Southern Region at Nine Elms in the spring of 1953, helping to cover for Bullied Pacifics withdrawn for examination and repair following the failure of 'Merchant Navy' No 35020 with a broken driving axle. The driver is applying sand to minimise the risk of slipping as the 'V2' gets its Waterloo–Bournemouth express away from Southampton Central. *Gresley Society collection*

the Eastern to the North Eastern, and in 1958, when the Great Central main line south of Heath was transferred from the Eastern to the London Midland along with 13 'V2s' based at Leicester, Woodford Halse and Neasden.

The 'V2s' were subject to very few modifications until in 1955 the Works Manager at Darlington drew attention to the large number of instances of cracked cylinder-block castings being suffered. This problem had first emerged as early as April 1939 and had led to a revision of some details in the large monobloc casting incorporating all three cylinders and the smokebox in a single large casting (the drawback of this design being that failure of any of these components necessitated an expensive replacement of the entire casting). A revised arrangement of three separate castings was designed, and from November 1955 Doncaster and Darlington were instructed to fit the new arrangement when replacement was required for all or part of the monobloc casting. This resulted in a visible change, as the new arrangement featured outside steam pipes.

the ER was reluctant to release ('B1s' and 'B17s' being the only available cover). Other, permanent transfers between Regions resulted from changes to regional boundaries, notably in 1956, when six 'V2s' based at Ardsley and Copley Hill moved from

ABOVE Fresh from a General Overhaul at 'The Plant', King's Cross-allocated 'V2' No 60862 (Darlington, June 1939) stands on display at a Doncaster Works open day in September 1953. The former No 4833 was a New England engine until its 1950-63 spell at King's Cross, returning briefly to New England in 1963 before withdrawn in June 1963 and cut up at Doncaster in November of that year. *J. M. Jarvis/ Kidderminster Railway Museum*

BELOW King's Cross-allocated 'V2' No 60814 (Darlington, October 1937) coasts through Woolmer Green on 11 July 1958 with a well-loaded up express goods. Originally LNER No 4785, this locomotive spent the vast majority of its career working from 'Top Shed', the exceptions being 19 months at St Margarets between 1951 and 1953 and a final allocation to Grantham from June 1962 until withdrawal on 9 April 1963. *E. R. Wethersett*

ABOVE Pioneer 'V2' No 60800 *Green Arrow* (Doncaster, June 1936) poses outside its home shed in 1961. Barring six weeks at Woodford Halse in 1953 the former No 4771 was allocated to King's Cross for its entire BR career, until withdrawal for preservation in August 1962. Here, more than a year after its last overhaul (at Darlington in January 1960), it still presents the smart appearance that typified 'Top Shed' locomotives, contrasting with the rather grubby prototype 'A4', No 60014 *Silver Link*, alongside. *W. Potter/Kidderminster Railway Museum*

BELOW Looking smart in BR green livery on 2 March 1962, having just emerged from its final overhaul at Doncaster Works, locally allocated No 60870 (Darlington, August 1939) nevertheless had just 16 months of service left, being destined for withdrawal in July 1963 and scrapping at Doncaster the following month. Following brief spells when new at New England and Grantham, the former No 4841 was a Doncaster engine from March 1940 until withdrawal in 1963. *G. Jones/Kidderminster Railway Museum*

LEFT Sunday engineering works have forced St Margarets-allocated 'V2' No 60882 (Darlington, October 1939) to haul the 2.40pm Edinburgh–Cowdenbeath local 'wrong line' over the Forth Bridge on 18 August 1963. New as LNER No 4853, it was always a Scottish engine, being allocated to Carlisle Canal, St Margarets and Haymarket sheds, returning to St Margarets ahead of withdrawal in July 1964 and scrapping at Cowlairs in February 1965. *W. A. G. Smith*

BELOW LEFT Ferryhill 'V2' No 60835 (Darlington, September 1938) awaits departure from Glasgow's Buchanan Street station on 30 March 1964 with the 11pm to Aberdeen. New as No 4806, it had been a North Eastern locomotive, working from York, Gateshead, Heaton and Tweedmouth, until transferred north to Ferryhill in June 1963 and would see out its career with a 15-month allocation to St Margaret's ahead of withdrawal in October 1965. The monobloc cylinder casting had been replaced in March 1962. *Paul Riley*

RIGHT Dundee 'V2' No 60919 (Darlington, September 1941) storms up the gradient between Inverkeithing and North Queensferry with the 09.10 Dundee–Blackpool holiday extra on 30 July 1966. New as LNER No 4890, it had been a North Eastern engine until transferred in October 1945 to Ferryhill; based at Dundee from May 1964, it would be withdrawn in September 1966. *C. E. Weston*

ABOVE The preserved No 4771 *Green Arrow* stands at the head of a rake of Gresley teak carriages at Bewdley, on the Severn Valley Railway, in October 2006. The locomotive would be withdrawn from main-line service in 2007. *Richard Hill*

Between May 1956 and March 1962 (after which any locomotive requiring such extensive repairs was automatically condemned) Darlington modified 71 examples, the last of these being No 60835, which emerged on 3 April 1962; none was altered at Doncaster, 'V2' overhauls having been concentrated at Darlington from January 1957.

Following the decision to fit the Kylchap double-chimney equipment to the 'A4' and 'A3' Pacifics, in October 1959 it was arranged for two 'V2s' to be fitted with plain double blastpipes and chimneys, without the Kylchap apparatus; this did little to improve steaming, however, and in the wake of positive results with the Kylchap 'A4s' and 'A3s' authorisation was obtained to fit the apparatus to 'V2' No 60881. Comparative tests were conducted from New England between this locomotive and No 60817, fitted with a plain double chimney, leading to a realisation that in performance terms No 60881 was now the equal of a Pacific and to a recommendation that all 'V2s' be fitted with the Kylchap double chimney. As if to vindicate this decision, shortly afterwards No 60881 was timed descending Stoke Bank at 101.5mph, but in view of the limited life expectancy of the 'V2s' only five further conversions were authorised, these being effected between February 1960 and November 1961.

The first 'V2' to be withdrawn was No 60823 from Perth in March 1962, and by the end of that year some 69 examples had been withdrawn, among them three locomotives (Nos 60815/63/90) which, somewhat surprisingly, had remained at the former GC shed at Leicester following its transfer to the LMR. The last 'V2' was No 60831, withdrawn from York on 6 December 1966, to be broken up by Drapers at Hull in February 1967. But this would not be the end of the 'V2' story, for upon its withdrawal in August 1962 from King's Cross – where, save for a five-week period on loan to Woodford Halse in 1953, it had spent its entire LNER and BR career – the class pioneer, by now numbered 60800, had been acquired for preservation.

Preservation of No 4771/60800 *Green Arrow*

Following cosmetic restoration as LNER No 4771, completed at Doncaster in April 1963, *Green Arrow* spent various periods in store at Hellifield, Leicester and Brighton before in 1971 being allocated to the proposed new National Railway Museum at York. In January 1972 the locomotive was moved to Norwich for restoration to working order by Bill Harvey; this took 14 months, and on 28 March 1973 the locomotive had a test run to Ely and back before moving to Tyseley for exhibition at the depot's open days on 2/3 June. After short trips to Stratford on Avon the first real challenge was working a 14-coach 'Gresley Commemorative' special from Tyseley to Didcot and back. The locomotive then moved to Carnforth, resuming a full main-line career on 6 October 1973 by hauling the A4 Locomotive Society's 'Hadrian' railtour between Carnforth and Barrow. There followed a seven-year stint on the main line, complemented by visits to a variety of heritage railways, following which a second overhaul permitted another period of main-line use between 1985 and 1992 before a further period 'out of ticket'.

NRM locomotives have to endure relatively long periods out of use, funds for overhauls being strictly limited, and thus it was not until 1999 that *Green Arrow* emerged from a third overhaul to resume its main-line career. This drew to a close on 3 March 2007 with a final run from Peterborough to Doncaster, a cracked monobloc cylinder casting and leaking tubes finally prompting the locomotive's withdrawal after a failure on the North Yorkshire Moors Railway on 31 March 2008, although temporary repairs permitted an NRM 'last run' special on 26 April, following which it was moved to Shildon for storage. At the time of writing the NRM is engaged in an as-yet-unresolved debate on the subject of cylinder-block repairs; a new monobloc casting is thought to be impracticable,

industry no longer having the capability of producing such large and complex castings, yet new three-part castings are regarded as non-authentic, notwithstanding the fact that 71 'V2s' were so modified by BR.

The 'K4' 5ft 2in mixed-traffic 2-6-0s

The allocation of two-cylinder 'K2' 2-6-0s to the West Highland line from 1925 allowed the unassisted load from Glasgow to Fort William to be increased from the 190 tons permitted for a 'D34' to 220 tons, thereby eliminating much double-heading. By 1934, however, loads were again increasing, and double-heading of the principal day trains had again become frequent, so work began on designing a more powerful locomotive to comply with the difficult restrictions that had precluded the use of the heavier 'K3', and on 21 February 1935 the Joint Traffic & Locomotive Committee agreed to the provision of one new 2-6-0, authority being obtained by reducing to 20 the approved Darlington 1936 order for 21 'K3s'.

On 28 January 1937 No 3441 *Loch Long* emerged from Darlington in mixed-traffic lined black, being worked up to King's Cross the next day for official inspection. The design followed a May 1936 proposal, the three-cylinder layout of the 'K3' being matched to a 'K2' boiler with pressure raised, in June 1937, to 200lb. This resulted in a powerful machine producing a tractive effort of 36,598lb and with an adhesion

BELOW An official works photograph of 'K4' No 3441 *Loch Long* (Darlington, January 1937) in 'shop' grey. Sent new to Eastfield, the locomotive would be withdrawn from Thornton Junction as BR No 61993 in October 1961 and cut up at Townhill. LNER

ABOVE Two generations of West Highland-line motive power are paired in this May 1956 view of a Fort William–Mallaig passenger train near Glenfinnan, the train engine, Eastfield-based 'K4' No 61995 *Cameron of Lochiel* (Darlington, December 1938), being piloted by Fort William 'K2' No 61791 *Loch Laggan* (Kitson, August 1921). *J. M. Jarvis/ Kidderminster Railway Museum*

factor of 3.54, allowing maximum loadings to be raised to 300 tons for a single locomotive. After it had demonstrated its mastery of its allotted tasks a further five locomotives were authorised on 16 February 1938 and ordered from Darlington the following day for inclusion in the 1938 building programme, No 3442 being delivered on 6 July 1938 and the final four locomotives, Nos 3443-6, in late December.

With the exception of the first, the 'K4s' bore the names of Scottish clan chiefs. No 3442 had been delivered to Eastfield in early July 1938 bearing *MacCailein Mor* nameplates, but in order to avoid causing offence (it being thought that the correct spelling was 'MacCailin Mor') the locomotive was impounded at Eastfield until replacement plates could be supplied from Darlington; in fact Gaelic authorities are not unanimous as to the correct version! By 20 July No 3442 had been named *The Great Marquess*, the revised *MacCailein Mor* plates being fitted

subsequently to No 3445. One other change involved No 3446, originally named *Lord of Dunvegan*, in honour of the chief of Clan MacLeod; the last of the male line had died in 1935, and his female successor requested that *MacLeod of MacLeod* be applied, this being implemented on 30 March 1939. Nos 3442-6 were all delivered in fully lined apple green, which livery was applied to No 3441 in April 1940.

In February 1945 Thompson produced outline drawings for rebuilding the 'K4s' as two-cylinder locomotives. The reconstruction of a single 'K4' was authorised in March, and on 18 August 1945 No 3445 entered Doncaster Works, duly emerging as a 'K1/1' and as such becoming the prototype for a new Class K1.

For 20 years the 'K4s' were used almost exclusively on West Highland-line passenger and freight services, although there were appearances on freights east from Glasgow to Niddrie. Workings from Fort William over the West Highland Extension line to Mallaig were relatively rare until 1947, when the gradual spread of new 'B1' 4-6-0s on passenger services from Glasgow saw the 'K4s' looking for other work, and from 1949 new 'K1' 2-6-0s began to appear on running-in turns from Eastfield (supplemented from 1950 by ex-LMS 'Black Five' 4-6-0s), although only from 1952 did these appear on a regular basis.

From May 1954 the 'K4s' were concentrated at Eastfield for West Highland freights – a reflection of the increasingly held view in the operating and maintenance departments that the high speeds required for West Highland passenger services south of Craigendoran were causing problems for the locomotives' running gear, which their use on freight trains would minimise. With the impending 'dieselisation' of the West Highland line Nos 61993/6 were transferred in April 1959 to Thornton Junction, where they were joined in December by the other three remaining 'K4s' and saw out their days on longer-distance freight workings to Aberdeen, finally being withdrawn in the closing months of 1961. The last 'K4' to be shopped was No 61994, at Cowlairs in May 1961, so when Viscount Garnock was looking for the best 'K4' to preserve it was this locomotive, formerly No 3442, that was selected.

Preservation of No 3442/61994
The Great Marquess

After withdrawal on 18 December 1961 No 61994 was sold to Viscount Garnock and given an overhaul and repaint into LNER livery as No 3442 at Cowlairs Works, moving south to Neville Hill on 29 April 1963. Over the next few years it

was used for a number of railtours, these including a visit to Darlington in October 1964 and a final BR special in March 1965 from Malton to Whitby, over what would later become the North Yorkshire Moors Railway, while in 1967 another special took it from London (Victoria) to Southampton via Brighton and the South Coast line. In 1969 it was joined at Neville Hill by 'K1' No 62005, purchased for spares. With the implementation in 1968 of BR's infamous steam ban the 'K4' found itself marooned, but eventually, in September 1972, it was moved to a new home on the Severn Valley Railway.

After running on the Severn Valley Railway for 10 years No 3442 resumed its main-line career in June 1989 and in July worked its way north from Hereford to Stockport and thence via Skipton to Carlisle before making a triumphant return to Fort William. Here, after working a special for

BELOW Having arrived in charge of a charter train, preserved 'K4' No 3442 *The Great Marquess* (Darlington, July 1938) is serviced at Worcester shed in 1965. Between 1963 and 1968 the locomotive operated from Neville Hill shed in Leeds, where, owing to BR's steam ban, it then went into hibernation, emerging only in 1972. *W. Potter/Kidderminster Railway Museum*

ABOVE From 1972 until 2005 No 3442 *The Great Marquess* was based on the Severn Valley Railway. This 1997 photograph shows the locomotive heading a complete Gresley train, consisting of five teak carriages, between Bridgnorth and Hampton Loade, en route for Kidderminster. The leading coach is recently restored Brake Composite No 24068. *Richard Hill*

LEFT On 10 April 2007 John Cameron's two preserved Gresley locomotives were used to power the Penzance–Thurso 'Great Britain' railtour between Perth and Inverness. Here 'K4' No 61994 *The Great Marquess* and 'A4' No 60009 *Union of South Africa* storm the last few yards to the 1,484ft summit of the Highland main line at Druimuachdar. The following day the 'K4' worked the train to Kyle of Lochalsh before handing over to Stanier '8F' 2-8-0 No 48151 for the run to Thurso, the 'K4'/'A4' combination returning the train south to Glasgow a couple of days later. *Bob Avery/Gresley Society Trust*

Viscount Garnock, it completed two weeks' successful operation of the 'West Highlander' service to Mallaig, marred only by the death of Viscount Garnock, who passed away a happy man shortly after riding on the footplate of his beloved No 3442 between Fort William and Glenfinnan. Not until four years later, in 1993, would the locomotive return to Fort William, during the course of a two-month Scottish visit that included several trips on the Fife Circle. Having returned south it remained in use on the Severn Valley Railway until a broken crank axle prompted its withdrawal, and thereafter it languished at Bridgnorth for several years before a change of ownership. Viscount Garnock's son did not share his father's enthusiasm for No 3442, and an approach was made to John Cameron, owner of 'A4' No 60009 *Union of South Africa*. Under the terms of the sale agreement the 'K4' was moved to Crewe Heritage Centre for repairs and a general overhaul, duly emerging in March 2007 and heading to its 'new' home at Thornton Junction, trips to Inverness in April and to Aviemore in June being followed by a return to Fort William in September. Since then it has become a popular and much-admired main-line performer besides making a number of visits to heritage railways.

The rebuilt 'W1' 4-6-4

Having languished at Darlington for more than a year, as described earlier No 10000 travelled under its own steam to Doncaster on 13 October 1936 for reconstruction as a three-cylinder locomotive with a conventional 250lb boiler (similar to the Diagram 108 design fitted to 'P2' No 2006) and 'A4'-style streamlining; indeed there is some evidence that Gresley intended to use No 10000 as a testbed for future development of the 'A4' design. Otherwise as much as possible was retained of the original locomotive, including the frames and the 1935-fitted Kylchap double chimney and exhaust, and the retention of the 4-6-4 wheel arrangement meant that the cab was larger than that found on a streamlined Pacific, so that, besides having to cover a firegrate of some 50sq ft, the fireman was faced with a greater distance between shovelling plate and firehole door. The work took a year, the locomotive emerging in rebuilt form on 6 November 1937 adorned in garter blue, with dark-red wheels and shaded gold lettering and numbers. Curiously, nameplates (this time *Pegasus*) were again cast but were never fitted.

In its new guise No 10000 was allocated initially to King's Cross, but the need to keep it under close scrutiny following a visit to Doncaster Works in February 1938 saw it transferred shortly afterwards to Doncaster shed, where it stayed for just over a year before returning in March 1939 to King's Cross. Here it was used on regular 'A4' diagrams, on occasion appearing on the streamliners, although the first of these was whilst it was still based at Doncaster, on 4 January 1939,

ABOVE No 10000 awaits departure from King's Cross following rebuilding (at Doncaster in November 1937) as a conventional locomotive. Aside from a two-week loan to Haymarket in 1942 it was to remain a 'Top Shed' machine, latterly as BR No 60700, until transferred to Doncaster in October 1953. Needing a new boiler, it would be condemned in June 1959 and cut up at Doncaster the same month. *Gresley Society collection*

when it was requisitioned at Grantham from a local train to replace No 4482 *Golden Eagle* on the down 'Coronation'; at Durham, however, the 'W1' disgraced itself by running hot and was replaced by nothing more prepossessing than 'G5' 0-4-4 No 1837, which took the train to Newcastle, there to be replaced itself by 'A1' No 2575 for the journey onward to Edinburgh. No 10000's second recorded appearance on a streamliner was on Monday 23 July 1939, when, having worked down to Newcastle from King's Cross on the previous day, it was put in charge of the up 'Silver Jubilee', arriving on time at King's Cross.

The locomotive's smooth riding and free-steaming characteristics made it popular with many drivers (even if it was less so with firemen), while its great power and adhesion, which qualities manifested themselves in its ability to accelerate heavy trains uphill, came in particularly useful during World War 2, when it hauled some prodigious loads over the East Coast route, trains of up to 21 carriages being recorded. Save for two weeks on loan to Haymarket in 1942 it remained a 'Top Shed' engine, latterly as BR No 60700, until October 1953, when it moved back to Doncaster. Thereafter it had a regular daily turn to King's Cross and back, and it was whilst working the return leg, the 3.50pm King's Cross–Doncaster, that the locomotive broke the leading bogie frame and was derailed at Peterborough (Westwood), coming to rest against the signal-box. Its unique 22-year-old boiler was deemed beyond economic repair, and on 1 June 1959 it was formally condemned, being broken up at Doncaster Works later in the month.

ABOVE Hull Dairycoates-allocated No 61435 (Darlington, November 1922) was the first Raven 'B16' 4-6-0 to be rebuilt by Gresley as a 'B16/2', in June 1937; then numbered 2364, it was reconstructed at Darlington with new cylinders, long-lap valves and two sets of Gresley/Walschaerts valve gear in place of the original three sets of Stephenson Link Motion. Here the locomotive, by now the last survivor of its class, poses in store at Hull Dairycoates shortly before being formally condemned in July 1964. *Gresley Society collection*

The rebuilt 'B16' 4-6-0s

Beginning in 1932 the 70 ex-NER Raven S3 4-6-0s (LNER B16) began to be subject to updating when visiting Darlington works. Clearly the locomotives were not responding well to their increasing use on fast work and were fitted with new solid bronze axleboxes, accompanied by cast steel horn guides and forged steel horn stays. Lubrication was enhanced as was wheel balancing and springing. However Gresley was still not satisfied with the general performance of this class and in June 1937 No 2364 was subject to a much more extensive reconstruction to implement what had been learned about the benefits of longer lap valves and increased valve travel. This included new one-piece cast cylinders and smokebox saddle with larger valves. Three independent sets of Stephenson's

link motion were replaced by two sets of Walschaerts gear to the outside valves with Gresley derived motion for the inside valve. Some cosmetic changes were made to the running plate and cab designs and a new Diagram 49 boiler was fitted giving the rebuild a new designation as B16/2. Evaluation of the changes took some time and it was over two years later before, between October 1939 and March 1940, a further six locomotives were similarly converted. Wartime priorities then intervened and no more conversions were undertaken before Gresley's death. Clearly the conversions were regarded as delivering good value for money so that Thompson resumed the programme in 1944, although with three sets of Walschaerts valve gear replacing the Gresley derived gear. Of the seven locomotives four survived to be withdrawn in June 1964, the last example being the first rebuild Dairycoates allocated No 61435(originally 2364) in July 1964.

The 'V4' mixed-traffic 2-6-2s

In 1939/40 design work was undertaken at Doncaster on a new lightweight 2-6-2 intended to 'solve the problem of passenger and freight working on sections of the line where heavier engines are not permitted owing to engineering restrictions' (quote from LNER Locomotive Committee minutes). Of the

LNER's 6,414 route miles its principal mixed-traffic locomotive, the 'V2', was permitted over just 2,752. By careful use of a variety of weight-saving features the 'V4' was reduced to just over 70 tons, leading to a Route Availability 4, which gave access to over 5,000 route miles. The combination of 5ft 8in driving wheels, three 15x26in cylinders and 250lb boiler pressure gave a tractive effort of 27,420lb and a load capacity which was similar to that specified for the Reid superheated North British Atlantics. On the West Highland route the maximum load was 250 tons, almost midway between the 220 tons of the 'K2' and the 300 of the 'K4'. Thus the 'V4', whilst not powerful enough for the heaviest trains, had the potential to be most useful addition to the locomotive fleet. An order was placed with Doncaster in October 1939 for two locomotives, delivered in February and March 1941, in time for the first, No 3401 *Bantam Cock*, to be inspected by Gresley at York on 11 February 1941, seven weeks before his death. No 3402 differed in being fitted with a steel firebox equipped with a thermic siphon, which it would retain until a visit to Doncaster in March 1945. With the change of CME there were to be no more 'V4s', the Thompson-designed 'B1' 4-6-0 emerging to take over most of the work envisaged for the 'V4s', although the fact that 'B1' production eventually ran to some 410 examples serves as an indication of what might have been, had Gresley survived.

As prototypes the two 'V4s' were to be evaluated in East Anglia and Scotland, the two LNER Areas with the greatest number of restricted routes. No 3401 was allocated initially to Doncaster for running-in and then spent a month at York, before arriving at Haymarket in May 1941 for six weeks of trials, including one on loan to Kittybrewster, during which it was noted at Ballater, Elgin and Peterhead; there then followed a five-month spell at Stratford, mainly on express passenger services to Cambridge, Norwich and Southend. No 3402, never officially named but known to all as 'Bantam Hen', was run in from Doncaster for five months before arriving in September 1941 at Eastfield, beginning the class's long-term association with the West Highland line. Meanwhile at the end of November 1941 No 3401 moved to Norwich, where it spent three months working London expresses, eventually returning to Haymarket in February 1942, but in October 1943 the logic of basing both locomotives at the same shed saw it join No 3402 at Eastfield. From 1949 the arrival of 'B1s' and then 'Black Fives' on the West Highland line displaced the 'V4s'

BELOW Brand-new 'V4' 2-6-2 No 3401 *Bantam Cock* (Doncaster, February 1941) poses for the official photographer at Doncaster Works. Following trials on the Great Eastern Section this locomotive would migrate north to Scotland, remaining there until withdrawn as BR No 61700 in March 1957. *Gresley Society collection*

ABOVE The second of the two 'V4s', No 61701 (Doncaster, March 1941), poses outside Waverley station on 6 June 1956, while based at Aberdeen. It had been new as LNER No 3402 and although never formally named was known unofficially as 'Bantam Hen'. Like its mate it spent the majority of its career in Scotland, being withdrawn in November 1957 and broken up at Kilmarnock in February 1958.
H. D. Ramsey/Initial Photographics

RIGHT One of 'V4' No 61700's *Bantam Cock* namplates — the only part of the locomotive to have survived. *Gresley Society Trust collection*

from their premier passenger turns to Eastfield's freight and light passenger turns, to Edinburgh, Perth and Kinross, and in May 1954 the pair moved to Aberdeen in exchange for two 'Black Fives', thereafter being used mainly on freights to Dundee, Edinburgh and Perth. Following a further influx of 'Black Fives' the 'V4s' were loaned to Kittybrewster (being allowed over all GNS Section routes save those to Boat of Garten and Banff), the heavy fish trains from Fraserburgh and Peterhead to Aberdeen being a regular task, although they also saw occasional use on the passenger service to Elgin, in substitution for a 'B1'. By September 1954 both locomotives were back at Ferryhill and had resumed their previous duties, also appearing occasionally at Edinburgh and Glasgow.

No spare boilers were constructed for the 'V4s', so their works visits to tended to be longer than those for other similar types. Both locomotives were 'shopped' exclusively at Cowlairs with the exception of No 3402's 1945 visit to Doncaster (for replacement of its steel inner firebox and removal of the thermic siphon) and one visit by each to Inverurie, in 1953 (3401) and 1955 (3402). By 1957 both locomotives needed replacement boilers and, comprising a small, non-standard class, were deemed surplus, No 61700 being withdrawn in March 1957 and No 61701 following in November, and with the scrapping of No 61701 at Kilmarnock in February 1958 one of Gresley's most attractive and potentially most useful designs became extinct.

The 1500V DC (later BR 'EM1') Bo+Bo electric

The prototype locomotive for the Manchester–Sheffield–Wath electrification was ordered on 16 January 1939 and delivered from Doncaster in February 1941 for display at York to the LNER's directors and the press. With electrical equipment supplied by Metropolitan-Vickers, No 6701 had been intended as the first of 70 such locomotives, but the others had been cancelled on 2 November 1939 following the outbreak of World War 2. Formally delivered and taken into stock on 20 September 1941, it was immediately subjected to three days of test running between Manchester London Road and Altrincham over the MSJ&A line (this being the only section of 1500V DC electrification then available), but thereafter it was

placed in store at Doncaster, where it stayed for the duration of the war.

With the war over but work on the Manchester–Sheffield scheme still on hold, it was decided that operating experience could be gained by sending the locomotive – which in 1946 had been renumbered 6000 – on loan to Nederlandse Spoorwegen (Netherlands Railways). Thus on 30 August 1947

BELOW The original Manchester–Sheffield 1500V DC-overhead electric locomotive, No 26000 (Doncaster, August 1940), rests outside its home shed of Reddish on 10 September 1956. Originally LNER No 6701, this was Gresley's first electric locomotive and the last design to emerge before his death in 1941. The electrification scheme having been deferred for the duration of World War 2, it was stored at Doncaster, and in 1947 it went on loan to Netherlands Railways. Named *Tommy* (formalising a nickname coined by Dutch railwaymen) following its return to the UK in 1952, it remained in service until March 1970, ultimately being cut up in November 1972. *W. Potter/Kidderminster Railway Museum*

it was shipped to Holland via the Harwich–Zeebrugge train ferry, and between September 1947 and March 1952 it covered some 310,000 miles on NS main lines, working both passenger and freight trains. Returned to the UK on 30 March 1952, it was given a General Overhaul at Stratford and put to work shunting at Ilford depot, and in a ceremony on 30 June 1952 at Liverpool Street station the locomotive (by now BR No 26000) was named *Tommy* to formalise the nickname which the locomotive had gained whilst operating in the Netherlands. By this time work had finally resumed on the Manchester–Sheffield electrification scheme, and a further 57 broadly similar electric locomotives were under construction at Gorton Works, but No 26000 had to wait until March 1953 for a transfer to Gorton shed, moving thence to its intended home of Reddish upon the commencement of electric services in June 1954. It would ultimately be withdrawn in March 1970 and cut up at Crewe in November 1972, although BR-built No 26020, dating from 1951, survives in preservation at the National Railway Museum.

Wagon design, 1923-41

At the Grouping the LNER inherited some 284,488 goods wagons, of which the North Eastern contribution was 123,823, the Great Northern 38,713, the Great Central 35,330, Great Eastern 27,213, North British 55,806 and Great North of Scotland 3,603. To be added to this huge fleet were innumerable privately owned wagons, mainly coal-carrying. Because the NER carried large volumes of coal to harbours for onward shipment in coastal vessels it had a proportionately larger fleet of company-owned coal-carrying wagons, the GNR and GCR in contrast serving largely the South Yorkshire and East Midlands coalfields, where privately owned coal wagons were much prominent and direct deliveries from colliery to customer were the norm. Some 52% of the NER fleet comprised mineral wagons, whereas on the GCR the proportion was 24% and on the GNR as low as 12%, reflecting the traffic base of the respective companies. By 1938 the total goods-wagon fleet had declined by 10%, to 258,236 vehicles, of which mineral wagons amounted to 30%, compared with 37% in 1923. These changes largely reflected the growth in productivity of the fleet as older all-timber coal wagons were replaced by higher-capacity wagons with steel underframes. At the Grouping 80% of the GNR's own mineral wagons had been below 12-ton capacity, the corresponding figure for the NER being only 45%. The 1938 LNER figure for wagons above 12-ton capacity was 52%, compared to 32% in 1923, reflecting the higher-capacity ex-NER fleet.

The LNER at the Grouping had acquired several large wagon works engaged as much on repairs as new construction. The NER had contributed the original Stockton & Darlington works at Shildon, which had concentrated on wagon work since losing locomotive work to Darlington in 1871. In 1920 the NER had opened the new Faverdale wagon works in Darlington and this became the principal LNER site for new wagon construction, finally closing in 1962. The GCR works at Duckinfield built carriages and wagons and was responsible in 1930 for the development of the first all-welded wagon underframes, before the transfer of new construction elsewhere. Shildon survived to become the last BR wagon works, building such iconic vehicles as the 'Merry-go-round' coal hoppers. Shildon finally closed in 1984, after a brief period of glory in 1975 as the location of the 'S&D 150' celebrations in 1975.

Most goods wagons complied with general standards laid down by the Railway Clearing House (RCH), but Gresley took exception to some of the details and was thereby responsible for improving standards. For example, the RCH design of cast-iron split axlebox was replaced from 1932 by Gresley's cast-steel open-fronted design. Large numbers of LNER wagons were built on wooden underframes, using the mass-production equipment at Darlington (Faverdale) Wagon Works, but as timber in large cuts was becoming more expensive the new Shildon Wagon Works was equipped to produce steel underframes, and the use of timber was much reduced. In 1936, in a similar vein, the Faverdale design office produced some all-steel hopper wagons to a new design with two doors, replacing earlier NER wooden hoppers with eight wooden doors, these being the forerunners of an eventual fleet of more than 60,000 coal hopper wagons built by the LNER and BR.

Gresley was at the forefront in introducing welding in lieu of riveting in the assembly of vehicle underframes, in order to reduce weight, and was responsible for both the first British all-welded wagon underframes (at Dukinfield, near Manchester, in 1930) and the first all-welded carriage underframes (at York, in 1934).

Britain's railways have always used a significant number of wagons constructed by contractors, many for private owners, and, over time, railway-company-built and -owned vehicles have declined in number, particularly since the closure of all the former railway-company-owned wagon works. As Britain's railways have lost the 'common carrier' obligation and been converted to air brakes the numbers of vehicles for freight service have reduced dramatically, leading to the replacement of virtually the entire wagon fleet.

Wagon preservation has neither the high profile nor the resources available to locomotive or even carriage preservation, and much effort has been expended on saving examples of pre-Grouping designs and more modern vehicles displaced by the adoption of the air brake. Preserved LNER goods vehicles are relatively rare, and even the North Yorkshire Moors Railway has only nine LNER freight vehicles, these being a 1923 box van, a 1946 open goods, two coal hoppers, two 'Lowmac' machinery-carrying wagons, a 1939 bogie 'Weltrol' wagon and two Darlington-built goods brake vans.

ABOVE Unfitted 12-ton van No 43365, with 9ft wheelbase, built at Shildon in 1925 to Diagram 10, one of a total of 25,000. *Peter Tatlow collection*

BELOW Unfitted 12-ton van No 151217, with 9ft wheelbase, built in 1927 as one of 250 completed to Diagram 14. Note the lamp bracket, unusual for an unfitted vehicle. *Peter Tatlow collection*

ABOVE Vacuum-fitted 10-ton large cattle wagon No 156415, with 10ft 6in wheelbase, built at Faverdale in 1929 as one of 200 to Diagram 39, on wooden underframes. A further 200 would be built later in the year, to Diagram 40. *R. Chorley collection*

BELOW Unfitted 20-ton convertible bulk-grain van No 156099, with 10ft 6in wheelbase. Built in 1929 as one of a batch of 25 constructed to Diagram 51 (based on a GWR design), it was equipped with hopper and side doors and was thus capable of being used as a conventional van for transporting bagged grain. Note the 'Return to Hull' legend. *R. Chorley collection*

ABOVE Unfitted 12-ton eight-plank sleeper open No 154906, with wooden underframe and 10ft 6in wheelbase; built at Faverdale in 1929, it was one of 350 built to Diagram 48, the overall production total being 1,749. Contamination from creosote would have rendered it unsuitable for other traffic, hence the 'Sleeper' branding. *R. Chorley collection*

BELOW Unfitted 12-ton seven-plank open No 158591, with 9ft wheelbase, built by W. H. Davies in 1930 to Diagram 63, one of 1,000 built. The stripe denotes an end door. *Peter Tatlow collection*

ABOVE Vacuum-fitted 8-ton insulated van No 165642, with 9ft wheelbase. Completed at Faverdale in 1931 (at a cost of £318) on a steel underframe supplied from Dukinfield, it was one of 35 built to Diagram 21, of an overall total of 297. *Peter Tatlow collection*

BELOW Unfitted 12-ton seven-plank open No 173362, with 9ft wheelbase, built at Faverdale in 1934 as one of 1,550 constructed to Diagram 91, total production amounting to 11,860. *R. Chorley collection*

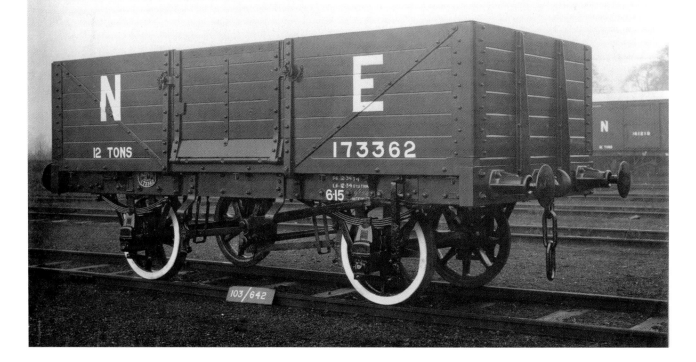

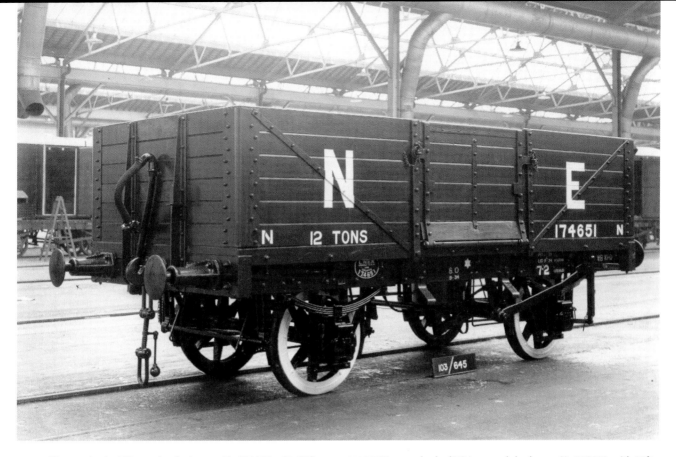

ABOVE Vacuum-braked 12-ton six-plank open No 174651, with 10ft wheelbase, built at Faverdale in 1934 as one of 1,250 constructed to Diagram 92, of an overall total of 6,630 turned out in the years 1934 40. *R. Chorley collection*

BELOW Vacuum-braked 20-ton goods brake van No 182922, with 16ft wheelbase, built in 1935 at Faverdale, as one of 50 to Diagram 61. The 'TOAD D', as it was coded, went on to become the standard BR goods brake van. *R. Chorley collection*

ABOVE Vacuum-braked 10-ton fish van No 184014, with 10ft wheelbase, built at Faverdale in 1936 (at a cost of £285) as of 250 constructed to Diagram 83, of an overall total of 550. *R. Chorley collection*

BELOW Unfitted 12-ton eight-plank open coal hopper No 188789, with 10ft 6in wheelbase, built by BRCW in 1936 as one of 1,400. *C. Roberts/Historical Model Railway Society/Peter Tatlow collection*

ABOVE Unfitted 20-ton hopper No 193254, with 12ft wheelbase. Dating from 1936, it was one of 500 built by Hurst Nelson of Motherwell (at a cost of £219 15s) to Diagram 100 as part of a larger batch of 2,000, construction of which was shared with Metropolitan-Cammell, BRCW and Head Wrightson. Production of this design would ultimately reach 13,645. *R. Chorley collection*

BELOW Built at Faverdale in 1938, 10-ton fish van No 229122 was one of 800 constructed to Diagram 134 (at a cost of £210 16s 4d each), the overall total being 1,940. With a 12ft wheelbase, it was vacuum-braked and steam-piped to facilitate inclusion in passenger trains, hence the XP branding. *Peter Tatlow collection*

ABOVE Vacuum-braked and steam-piped to facilitate use in passenger trains, 10 ton insulated fish van No 230653, with 12ft wheelbase, was built in 1938 as one of 800 completed to Diagram 134.
Peter Tatlow collection

BELOW Vacuum-braked 12-ton van No 238263, with 10ft wheelbase and steel ends, built at Faverdale in 1940 (at a cost of £258 3s 5d) as one of 1,000 constructed to Diagram 116, the overall total being 7,750.
R. Chorley collection

Gresley carriages, 1923-41

Shortly after the Grouping Gresley appointed as his personal assistant O. V. S. Bulleid, and it is clear that the latter assumed much responsibility for carriage and wagon matters. In 1976 Gresley's former assistant, Norman Newsome, presented to the Gresley Society a paper entitled 'Fourteen Years with Gresley on Carriages and Wagons' wherein he confirmed the key role played by Bulleid in supervising carriage design matters, only the most important decisions being referred to Gresley himself. Newsome summed up Gresley's philosophy for carriage design as incorporating five key principles:

1. The maximum use of articulation, in order to save weight
2. The maximum use of India-rubber springs, to reduce requirements for replacement in buffing and drawgear
3. Buckeye knuckle couplings, to prevent telescoping in accidents
4. The elimination of oil gas, to reduce fire risk
5. The Gresley double-bolster bogie with pressed steel frame and 8ft 6in wheelbase for long-distance carriages, because of its good riding qualities

In addition Gresley was an early advocate of pressure ventilation and double-glazing for prestige stock.

In the early days of the LNER new carriages had been built to the designs of the constituent companies; LNER standards would be 60ft underframes for corridor main-line stock and 51ft for non-corridor stock; articulated stock was based on 43ft bogie centres for general running, but 47ft was permitted over certain routes. The GE Section, however, would not accept 60ft carriages on some of its main-line services, on the basis that it had so many separate portions on trains from Liverpool Street in order to serve multiple destinations that it could not accept this length. Gresley was therefore compelled to build 51ft corridor carriages solely for the GE – one of numerous instances wherein he was flexible enough to accept local requirements as of greater priority than the need for standardisation. The old GER carriages were 54ft long, and every year, when the carriage-building programme was being discussed, Gresley tried to persuade the GE authorities to accept 60ft vehicles, but the operators consistently refused; they did relent in 1925 for a new 'Hook Continental' set, in 1929 for a 'Cromer' set and 1937 for the 'East Anglian' and a replacement set for the 'Hook Continental', but only after nationalisation and the introduction of the BR Mk 1 vehicles would the GE be forced to accept 60ft stock for general use.

The LNER's carriage-building policy was to produce completely new sets of specially designed vehicles for the premier services, older vehicles being displaced to less important services, in a process that would later be known as 'cascading'. Each of the three Areas was largely autonomous in the deployment of its passenger rolling stock and submitted its own bid for new construction in the annual carriage-building programme, centralised control not being established until 1942.

The 1923/4 programme represented merely the summation of the constituent companies' proposals for new construction in 1923 and the completion of outstanding orders from 1922, several new Royal Train vehicles being included. There were as yet no carriages to LNER standard designs; these would have to wait until December 1923, when the details of the new 'standard' designs were confirmed for implementation from the 1924/5 programme. This would see the construction of more than 100 vehicles to re-equip the East Coast sets and provide new vehicles for Newcastle–South Wales and the Continental boat train. Also included for 1924 were five-car articulated commuter sets for GE services, designed along the lines of the 'Quad-Art' sets already in use on GN inner-suburban services. These 'Quint-Art' sets had to be modified with stronger frames, as the crush-load conditions to which they were subjected caused deflection in the frames and difficulty in closing doors. Demonstrating his interest both in economy and in planning for the future, Gresley designed the outer underframes of these vehicles so that they could be fitted with motor bogies in the event of electrification of the GE suburban lines, although the intended 'Quad-Art' sets for the GN were deferred until the decision on GN suburban electrification had been taken. Only two vehicles from this year survive, one (No 10155) at the Great Central, the other (10021) with the SRPS at Bo'ness, neither as yet restored. However, a unique and most fortunate survivor from the 1923 Doncaster build programme, carried forward from the GNR, is 'Quad-Art' set No 74. After 43 years' service on GN commuter services this was already at King's scrapyard at Wymondham and just hours away from destruction when it was saved for the North Norfolk Railway, arriving there in June 1967. Following 10 years of use and outdoor storage in all weathers it was withdrawn for restoration, but although a start was made this proved beyond the available resources until a Heritage Lottery Fund grant was secured, whereupon the set moved to Carnforth for a £½ million restoration, begun in 2003. The fully restored set returned in 2008 and is now housed in its own shed at Holt, from which it emerges on special occasions as befits a unique set of carriages.

The 1925/6 programme was noteworthy in that it relied on outside contractors for the major part, comprising 353 contractor-built vehicles and only 248 built in-house. Included within the total were large number of non-vestibuled carriages for use in the London suburbs, the North East and southern Scotland, although tight finances led to the cancellation of 101 vehicles, along with the GN suburban electrification.

ABOVE Four-wheel vacuum-braked parcels van No 70203 (originally 6890), built to Diagram 120 at Stratford in 1928 as one of batch of 29. *Peter Tatlow collection*

The 1926/7 programme carried on from that of the previous year and included a significant number of non-vestibuled carriages, although the unfavourable economic climate saw 145 vehicles deferred to 1927. Three vehicles from 1926/7 survive, all as yet unrestored, at Bere Ferrers (3107) and Mangapps Farm (3641 and 61684).

The 1927/8 programme of 313 vehicles included the deferred non-vestibuled sets from the previous year and included two completely new sets for the new non-stop 'Flying Scotsman' service. Innovations introduced were the first application of armrests in Third-class compartments and subsequent provision of a ladies' hairdressing compartment, a separate ladies retiring room and a cocktail bar. Gresley was personally involved in the detailed design features of these vehicles and chose Sir Charles Allom to undertake interior design of the restaurant cars, following his work on interior design of the new 1924 LNER Royal Train vehicles. Gresley also was strongly in favour of the widespread use of electricity on trains for water heating in toilet washbasins and for cooking and refrigeration in restaurant cars when most railways still used oil

gas for cooking. The GE Section bid successfully for 30 vehicles for Cromer services, built on 60ft underframes. No vehicles from the 1927/8 programme have survived.

The 1928/9 programme was principally concerned with the construction of new suburban 'Quad-Art' or 'Quint-Art' sets for the GN and GE suburban services but did include for East Coast services two triplet restaurant car sets, seven restaurant cars with electric cooking and 100 vestibuled carriages. As the main line companies (excluding the SR) had decided to introduce third class sleeping cars, 16 of the 48 corridor thirds in this programme were approved for construction as convertible third class sleepers, with a further 12 approved in advance of the 1929/30 programme. One survivor from this year is Restaurant First No 1222, waiting restoration from departmental condition at the Great Central Railway.

The 279 passenger vehicles envisaged in the 1929/30 programme were intended to replace 437 withdrawn vehicles, including some vans and milk tanks, and included a further 14 suburban sets. Three vehicles from 1929/30 have survived – an unrestored Restaurant First (42969) at the North Yorkshire Moors Railway, a partially restored Pantry Third (42972) at Mangapps Farm, and a fully restored pigeon van (6843) on the North Norfolk Railway, where it usually runs attached to the preserved 'Quad-Art' set.

ABOVE First-class sleeper No 1210, built Doncaster in 1925 to Diagram 17. The very similar No 1211, built in 1935 to Diagram 157, remained in traffic for an amazing 37 years, having become by the time of its withdrawal in 1972 the last wooden-bodied sleeping car in BR service; acquired for preservation by the Strathspey Railway, it was then used as accommodation for volunteers, finally being moved to Bo'ness early in 2015 for restoration. *Ian Allan Library*

RIGHT This vehicle was built at York in 1935 as a Tourist Open Third to Diagram 186. After withdrawal from normal service it served in the Eastern Region Mobile Control Office train — intended for use in the event of nuclear war. It arrived on the Severn Valley Railway in 1980. Restoration of the interior is proceeding, and this view shows the recently fitted mirrors, luggage racks and coathooks. Subsequent work will concentrate on the replacement of the BR Mk 1 seats with correct LNER-design bucket seats. *Richard Hill*

The 1930/1 programme comprised 280 carriages, intended to replace 369 older vehicles. Plans for suburban GN and GE electrification initially saw no further orders placed for suburban stock but as doubts emerged the urgency of replacement of elderly stock saw four 'Quint-Art' sets for Enfield services ordered.

The 1931/2 programme was ambitious with over 400 vehicles that included many sets for front-line services off the East Coast main line and twin sets for local services on the main line and in Lincolnshire. The financial situation was deteriorating and cutbacks became the order of the day so that only 312 orders survived. Despite this 1931 saw Doncaster build the first pressure-ventilated carriage in the form of No 1134, a 'Super First'; until the streamliner era full pressure ventilation (an early version of air-conditioning) was

LEFT Built at Doncaster in 1936, No 7960 is the last surviving LNER Kitchen Composite built to Diagram 187, with an 18 seat Third-class saloon and a 12 seat First-class saloon. This vehicle was designed for (and spent most of its working life on) the Great North of Scotland Section, between Aberdeen and Inverness. Withdrawn in 1961, it saw several years' use in departmental service and was semi-derelict when saved for future use on the Severn Valley Railway. Restoration took from 1990 until 2012, and the kitchen has still to be fully equipped before the coach can take its intended place in a quality charter dining set. *Richard Hill*

BELOW The restored 12-seat First-class saloon in No 7960. *Richard Hill*

applied only to First-class vehicles for the premier services and to sleeping carriages.

The year 1932 was blighted by the poor economic situation, which led in August to the suspension of all carriage construction included in the 1931/2 programme. Despite the suspension of new construction, scrapping of obsolete vehicles continued so that the stock of passenger rated vehicles declined by 1,300 vehicles to 12,800 by the end of 1932.

Despite the poor financial background, in 1932 Gresley proposed to Wedgwood a new design of all-steel carriage, using fittings of a commercially produced steel material known as 'Alpax'; the detailed design work on No 65000 was carried out by Norman Newsome and resulted in a vehicle 2 tons lighter than its teak equivalent. Finances were little improved in the 1933 programme so five 12-vehicle trains of vestibuled open 'Tourist' stock for excursion service were authorised, as partial replacements for 36 sets of elderly GNR close-coupled four-wheel suburban stock which had been retained for such workings, and the dramatic improvement in the quality of the stock employed

ABOVE Built in 1936 at York to Diagram 216, this short-frame Open Third was designed for use on the Great Eastern Section. After withdrawal it saw use in departmental service, with a largely gutted interior. After several changes of ownership and location it arrived at Kirkby Stephen in 2000, following which external restoration has been completed, and restoration of the interior is now proceeding rapidly, new replica bucket seats having been installed in 2013. *Mike Thompson*

led to an immediate increase in business. Built to run with these sets were the first Buffet cars, another Gresley innovation. Only two vehicles from 1931 survive, these being an unrestored Corridor Third (3395) on the North Norfolk Railway and a restored Post office van (6777) on the Great Central.

By 1933 the economy was beginning to recover, and a modest start, in the shape of 270 vehicles for the 1934 programme, was made to recover from the backlog caused by the hiatus in construction. Among these were a further two 'Tourist' sets, along with sets for Cromer and Clacton and some First-class sleeper and restaurant cars. From 1934 two

Open Thirds (43600 and 43612) survive, both now fully restored as part of the Severn Valley Railway's magnificent LNER set. These vehicles, incidentally, were among the first to feature a fully welded underframe.

Chairing a special Line Traffic Committee meeting in November 1934, Gresley outlined an objective for the replacement of all four- and six-wheeled stock, except from 'third-rate branch lines [and] miners' and workmen's trains'. The upturn in the economy – and the availability of Government funding for some projects, particularly where work was out-sourced to contractors – now permitted a supplementary 1935 programme for some 647 vehicles, beyond the original £700,000 budget (itself reduced from an original £1.93 million). This allowed many main-line sets to be replaced, and further 'Tourist' stock provided, while provision for the new 'Silver Jubilee' stock was made in April 1935 by corresponding reductions in other orders. The programme also provided for the conversion of 593 gas-lit carriages to electric lighting. There are eight survivors from 1935 comprising four vehicles as yet unrestored – two Corridor Thirds (23890, 23896) and a Tourist Open Third (43632) on the North Yorkshire Moors Railway and a Sleeper First (1211), now at Bo'ness – and four fully restored, these being a Tourist Open Third (52255) on the Severn Valley Railway, Open Brake Third (43567) and a Tourist Open Third (43654) on the NYMR and another Open Brake Third (43571) on the Colne Valley Railway.

ABOVE No 88275 (originally 24585), a steel-panelled composite articulated twin built by Metro-Cammell in 1938 for use on the Darlington–Saltburn service. *Ian Allan Library*

TOP RIGHT 'Beavertail' observation car No 1729, one of two (the other being No 1719) built at Doncaster in 1937 to Diagram 232 for use on the 'Coronation' streamliner. Furnished with just 16 seats, it commanded a supplementary fare but was not used during the winter months, when the train ran mainly in darkness. Stored for the duration of World War 2, it would eventually be adapted by BR for more-typical observation-car use in Scotland. Acquired for preservation by the Gresley Society in 1967, it was kept initially on the Keighley & Worth Valley Railway before being moved in 1974 to Ashford and thence in 1978 to Carnforth. Eventually sold to RVP (Railway Vehicle Preservations) in 2006, it was moved to Barrow Hill for restoration to original condition, which at the time of writing (2015) was still in progress at Nemesis Rail, Burton-on Trent. *Ian Allan Library*

BOTTOM RIGHT Built at York in 1937 to Diagram 167, Tourist Restaurant Buffet No 643 was one of six built for Liverpool Street–Cambridge services. Modernised by BR in 1959, it was one of the last Gresley carriages to remain in regular use, finally being withdrawn in 1977, after 40 years' service. Pressed straight into use on the Severn Valley Railway, it had to wait until 1987 for withdrawal for full restoration. *Richard Hill*

The 1936 programme of 596 vehicles included four high-speed sets (including a spare) for the 'Coronation' and 'West Riding Limited' and a conventional set for the 'East Anglian', as well as a number of restaurant and buffet cars and some more non-vestibuled sets for Marylebone commuter services. Of the 15 1936 survivors eight are unrestored, these being a Corridor Third (3857) and an almost-completed Tourist Open Third (60505) at Kirkby Stephen, a Restaurant Buffet (24082) on the Epping–Ongar Railway, an Inspection Saloon (900580) at Carnforth, an Open Third (23953) at the East Anglian Railway Museum, an Open Third (23981), Buffet (24080) and a Gangwayed Brake Pigeon (4149) on the Great Central; the seven restored vehicles comprise a Kitchen Composite (7960) and a Tourist Open Third (24105) on the Severn Valley Railway, two Tourist Open Thirds (23956 and 24109) on the NYMR and a Restaurant Buffet (24079) at Croughton Manor plus the two SLF cars (1591 and 1592) from Eisenhower's HQ train at Green Bay Wisconsin.

In 1937 passenger traffic increased by 6.7% over that seen the previous year, and the LNER responded by building 711 vehicles in the 1938 programme, construction including two new sets for the 'Flying Scotsman' and another for the 'Hook Continental' as well as 105 other new vehicles for the East

Coast plus many other vehicles, vestibuled and non-vestibuled, among them nine articulated sets for the Darlington–Saltburn service. One rather special vehicle was a Corridor Third (1587) constructed to expand an articulated twin to a triple set for enhanced capacity of the 'Silver Jubilee'.

Survivors from 1937 are the most numerous and include three under restoration – two Restaurant Buffets, one at Rushden (24279) and one on the NYMR (649), and a 'Coronation' observation car (1729), currently at Burton-on-Trent. Whilst both of the 'Coronation' observation cars survived it was with modified (1959) observation ends; the work on 1729 involves restoration of the original 'beaver-tail' shape. The 10 restored vehicles include two Restaurant Buffets (24278, 24280), a Post Office van (2441) and the other 'Coronation' observation car (1719), all on the Great Central Railway, a Restaurant Buffet (643) and a Brake Composite (24068) on the Severn Valley Railway, further Restaurant

Buffets on the NYMR (641), at the North Norfolk Railway (51769), at Bo'ness (644) and the NRM (650).

Having received a boost in 1938 the economy was now showing signs of overheating, significant inflation in contractors' prices leading to a severe cutback in orders from contractors, who in 1939 delivered only 96 vehicles, in contrast with the 286 supplied by the LNER's own workshops. New sets for secondary non-London routes featured heavily, although there were odd vehicles for individual East Coast services; there were also numerous conversions of existing stock to form new push-pull sets for branch-line services on the GN and GE Sections and in Scotland. There are only five survivors from 1938. Two are about to be fully restored, these being the Gresley Society's 'Flying Scotsman' Buffet Lounge (1852) at Kirkby Stephen, and an Open Brake Third (43556) on the NYMR; the three restored vehicles are a pigeon van (4247) on the Keighley & Worth Valley Railway, an Open Third (56856) at the NYMR and Brake Third (41384) at Quainton.

In 1939 deliveries tailed off, new construction running at less than 30% of the rate of withdrawals; reflecting the general uncertainty in the run-up to war, orders for 1940 were down to 179 passenger vehicles and 34 brake vans. Part-restored survivors are a Restaurant Buffet (24287) in use as a shop/café at Kirkby Stephen and a Brake Third (57451) awaiting further attention on

the Great Central Railway, having earlier run on the Keighley & Worth Valley, as well as the GC; the only restored vehicle is a covered carriage truck (1298), at Monkwearmouth.

With the onset of war, 1940 saw further retrenchment (not helped by a devastating non-war-related fire at Doncaster Carriage Works), and the construction programme of only 155 vehicles included 28 passenger brake vans. Two of these survive, at Llangollen (4268) and Bo'ness (4271), as do similar vans from 1941, Nos 4050 recently restored on the Great Central and 70754 at the North Tyneside Museum. Additionally Bogie passenger brake No 70759 of 1940 is being restored by the LNER Coach Association on the Severn Valley Railway as a Brake Third with four compartments, to re-create a type of vehicle poorly represented in preservation.

BELOW This Corridor Brake Third was built at York in 1939 for use on the Great Central Section. Acquired straight from regular service in 1965, it was preserved by the Gresley Society on the Keighley & Worth Valley Railway, where it was used for some years (notably starring in the film of *The Railway Children*) before the need for extensive repairs saw it moved to the Great Central Railway in 1978 and eventually sold to RVP in 1986. However, only minor work has been undertaken, and the vehicle still awaits the resources necessary for full restoration and, ultimately, a return to passenger service. *RVP*

During the 18-year period from 1923 to 1941 more than 4,000 carriages were built to Gresley designs by LNER workshops at Stratford, Doncaster, York and Dukinfield, and a further 2,329 by contractors, principally BRCW, Metro-Cammell and R. Y. Pickering. Of an overall total that thus exceeds 6,300 vehicles, only 86 survive in preservation, and of these only 34 can reasonably be described as 'restored'. For readers wishing to admire these beautiful vehicles, the principal sites are the Severn Valley Railway, the North Yorkshire Moors Railway and the Great Central Railway, although there are smaller collections at Kirkby Stephen, Mangapps Farm (Essex) and the SRPS site at Bo'ness. What is surprising, particularly in view of its relatively healthy collection of locomotives, is the poor collection of LNER carriages to be found at the National Railway Museum. Almost 25% of all restored vehicles are catering vehicles, reflecting the fact that the last Gresley vehicles in BR service were buffet cars, some surviving until as late as 1970. Particular cause for regret is the fact that there are no surviving articulated coaches from the five streamlined trainsets, even though some lasted as late as 1964 – well in to the era of preservation – so that now we have only photographic records and short film clips to remind us of the elegance of these trend-setting vehicles. How many people travelling in today's Eurostar and TGV sets realise how much the experience of air-conditioned, articulated lightweight trains and at-seat dining service owes to the innovative genius of Sir Nigel Gresley?

The end of the Gresley Era

As the war progressed, Gresley began to exhibit the classic signs of overwork, and his health deteriorated. Chronic bronchitis set in, and his heart began to fail. He managed to make it to York on 19 February 1941 to witness the unveiling of both his last steam-locomotive design, the 'V4', and his first electric locomotive, No 6701. A month later he was not well enough to attend the first showing at Waterloo of the new 'Merchant Navy' Pacific *Channel Packet*, designed by his former assistant, Oliver Bulleid. Shortly afterwards, on 5 April 1941, he died at his home at Watton-at-Stone, in Hertforshire.

Following Gresley's death the LNER Chairman, Sir Ronald Matthews, reportedly approached both the Southern, in an effort to entice Bulleid back, and the LMS, to enquire as to the availability of R. C. Bond. Failure in both these endeavours meant that the choice of successor fell to the Mechanical Engineer at Doncaster, Edward Thompson.

Thompson envisaged far-reaching changes to the LNER's locomotive policy as established by Gresley and convinced Matthews that a review should be undertaken by an independent adjudicator — who turned out to be none other than Sir William Stanier, of the LMS! Apparently the report was non-committal, Stanier not actually condemning the conjugated

valve gear but merely commenting that he would not use it himself. But from the many changes implemented by Thompson – not the least of which would be his choice for extensive and unsympathetic rebuilding of his predecessor's very first Pacific, No 4470 *Great Northern* – it soon became clear that the Gresley era had passed.

Nonetheless, we are fortunate that many of Gresley's successful and graceful locomotives have survived, including the world's most famous steam locomotives, *Flying Scotsman* and *Mallard*, alongside many of his carriages which were the ultimate in style and comfort. Almost three quarters of a century after his death, these vehicles can still be admired by all of those who have come to appreciate the beauty and efficiency of his designs.

'Mallard75'

When the then Head of the National Railway Museum, Steve Davies, reviewed the possibilities for appropriate celebrations of the 75th anniversary of Mallard's record run in 2013 he came up with a highly imaginative proposal – to reunite all of the six surviving 'A4' Pacifics by repatriating Nos 60008 and 60010 from the USA and Canada respectively! Despite the many logistical challenges, plans were made and agreements obtained so that by 25 September 2012 both locomotives set sail from Halifax for Liverpool.

The extraction of both locomotives was not without its difficulties, particularly for No 60008. International haulage expert Andrew Goodman used all his talents to move other exhibits and facilitate the release of the locomotive which had initially seemed to offer insuperable problems. Both locomotives demonstrated the huge difference between the UK and North American rail structure gauges by being moved to Halifax on rail flat cars.

Arrival in Liverpool was on 3 October 2012, after which both locomotives moved by road to the NRM 'Locomotion' base at Shildon for restoration. No 60008 was to be restored to its current identity in 1960s BR Brunswick green. No 60010 was to be transformed back to the condition in which it was in March 1938 – garter blue livery, No 4489, side valances, CPR Bell and single chimney (not, as incorrectly described elsewhere, as original condition which was as *Woodcock*, silver grey with green wheels and no bell).

The exhibition at the NRM was to be referred to as 'The Great Gathering' and ran from 3 to 17 July and 26 October to 8 November 2013. In between *Mallard* and more modern East Coast motive power featured in an exhibition at Grantham over the weekend of 7-8 September. The last piece in the jigsaw was the triumphant arrival of No 4464 after its 90mph run from London on 29 June. The Great Gathering was an unprecedented success with total numbers on site having to be controlled after a few hours on day one, repeated on all other

ABOVE On 19 February 2014, to mark the end of 'The Great Farewell' at 'Locomotion', NRM Shildon, all six 'A4s' were lined up, left to right No 60007 *Sir Nigel Gresley*, No 60008 *Dwight D. Eisenhower*, No 60009 *Union of South Africa*, No 4489 (60010) *Dominion of Canada*, No 4464 (60019) *Bittern* and No 4468 (60022) *Mallard*. *Jack Beeston/Gresley Society collection*

days in order to restrict numbers. Total attendance was 244,500, breaking all records for an event at the NRM. The costs of the complete project was £530,700 and at the end the NRM announced a profit of £404,500.

In addition a 'Great Farewell' was organised at 'Locomotion', Shildon between 15 and 22 February 2014, before which Nos 4489 and 60008 plus No 4489 had visited Barrow Hill over the weekend of 8/9 February. At the end of February both locomotives were returned by road to Liverpool docks, arriving back in North America at Halifax on 11 May 2014. Return home was as outwards on rail flat cars, No 4489 arriving back at Delson on 3 June and No 60008 at Green Bay on 6 June.

Gresley Replicas

The successful completion of the project to build a new 'A1' Pacific, *Tornado*, has created much interest and inspired others to fill gaps in the portfolio of preserved steam. Gresley designs feature prominently in this process with no fewer than four locomotives of two designs among the new construction projects.

1. The 'P2' Steam Locomotive Company. 2-8-2 No 2007 *Prince of Wales*

This subsidiary of the 'A1' Steam Locomotive Trust (builders and operators of 'A1' No 60163 *Tornado*) had already by 2014 engaged on the assembly of the frames of No 2007 *Prince of Wales* at Hopetown works, Darlington. Using the tried and tested formula undertaken for No 60163, the P2SLC has already raised over one half of the funds required, at a faster rate than for *Tornado*. Total costs are estimated as £5 million, with construction taking place over a 7-10 year period. No 2007 is planned to be aesthetically similar to the original 'P2' No 2001

Cock o' the North with an enhanced and modernised version of the Lentz poppet valve gear. Using experience gained from the operation of *Tornado*, No 2007 will incorporate detailed design changes where operation of the original locomotives revealed some design weaknesses, the objective being to demonstrate the general validity of the original design and reveal to the modern world the majesty of Gresley's most powerful express passenger locomotive design.

Spurred on by its success, the 'A1' Trust has already begun the debate on which designs should feature in subsequent projects after the completion of No 2007. At present favourites are the 'V3' 2-6-2T, the 'V4' 2-6-2 and the 'K3' 2-6-0.

2. The Doncaster P2 Locomotive Trust.
2-8-2 No 2001 *Cock o' the North*

This Doncaster-based group plans to build a replica of No 2001 as rebuilt by Gresley in 1938 with 'A4' 'Bugatti'-style front end and Walschaerts valve gear. The Doncaster P2 Trust dismisses the concept of the original 'P2' design and believes that the subsequently modified locomotive will offer a better opportunity for a robust and practical design – differing markedly in the approach adopted by the P2SLC. Although hoping to find premises in Doncaster for the final assembly of the locomotive, the Doncaster P2 Locomotive Trust has temporarily set up the new main frames for the locomotive at the Great Western Society's site at Didcot. Fundraising is proceeding at a much slower pace than for No 2007.

3 The 'B17' Steam Locomotive Trust.
No 61673 *Spirit of Sandringham*

This organisation achieved charitable status in 2011 and plans to construct a new 'B17' 4-6-0 to the latest group standards for operation on the main line. The locomotive is planned to be equipped with both designs of tender with which the original class operated. Examples of both design of tender have been acquired. Because of its proven expertise in new-build construction the 'B17' locomotive Trust has selected the Llangollen Railway as its base and profiled the new locomotive frames in April 2015 at Wolverhampton, the process being initiated by Sir Nigel Gresley's grandson Tim Godfrey.

4. 'Engine 61662 Appeal'. 'B17' 4-6-0
No 61662 *Manchester United*

This subsidiary of the NBL Preservation Group Ltd was created in 2008 in order to build a new 'B17' No 61662 *Manchester United*. Construction thus far has included the cab and an appropriate LNER group standard tender has been acquired from a scrapyard in Doncaster. The estimated budget for the scheme is £1.8 million.

RIGHT Gresley's Class P2 locomotive No 2002 *Earl Marischal* stands at King's Cross on 9 November 1934. The construction of two new examples of this class will allow us the opportunity to ride behind a mighty 'P2' once again – for the first time since 1944. *S. Osborne*

The Gresley Legacy

Sir Nigel Gresley was responsible for the new construction of 1,536 locomotives of 23 different classes. A further 445 locomotives of 13 classes were substantially reconstructed (and there were a further 169 new builds to these modified designs), a grand total of 2,150 locomotives over a period of 30 years (1911 to 1941) in harness as Chief Locomotive Engineer of the Great Northern and then LNER. During the same period he was responsible for the design of over 6,300 carriages and countless freight wagons. Of the locomotives only 11 (less than 0.5%) have survived, of which five are currently operational – two 'A4's, No 60007 *Sir Nigel Gresley* and No 60009 *Union of South Africa*, the 'K4' 2-6-0 *The Great Marquess*, the 4-4-0 *Morayshire* and the only preserved Gresley tank engine 'N2' 0-6-2T No 1744. Of the two Gresley rebuilds, only the 'B12' 4-6-0 No 1572 is currently operational. On the carriage front, the 86 survivors (1.4%) include only 34 which can properly be described as 'restored'.

Despite this it is still possible to ride behind a Gresley designed locomotive inside a fully restored Gresley carriage regularly on the North Yorkshire Moors Railway and occasionally on the Severn Valley Railway also, both railways operating full rakes of magnificently restored Gresley teak-bodied carriages. Other examples are more widespread but the progress of restoration proceeds apace and over time the delights and comfort of these vehicles will continue to enchant passengers anew. The construction of new examples of Gresley locomotive designs will give fresh opportunities to ride behind, listen to and take in the aroma of unfortunate gaps in history. Who could not look forward in great anticipation to the opportunity in but a few years time of riding in a Gresley carriage behind the mighty 'P2', a treat denied to all since 1944?

INDEX